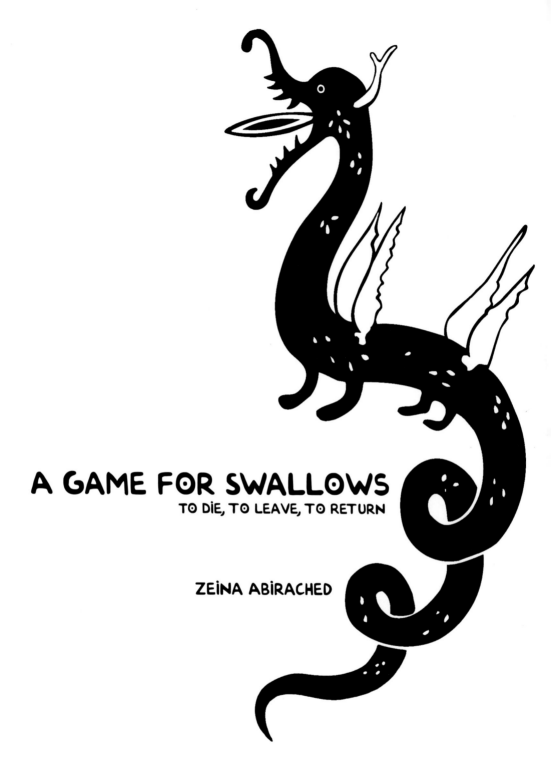

A GAME FOR SWALLOWS
TO DIE, TO LEAVE, TO RETURN

ZEINA ABIRACHED

GRAPHIC UNIVERSE™ • MINNEAPOLIS • NEW YORK

FRENCH VOICES

THIS WORK, PUBLISHED AS PART OF A PROGRAM PROVIDING PUBLICATION ASSISTANCE, RECEIVED FINANCIAL SUPPORT FROM THE FRENCH MINISTRY OF FOREIGN AFFAIRS, THE CULTURAL SERVICES OF THE FRENCH EMBASSY IN THE UNITED STATES, AND FACE (FRENCH AMERICAN CULTURAL EXCHANGE). WWW.FRENCHBOOKNEWS.COM

FRENCH VOICES LOGO DESIGNED BY SERGE BLOCH

STORY AND ART BY ZEINA ABIRACHED
TRANSLATION BY EDWARD GAUVIN

FIRST AMERICAN EDITION PUBLISHED IN 2012 BY GRAPHIC UNIVERSE™.
PUBLISHED BY ARRANGEMENT WITH ÉDITIONS CAMBOURAKIS.

QUOTATIONS FROM EDMOND ROSTAND'S *CYRANO DE BERGERAC* ADAPTED FROM THE 1899 TRANSLATION BY GLADYS THOMAS AND MARY F. GUILLEMARD.

MAP P. 8 ©LAURA WESTLUND/INDEPENDENT PICTURE SERVICE

GRAPHIC UNIVERSE™
A DIVISION OF LERNER PUBLISHING GROUP, INC.
241 FIRST AVENUE NORTH
MINNEAPOLIS, MN 55401 U.S.A.

WEBSITE ADDRESS: WWW.LERNERBOOKS.COM

LIBRARY OF CONGRESS CATALOGING-IN-PUBLICATION DATA

ABIRACHED, ZEINA, 1981-
(JEU DES HIRONDELLES. ENGLISH)
A GAME FOR SWALLOWS : TO DIE, TO LEAVE, TO RETURN WRITTEN BY ZEINA ABIRACHED ; ART BY ZEINA ABIRACHED ; TRANSLATION BY EDWARD GAUVIN.
P. CM.
TRANSLATION OF LE JEU DES HIRONDELLES.
ISBN 978-0-7613-8568-4 (LIB. BDG. : ALK. PAPER)
1. ABIRACHED, ZEINA, 1981-—COMIC BOOKS, STRIPS, ETC. 2. LEBANON—HISTORY—CIVIL WAR, 1975-1990—COMIC BOOKS, STRIPS, ETC. 3. BEIRUT (LEBANON)—COMIC BOOKS, STRIPS, ETC. 4. GRAPHIC NOVELS. I. TITLE.
PN6790.L43A2513 2012
741.5—DC23 2011003891

MANUFACTURED IN THE UNITED STATES OF AMERICA
1 - DP - 7/15/2012

iNTRODUCTiON

A song I used to love back in 1969 asks what war is good for. The answer: absolutely nothing. My politics are pretty simple: people have the right to love one another, regardless of gender; basic health care is a human right; women have the right to control over their own bodies; it is unfair for 1 percent of the population to have all the wealth while 99 percent have nothing; and war is bad.

But I don't understand wars. OK, I get the reasons for World War II and the American Civil War, but I will never understand World War I. What was Bosnia all about? Why did Iran and Iraq fight with each other? And what was the reason for the Lebanese Civil War? Are there *justifiable* reasons for wars?

From my untutored viewpoint, a bunch of old guys send a bunch of young guys out to kill and die while ordinary people like you and me, caught in the middle, simply try to survive. And sometimes, in the course of surviving, we do beautiful things.

In a crisp, accessible black-and-white style, reminiscent of Marjane Satrapi's *Persepolis*, Zeina Abirached shows us both the horror and the beauty that can emerge from war. It's 1984 in East Beirut. Very young Zeina has never known anything but war. She lives in the middle of the war zone with her parents and her even younger brother. The family has closed off most of their apartment and moved into the foyer, the only safe room in the house. They've dragged in their mattresses, their chairs and rugs. Hanging on the wall is the family heirloom, a tapestry depicting Moses and the Hebrews fleeing Egypt. The tapestry is separated into panels, like the comic page that contains it: a comic within a comic.

Zeina's parents have gone out to visit her grandmother, who lives a few blocks away—and they have not returned, although they left for home an hour ago. And here's where the beauty comes in.

The neighbors all filter down in ones and twos, to stay with the kids. Soon, nine people fill the tiny foyer. Some of them have lost loved ones to the war. Some of them are preparing to flee to Canada, like Moses and the Hebrews in the tapestry.

They drink strong Turkish coffee and listen to the bombardment outside. Anhala, an old woman, makes a Lebanese cake called *sfouf* that sounds delicious. Should the worst happen, these kids will be loved and cared for!

As I write this, the newspapers and the Internet are full of tributes to Marie Colvin, the journalist who was killed by shelling in Syria on February 22, 2012, along with a French photojournalist named Rémi Ochlik. With her black eye patch, which she wore after losing her eye to shrapnel while covering conflicts in Sri Lanka in 2001,

she cut a dashing figure. She always seemed to me like the heroine of a comic book. The *Washington Post* describes her as risking her life "to cover wars from the perspective of ordinary people, particularly women and children." In other words, people like Zeina and her neighbors.

Here is an excerpt from Colvin's last dispatch, to the *Sunday Times* of London three days before she was killed:

> *They call it the widows' basement. Crammed among make-shift beds and scattered belongings are frightened women and children trapped in the horror of Homs, the Syrian city shaken by two weeks of relentless bombardment. . . .*
>
> *Snipers on the rooftops . . . shoot any civilian who comes into their sights. Residents were felled in droves in the first day of the siege . . . but have now learnt where the snipers are and run across junctions where they know they can be seen. . . .*
>
> *No shops are open, so families are sharing what they have with relatives and neighbours.*

The story sounds so much the same as Zeina's.

I found a recipe for *sfouf* on the Internet. It looks pretty easy to make, but you need semolina flour and turmeric. I shall walk two blocks to the supermarket for the flour and spice, and nobody will shoot at me. Doesn't everybody deserve to live like that?

—Trina Robbins
March 2012

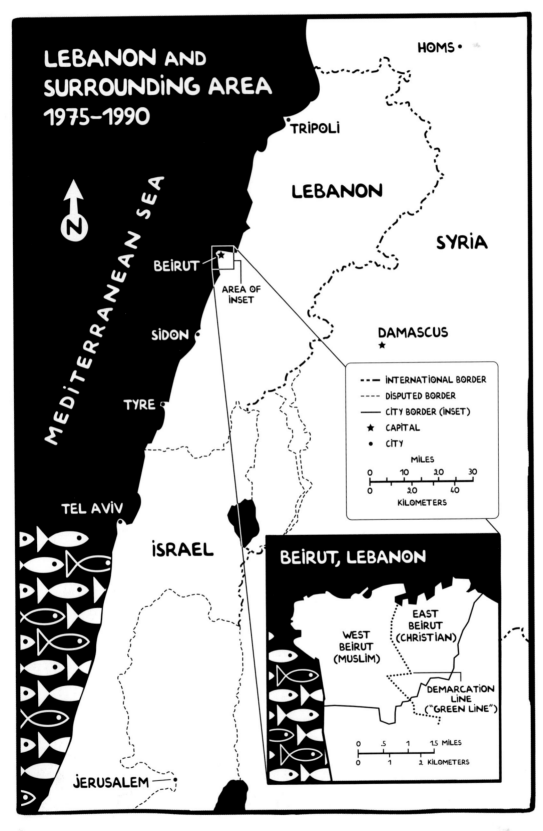

LEBANON AND SURROUNDING AREA 1975–1990

MEDITERRANEAN SEA

HOMS •

TRIPOLI

LEBANON

SYRIA

BEIRUT

AREA OF INSET

DAMASCUS ★

SIDON ○

TYRE ○

---- INTERNATIONAL BORDER
---- DISPUTED BORDER
—— CITY BORDER (INSET)
★ CAPITAL
• CITY

MILES
0   10   20   30
0   20   40
KILOMETERS

TEL AVIV

ISRAEL

BEIRUT, LEBANON

WEST BEIRUT (MUSLIM)

EAST BEIRUT (CHRISTIAN)

DEMARCATION LINE ("GREEN LINE")

0   .5   1   1.5 MILES
0   1   2 KILOMETERS

JERUSALEM •

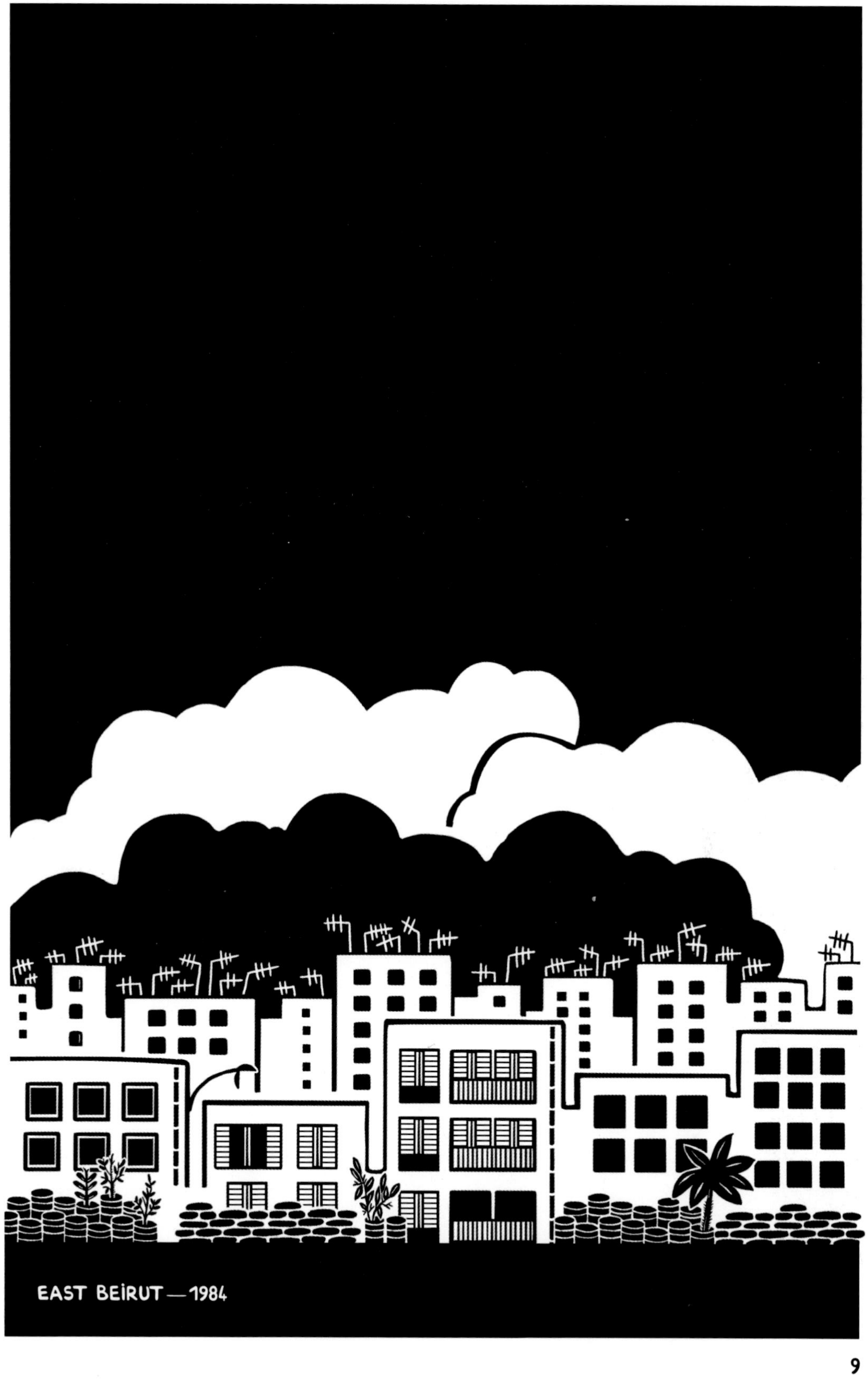
EAST BEIRUT — 1984

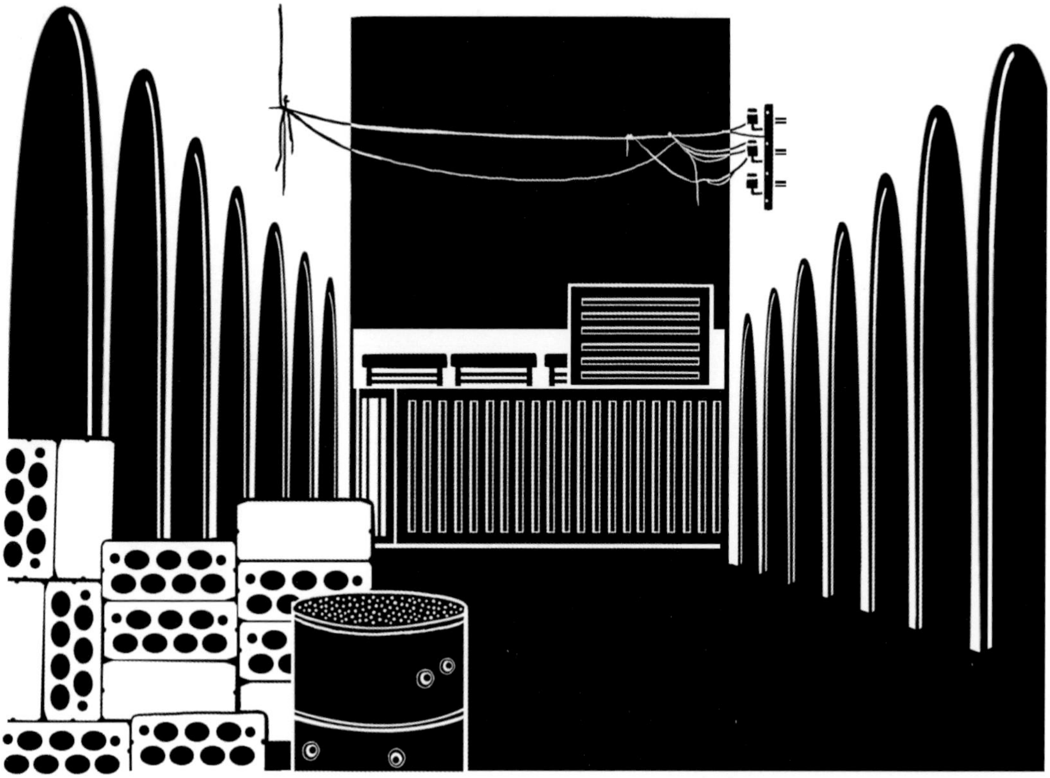

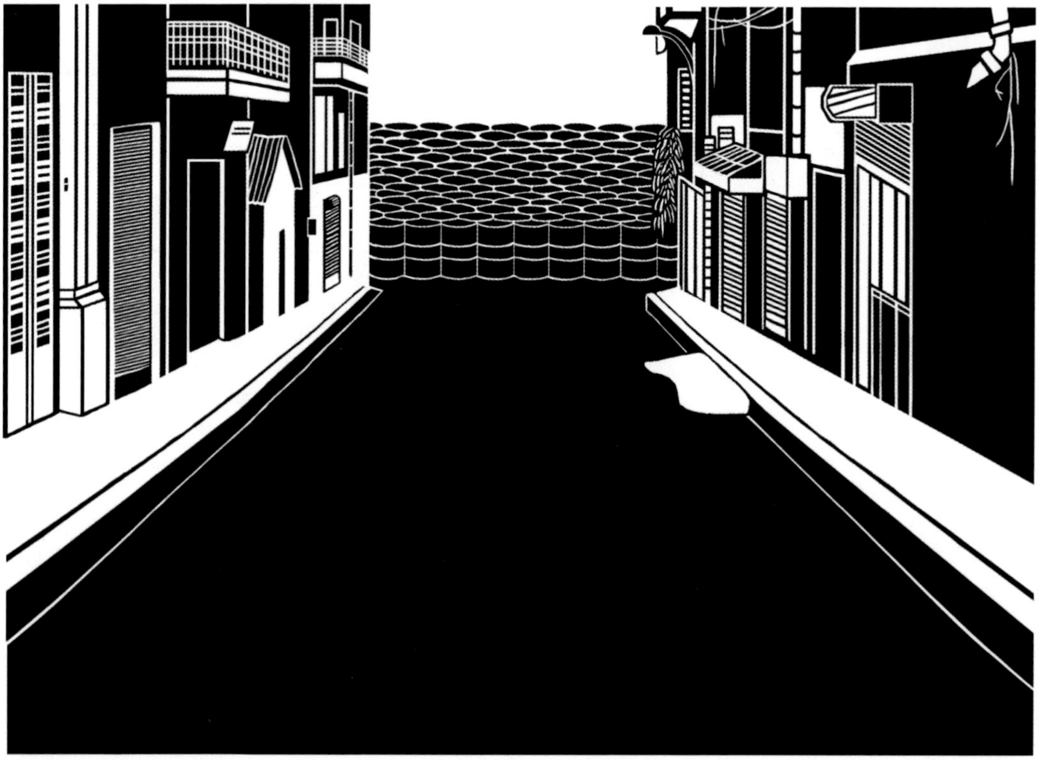

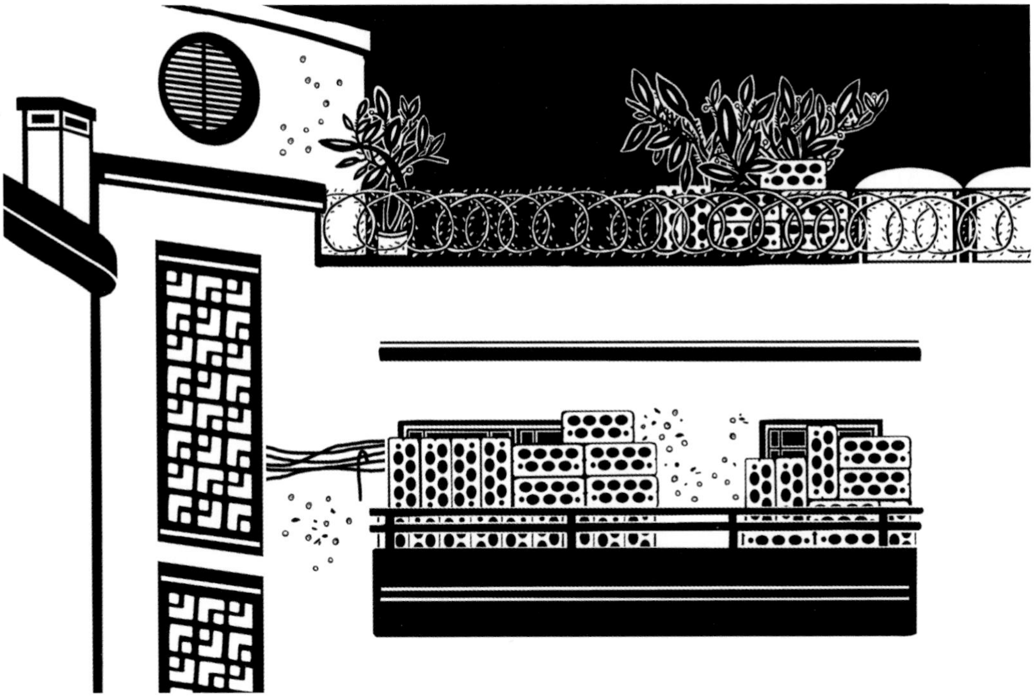

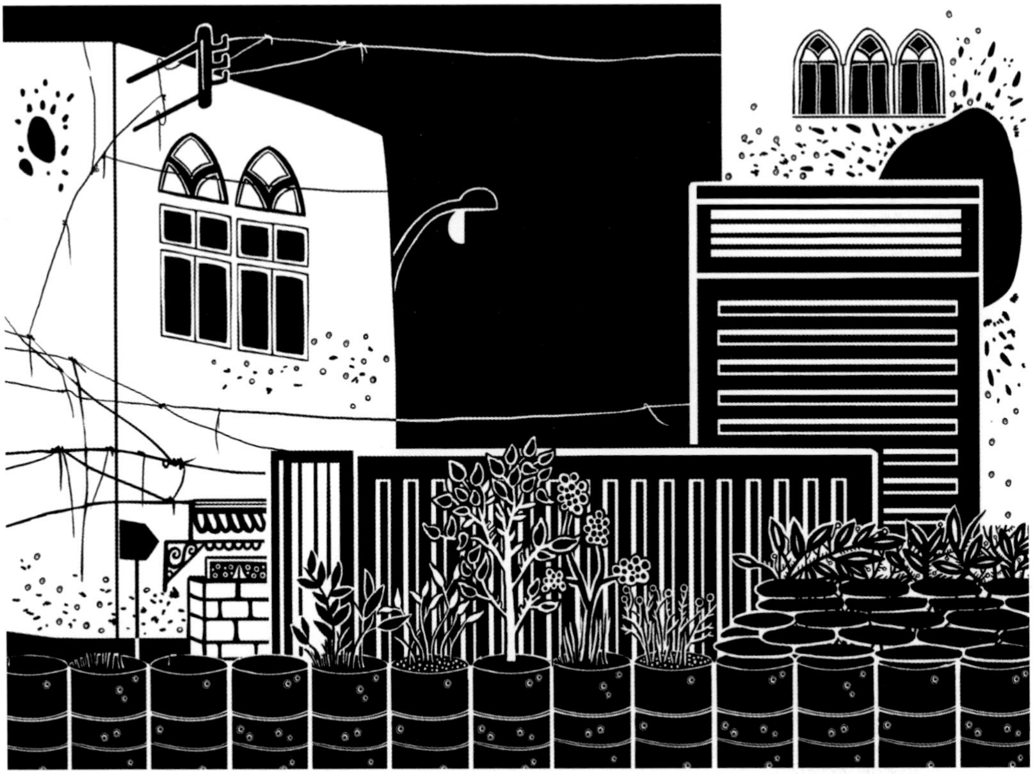

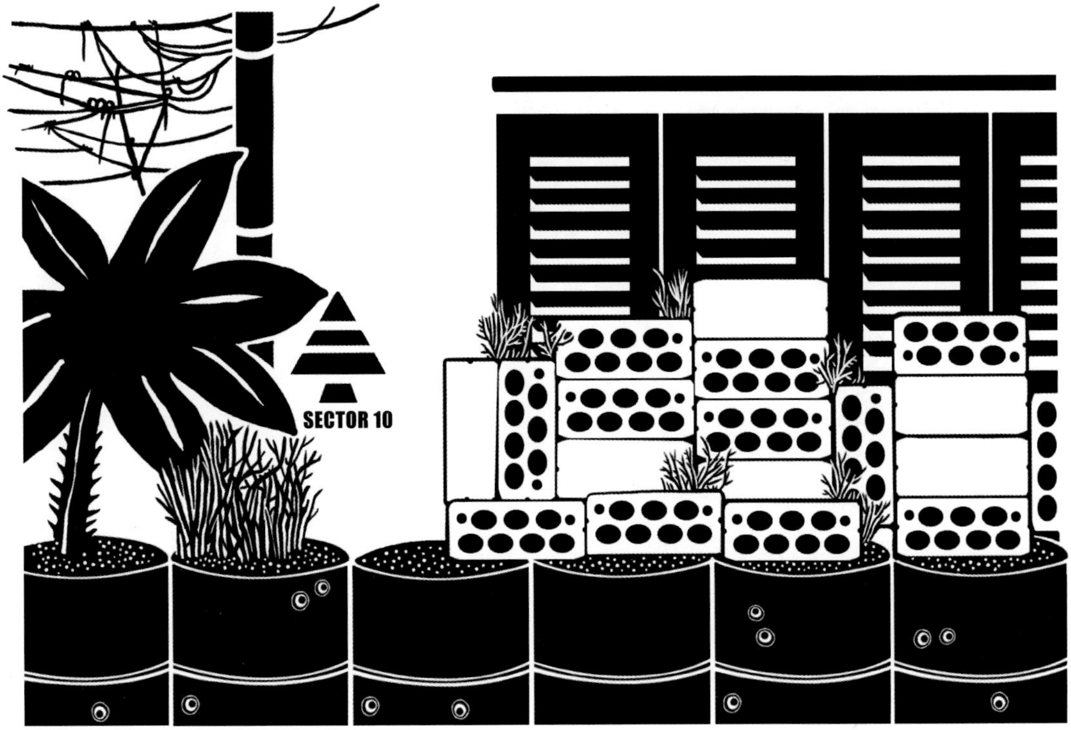
SECTOR 10

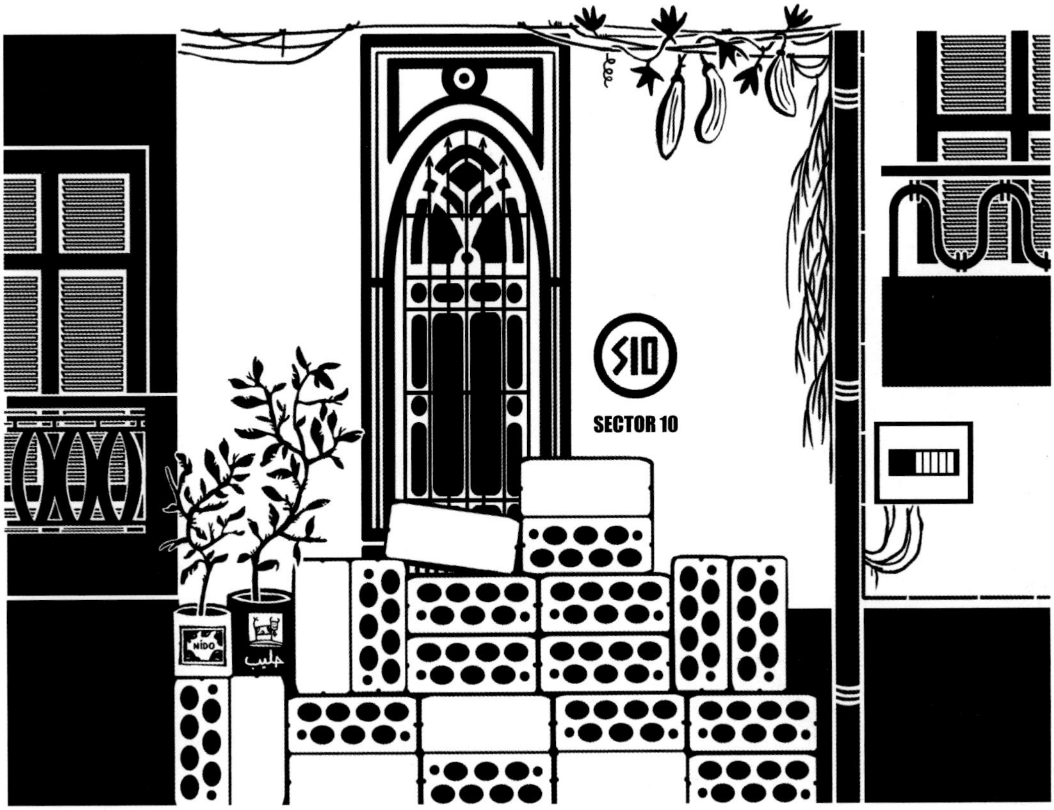
S10
SECTOR 10
NIDO
حليب

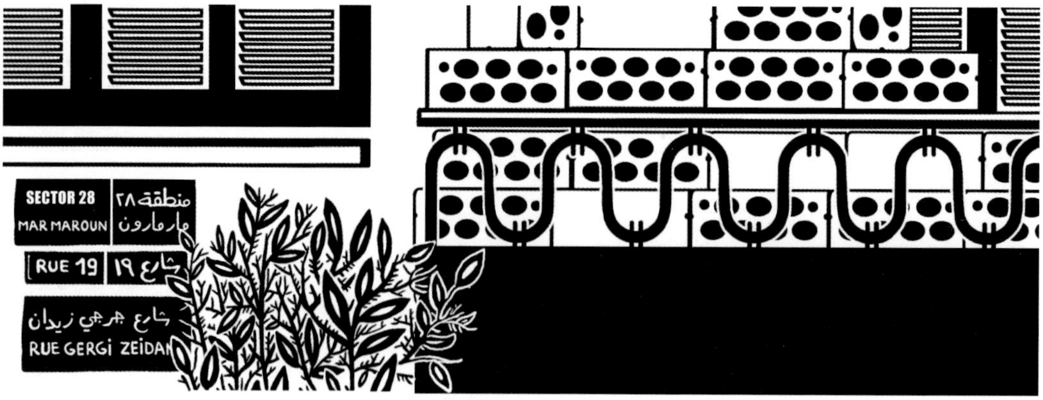
SECTOR 28
منطقة ٢٨
MAR MAROUN
مار مارون
RUE 19
شارع ١٩
شارع جرجي زيدان
RUE GERGI ZEIDAN

IN THE NEIGHBORHOODS ALONG THE DEMARCATION LINE, WALLS OF SANDBAGS SEVER THE STREETS.
CONTAINERS TAKEN FROM THE DOCKS OF THE DESERTED PORT STAND IN THE MIDDLE OF ALLEYS TO PROTECT RESIDENTS FROM SNIPERS' BULLETS.
BUILDINGS SHUT THEMSELVES AWAY BEHIND WALLS OF CINDER BLOCKS AND METAL DRUMS.
INSIDE THESE DIVIDED SECTORS, LIFE IS ORGANIZED AROUND THE CEASE-FIRES.

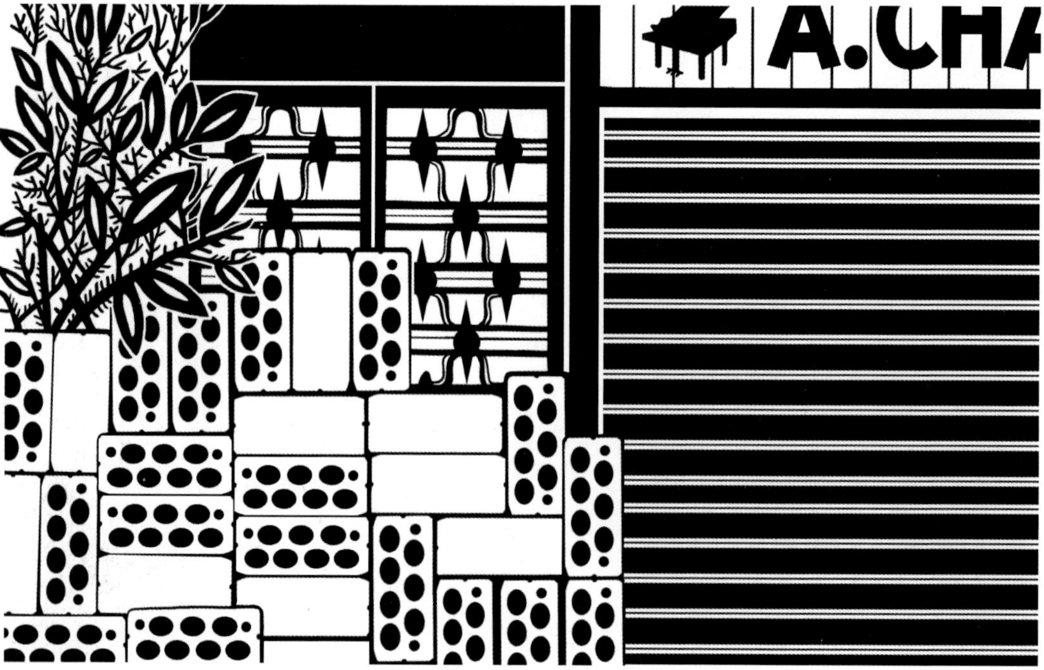
A.CH

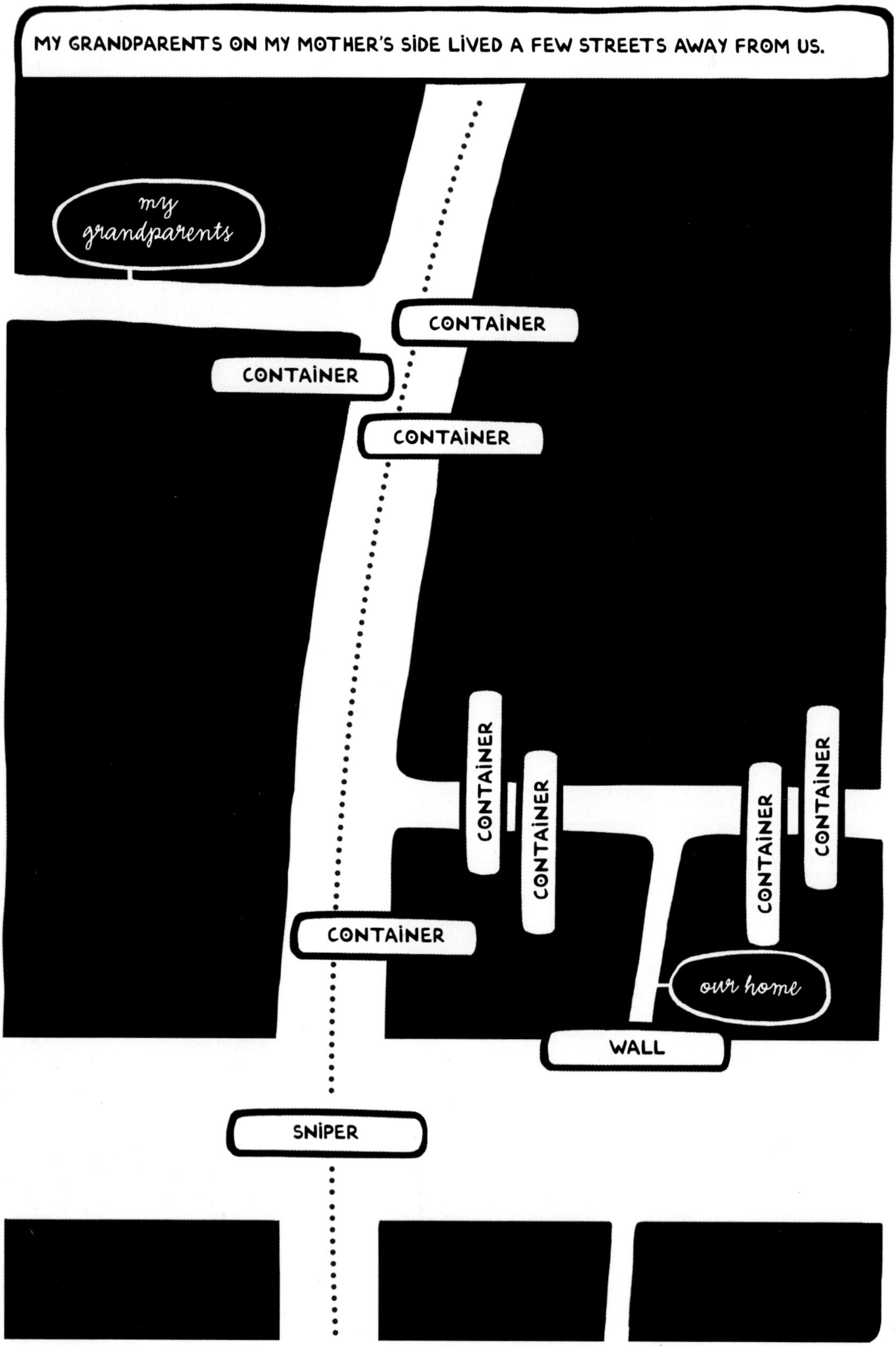

MY GRANDPARENTS ON MY MOTHER'S SIDE LIVED A FEW STREETS AWAY FROM US.
my grandparents
CONTAINER
CONTAINER
CONTAINER
CONTAINER
CONTAINER
CONTAINER
CONTAINER
CONTAINER
our home
WALL
SNIPER

TO AVOID THE SNIPER, PEOPLE HAD PERFECTED A WAY OF MOVING BETWEEN BUILDINGS.

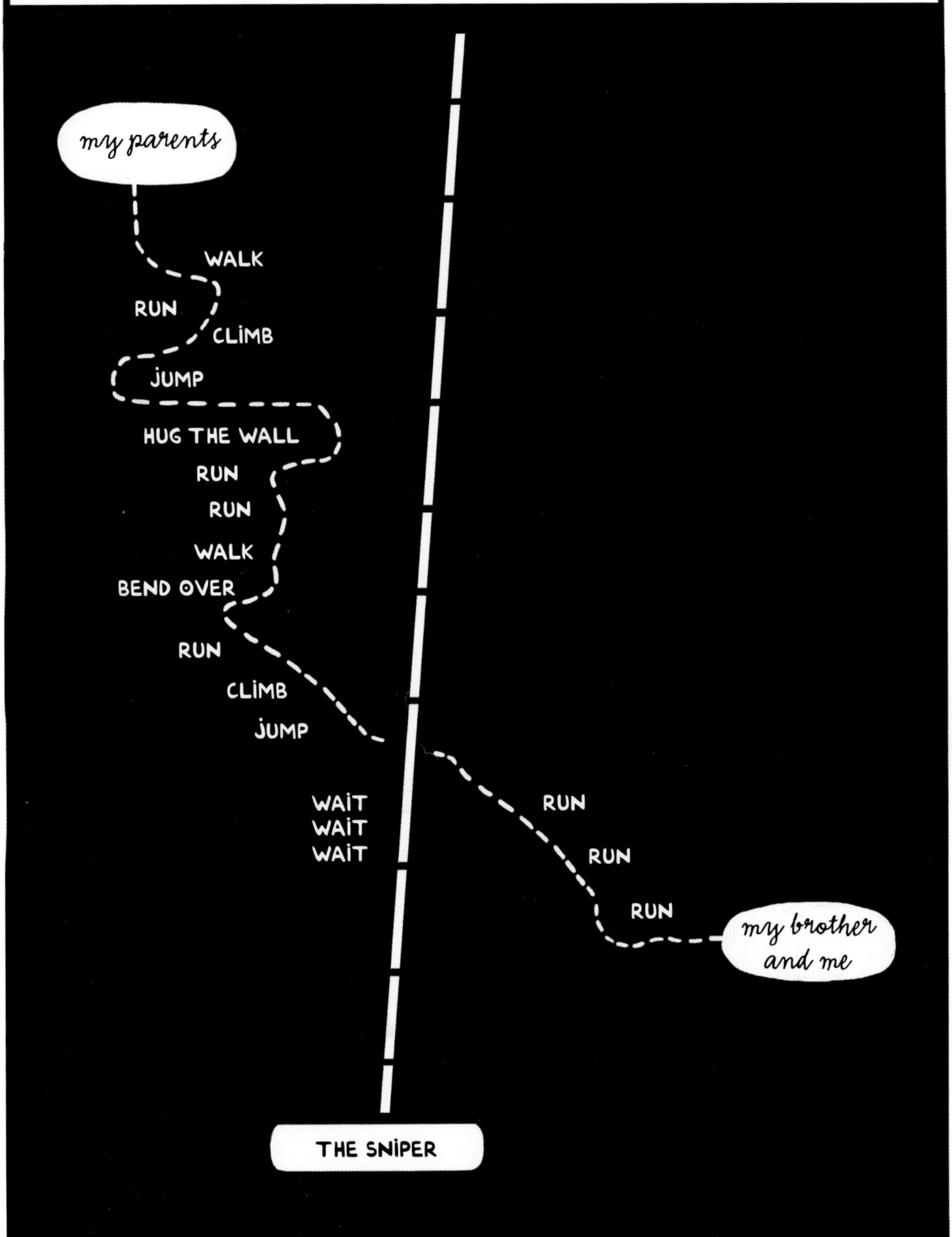

CROSSING THE HANDFUL OF STREETS BETWEEN US MEANT FOLLOWING COMPLICATED AND PERILOUS CHOREOGRAPHY.

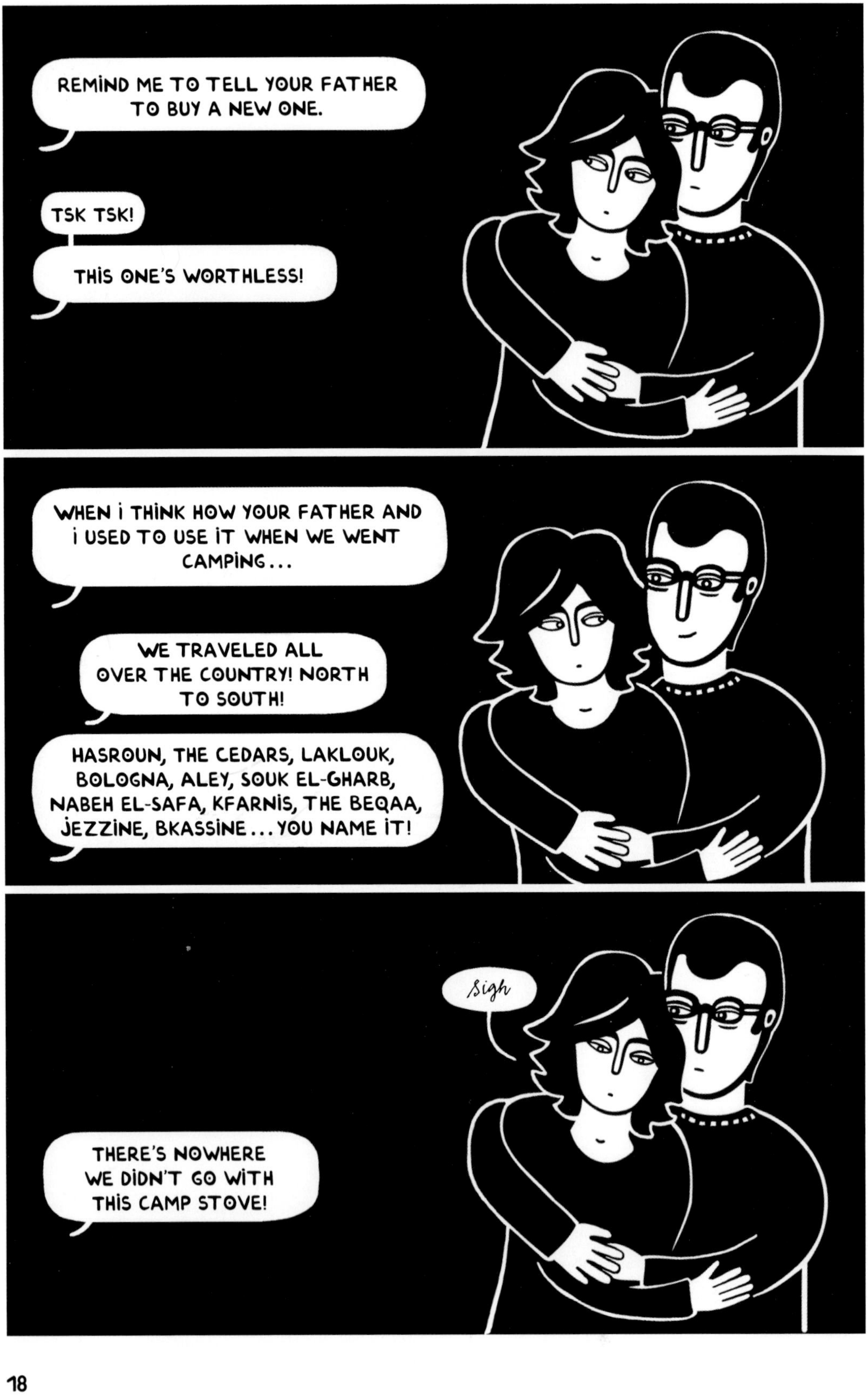
REMIND ME TO TELL YOUR FATHER TO BUY A NEW ONE.
TSK TSK!
THIS ONE'S WORTHLESS!
WHEN I THINK HOW YOUR FATHER AND I USED TO USE IT WHEN WE WENT CAMPING...
WE TRAVELED ALL OVER THE COUNTRY! NORTH TO SOUTH!
HASROUN, THE CEDARS, LAKLOUK, BOLOGNA, ALEY, SOUK EL-GHARB, NABEH EL-SAFA, KFARNIS, THE BEQAA, JEZZINE, BKASSINE... YOU NAME IT!
Sigh
THERE'S NOWHERE WE DIDN'T GO WITH THIS CAMP STOVE!

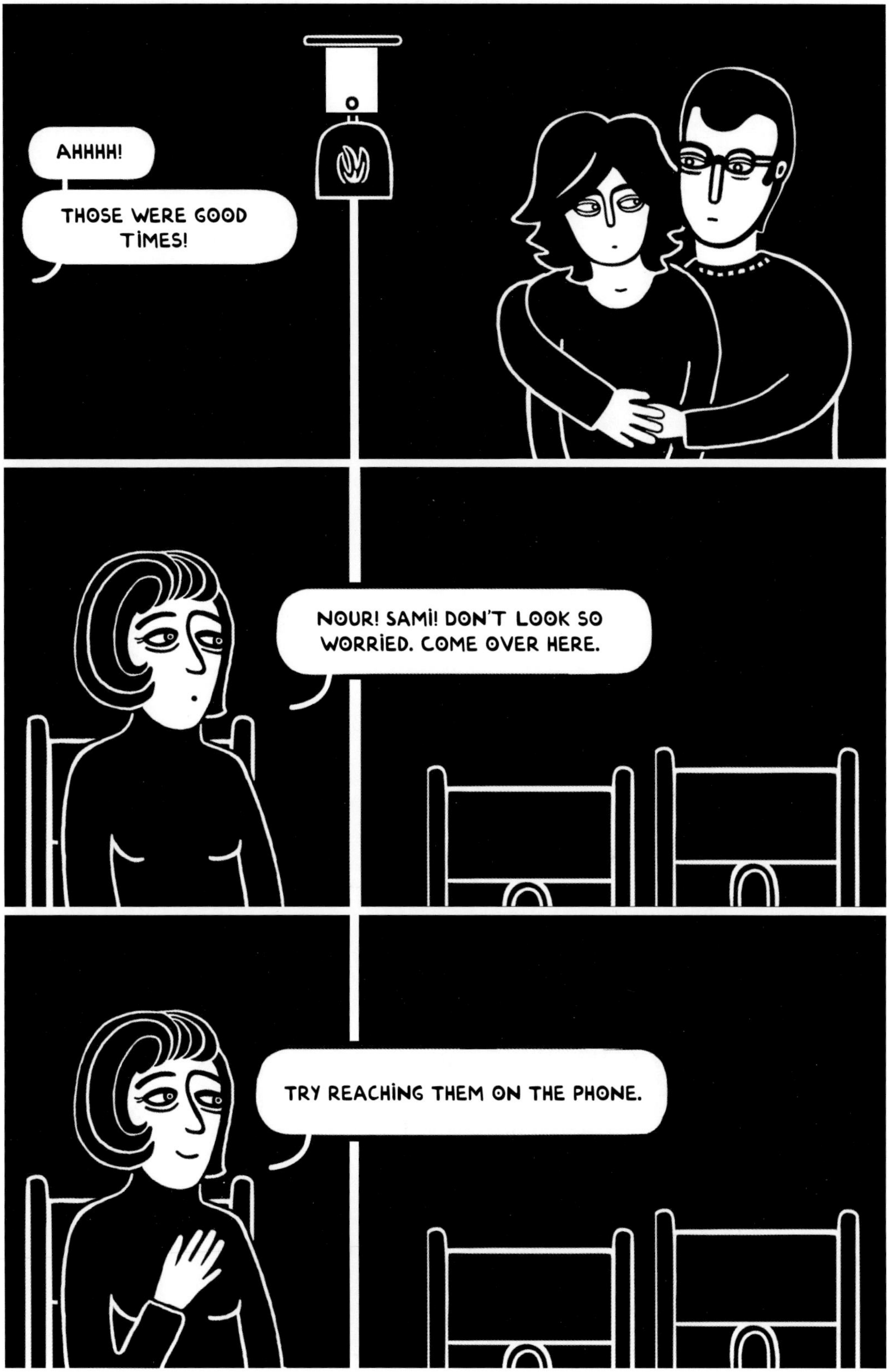
AHHHH!
THOSE WERE GOOD TIMES!
NOUR! SAMI! DON'T LOOK SO WORRIED. COME OVER HERE.
TRY REACHING THEM ON THE PHONE.

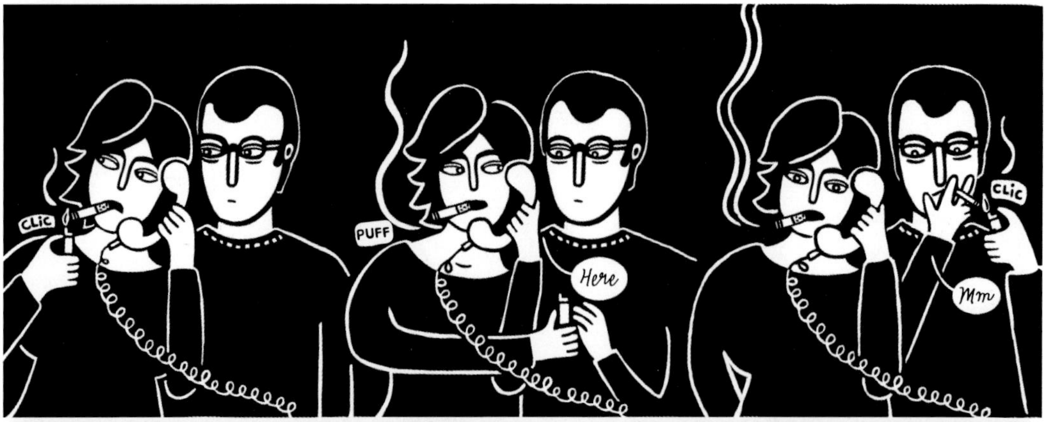
CLIC
PUFF
Here
CLIC
Mm

BACK THEN, IT WAS VERY HARD TO REACH SOMEONE BY PHONE.

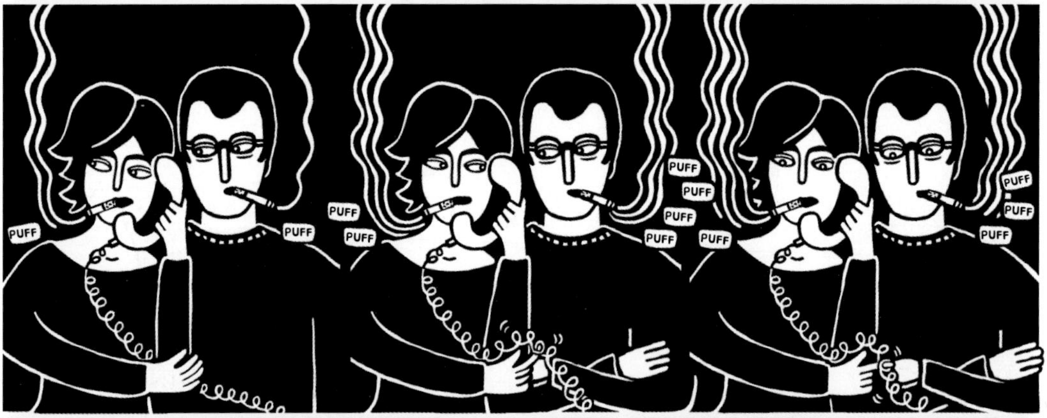
PUFF
PUFF
PUFF
PUFF

YOU COULD WAIT HOURS ON END JUST FOR A DIAL TONE.

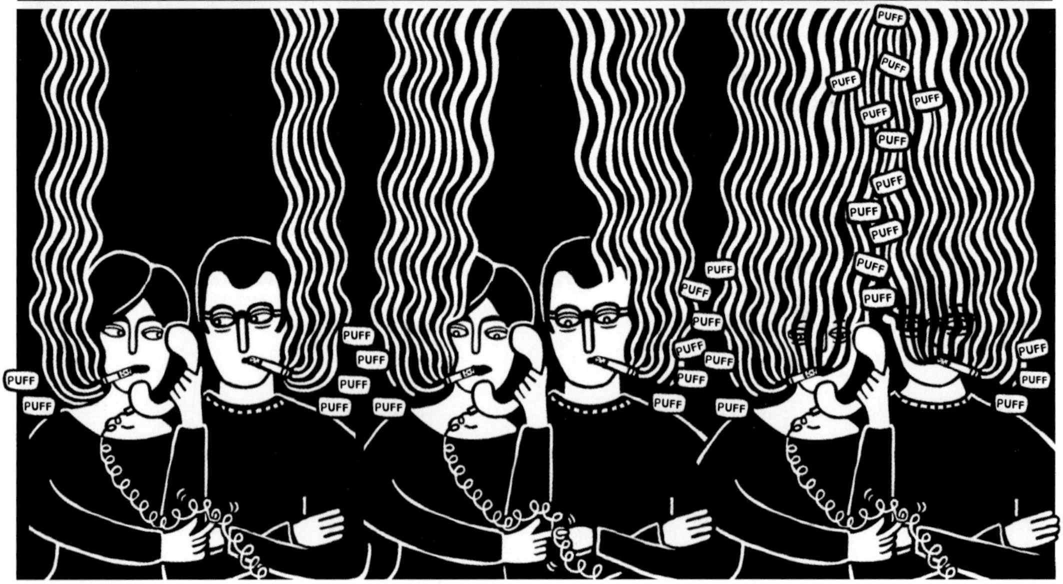
PUFF
PUFF
PUFF

SOMETIMES, WHEN MY MOTHER HAD AN IMPORTANT PHONE CALL TO MAKE, SHE'D ASK ME AND MY BROTHER TO WAIT FOR THE "KHATT" (DIAL TONE) SO SHE COULD DO SOMETHING ELSE IN THE MEANTIME.

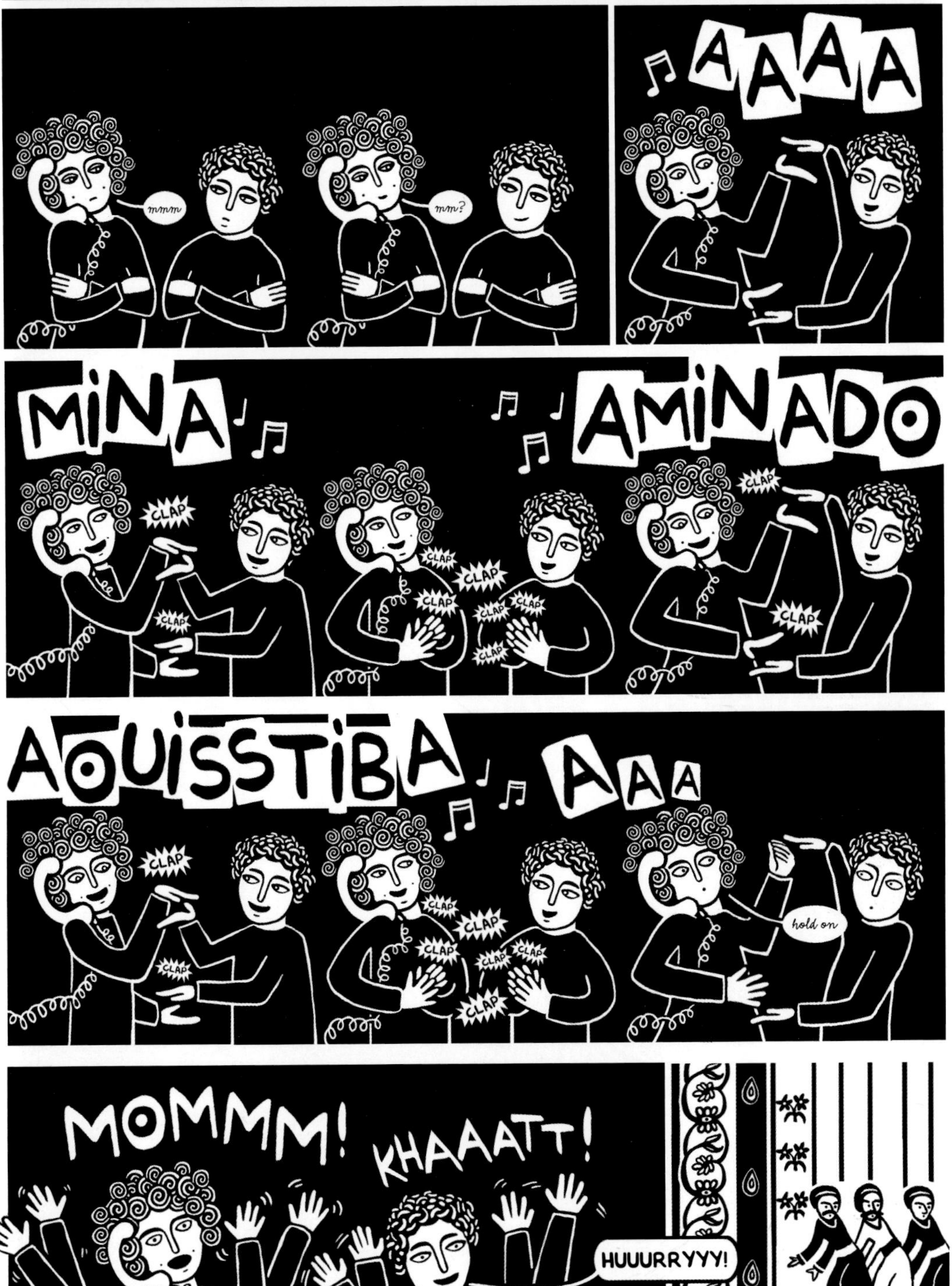

mmm
mm?
AAAA
MINA
AMINADO
CLAP
CLAP
CLAP
CLAP
CLAP
CLAP
CLAP
CLAP
CLAP
CLAP
AOUISSTIBA
AAA
CLAP
CLAP
CLAP
CLAP
CLAP
CLAP
CLAP
CLAP
hold on
MOMMM!
KHAAATT!
HUUURRYYY!

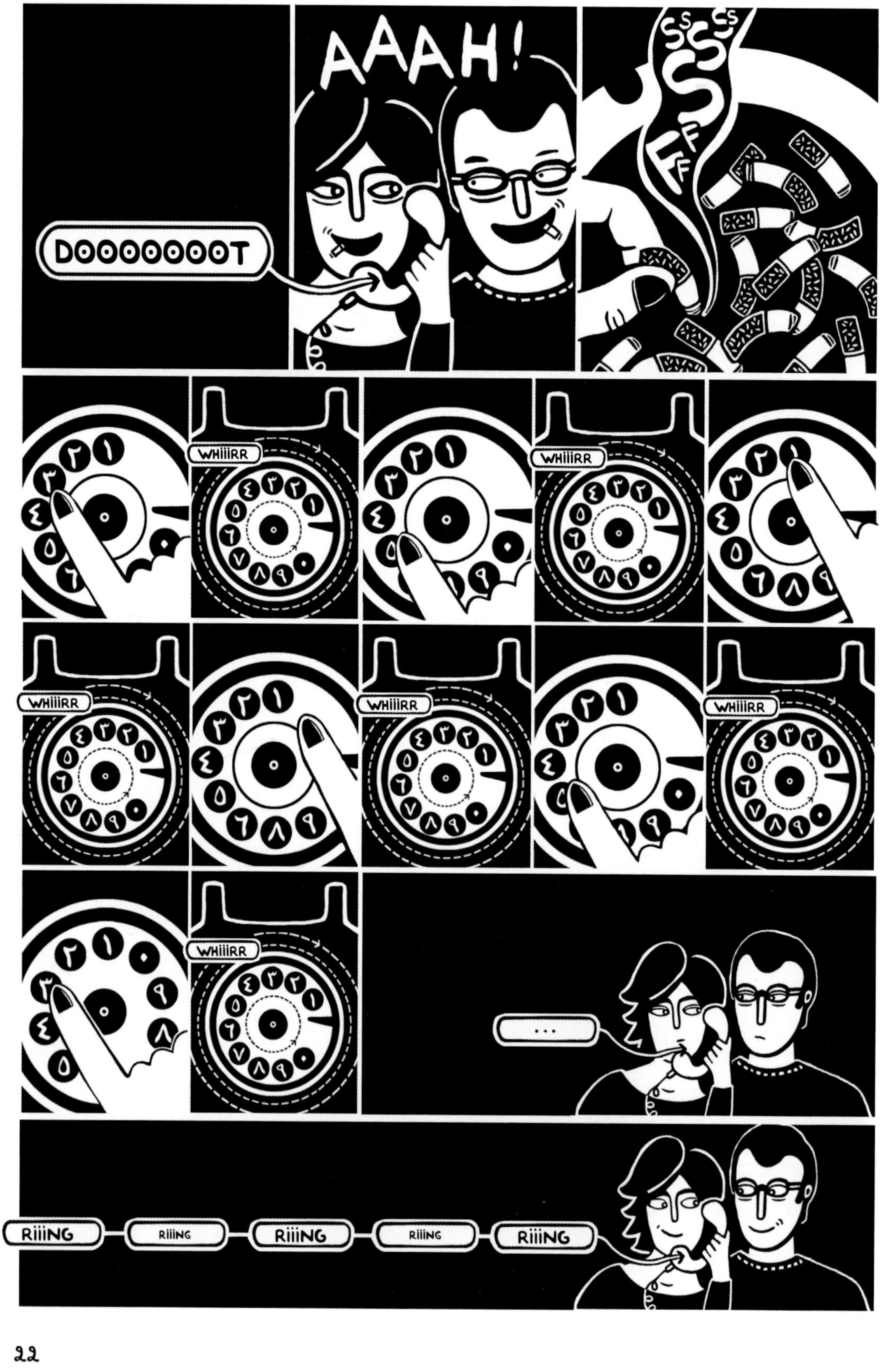
DOOOOOOOT
AAAH!
SSSSS
FFF
WHiiiRR
WHiiiRR
WHiiiRR
WHiiiRR
WHiiiRR
WHiiiRR
...
RiiiNG
RiiiNG
RiiiNG
RiiiNG
RiiiNG

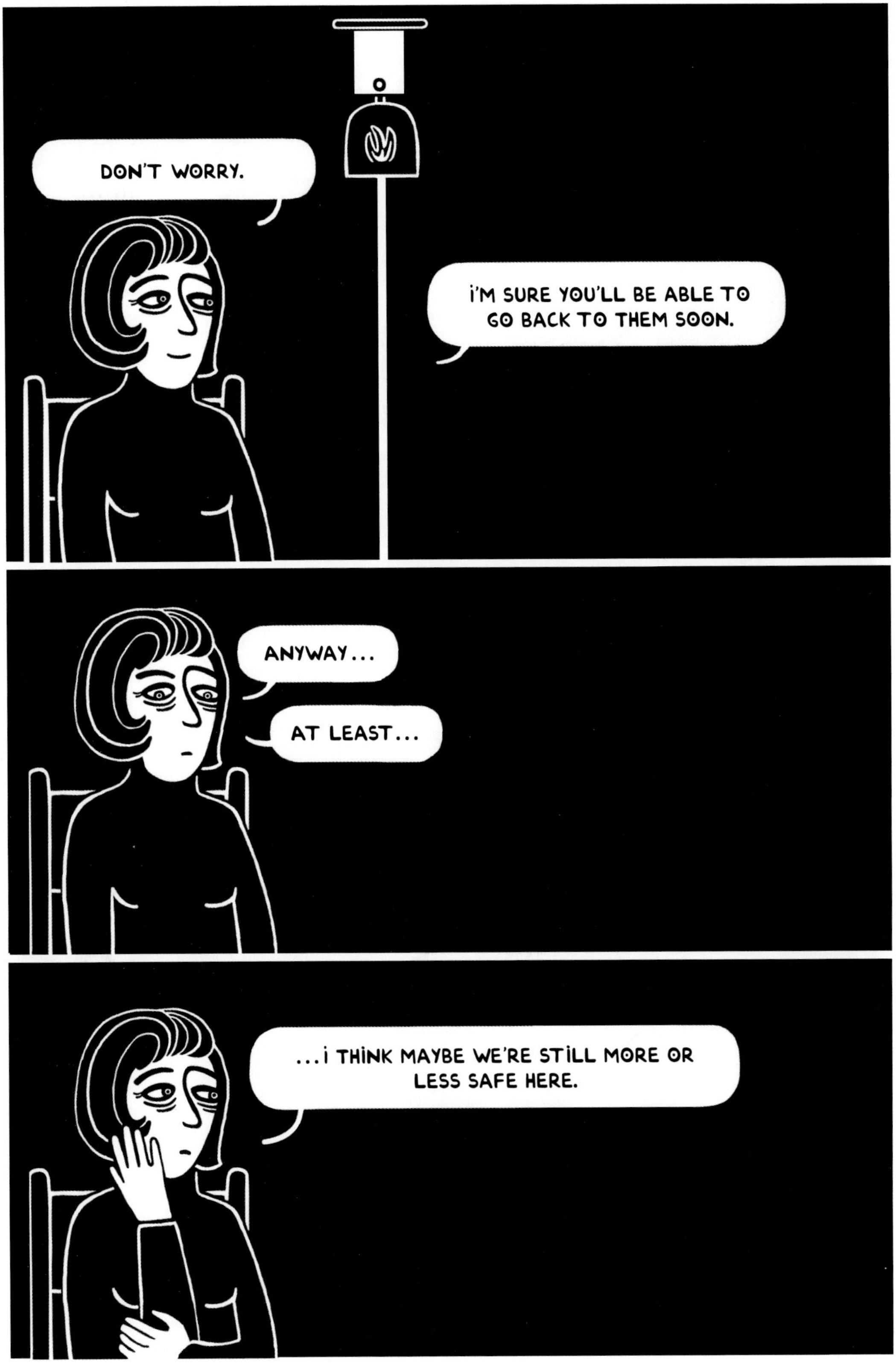
DON'T WORRY.
I'M SURE YOU'LL BE ABLE TO GO BACK TO THEM SOON.
ANYWAY...
AT LEAST...
...I THINK MAYBE WE'RE STILL MORE OR LESS SAFE HERE.

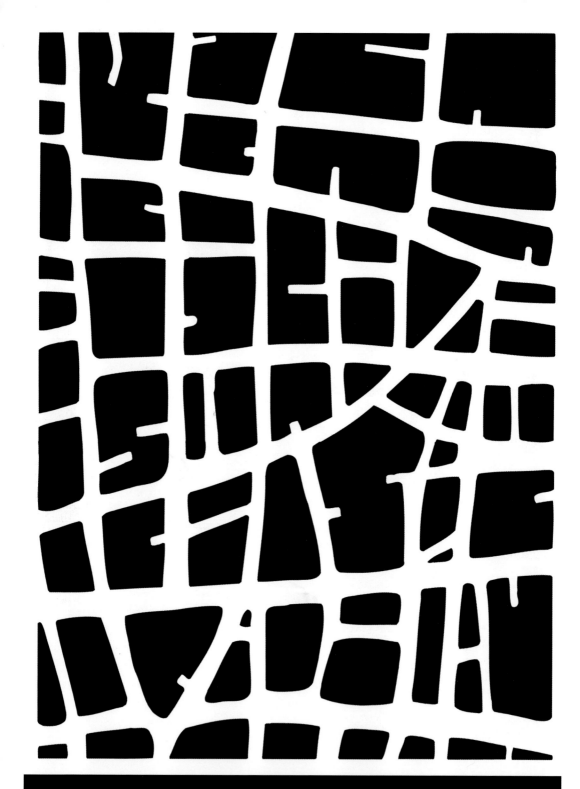

HERE IS ALL THE SPACE WE HAVE LEFT ...

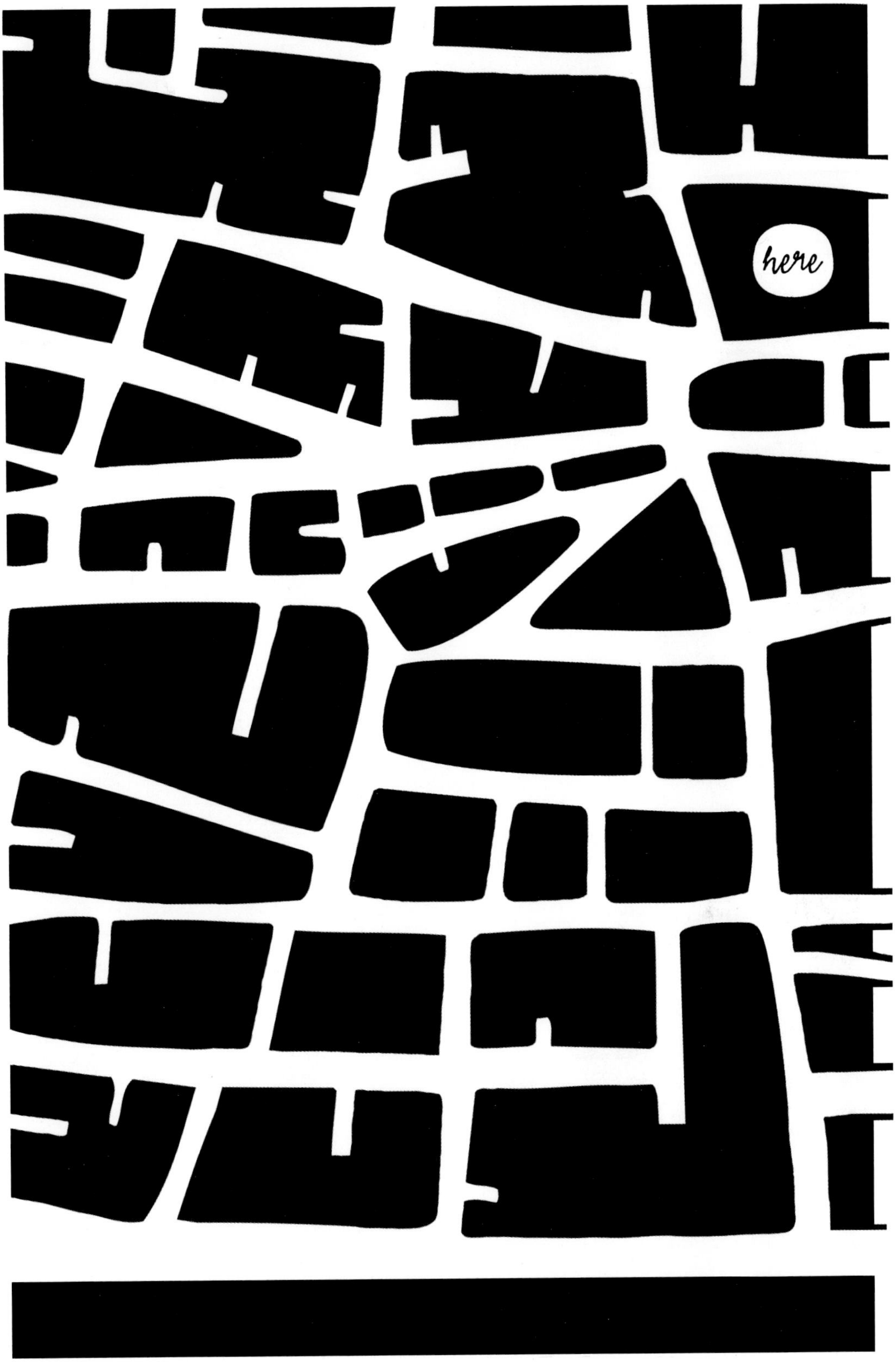
here

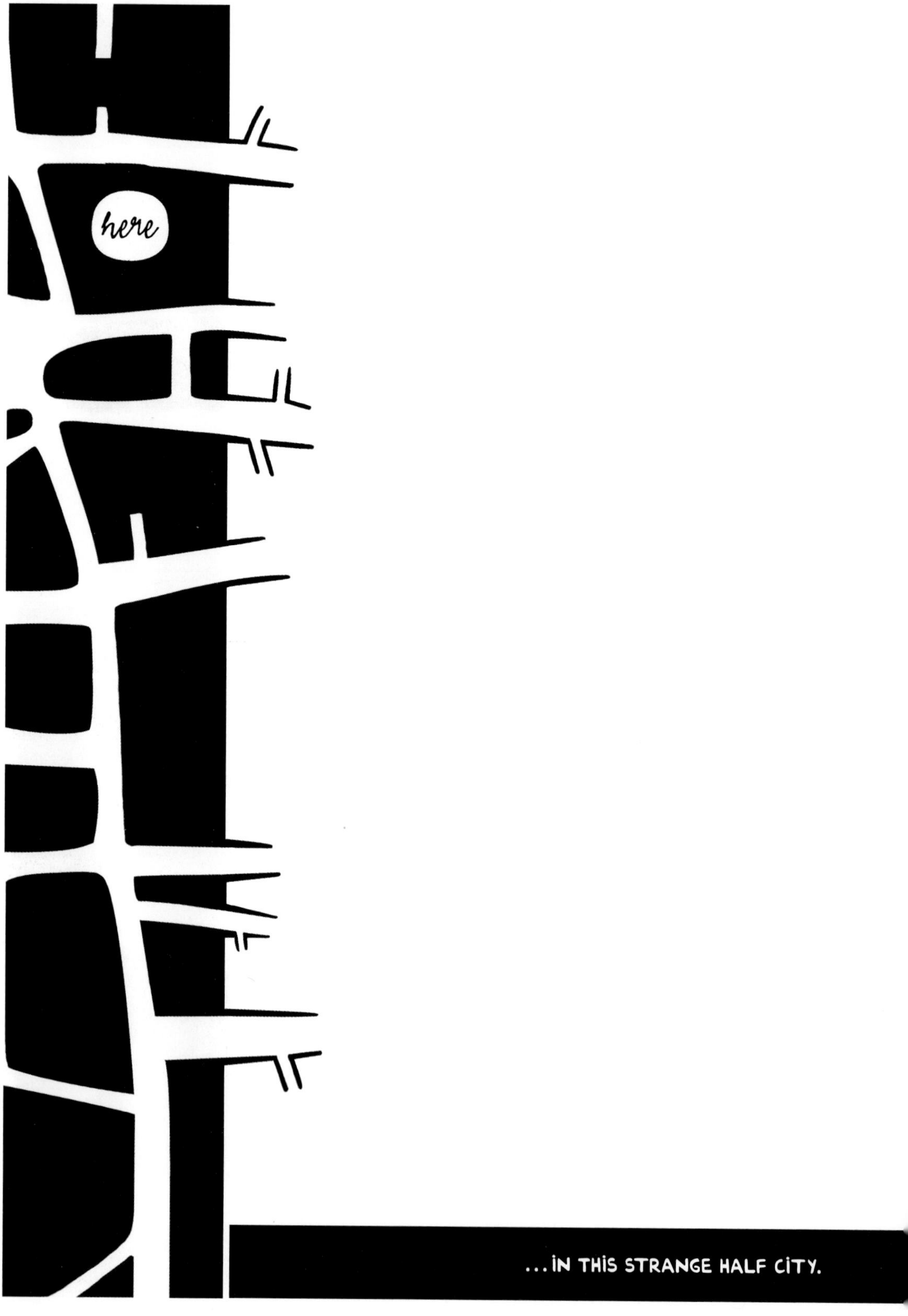
here
...IN THIS STRANGE HALF CITY.

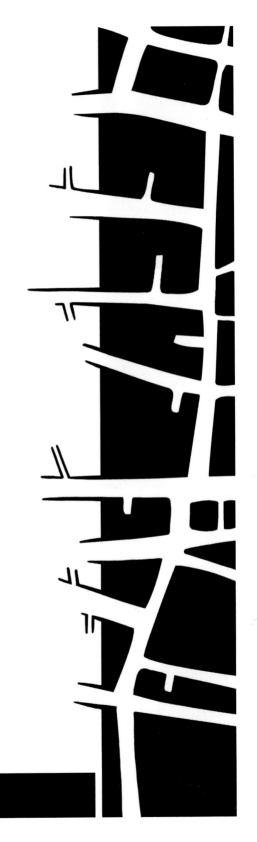

SNIPERS,

OIL DRUMS,

CONTAINERS,

BARBED WIRE,

SANDBAGS

CARVE OUT A NEW GEOGRAPHY.

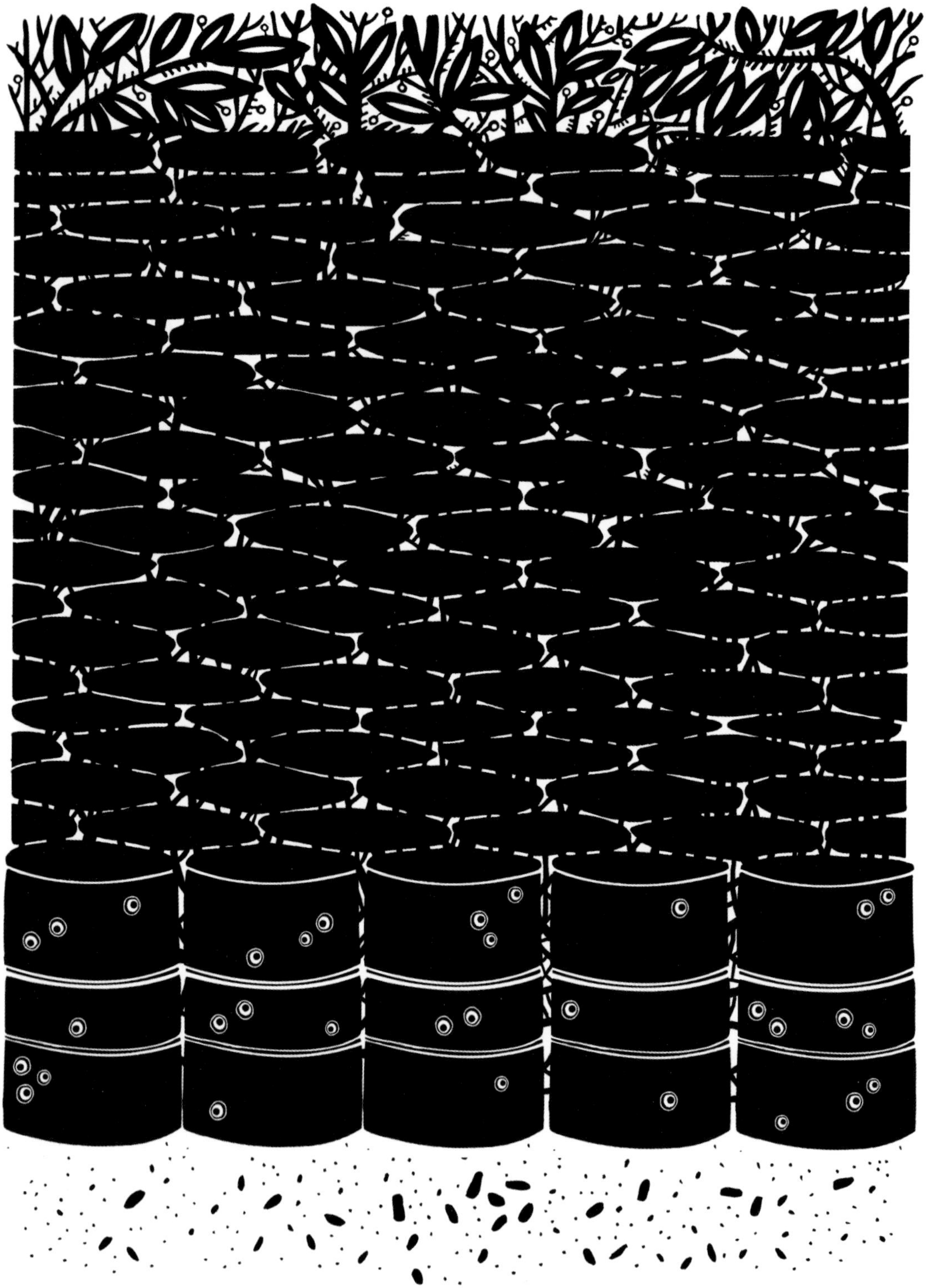

OUR APARTMENT BUILDING LOOKED OUT ON THE DEMARCATION LINE.

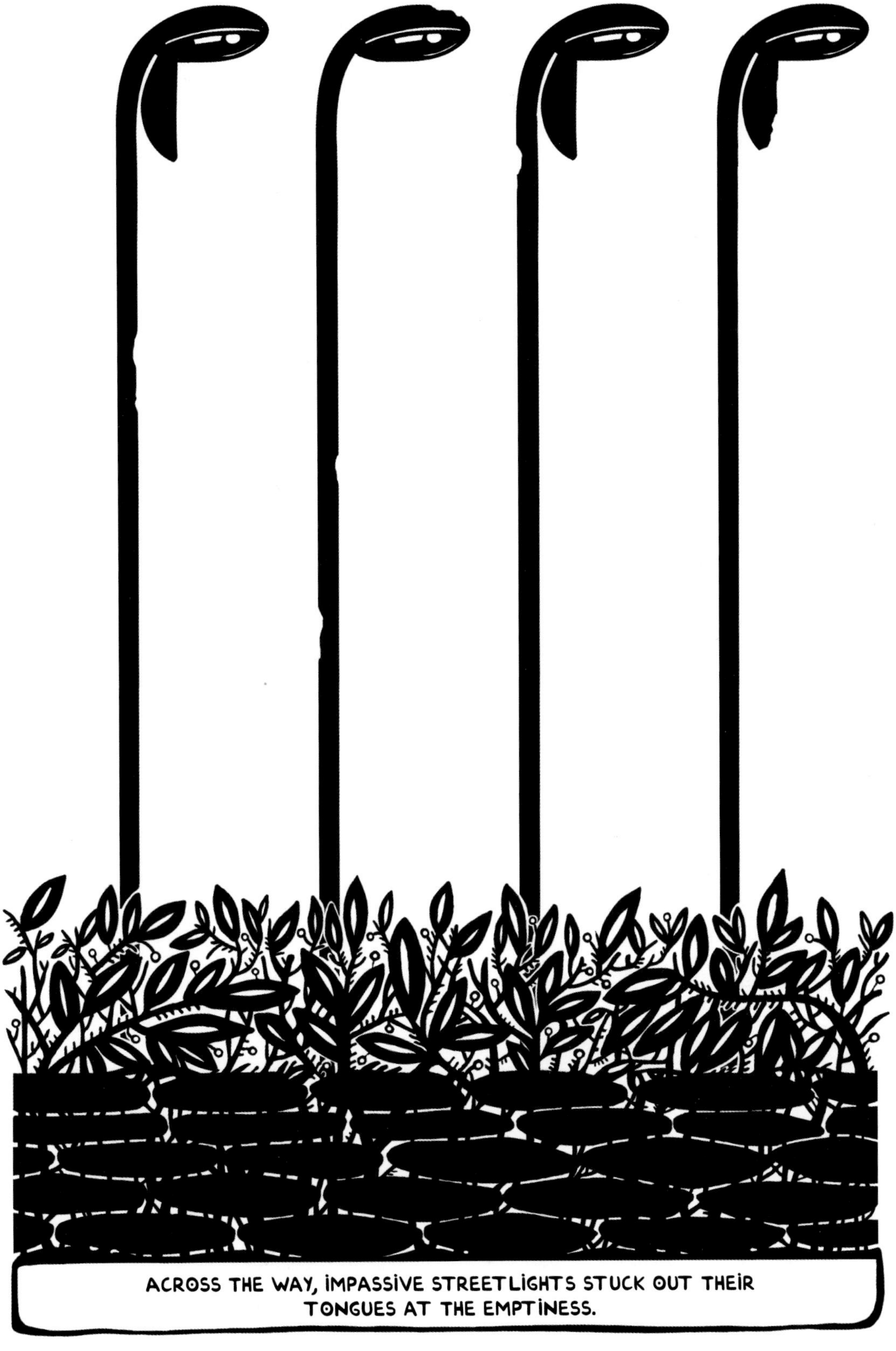
ACROSS THE WAY, IMPASSIVE STREETLIGHTS STUCK OUT THEIR TONGUES AT THE EMPTINESS.

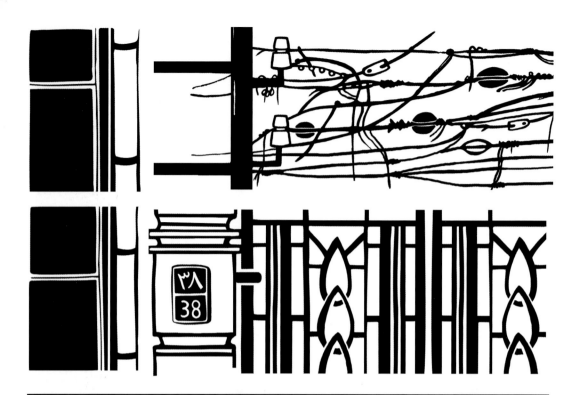

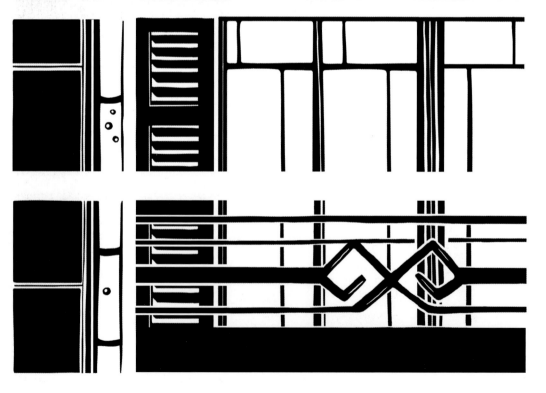

IT WAS A BUILDING FROM THE 1940S. MY FATHER'S PARENTS HAD LIVED THERE ALL THEIR LIVES.

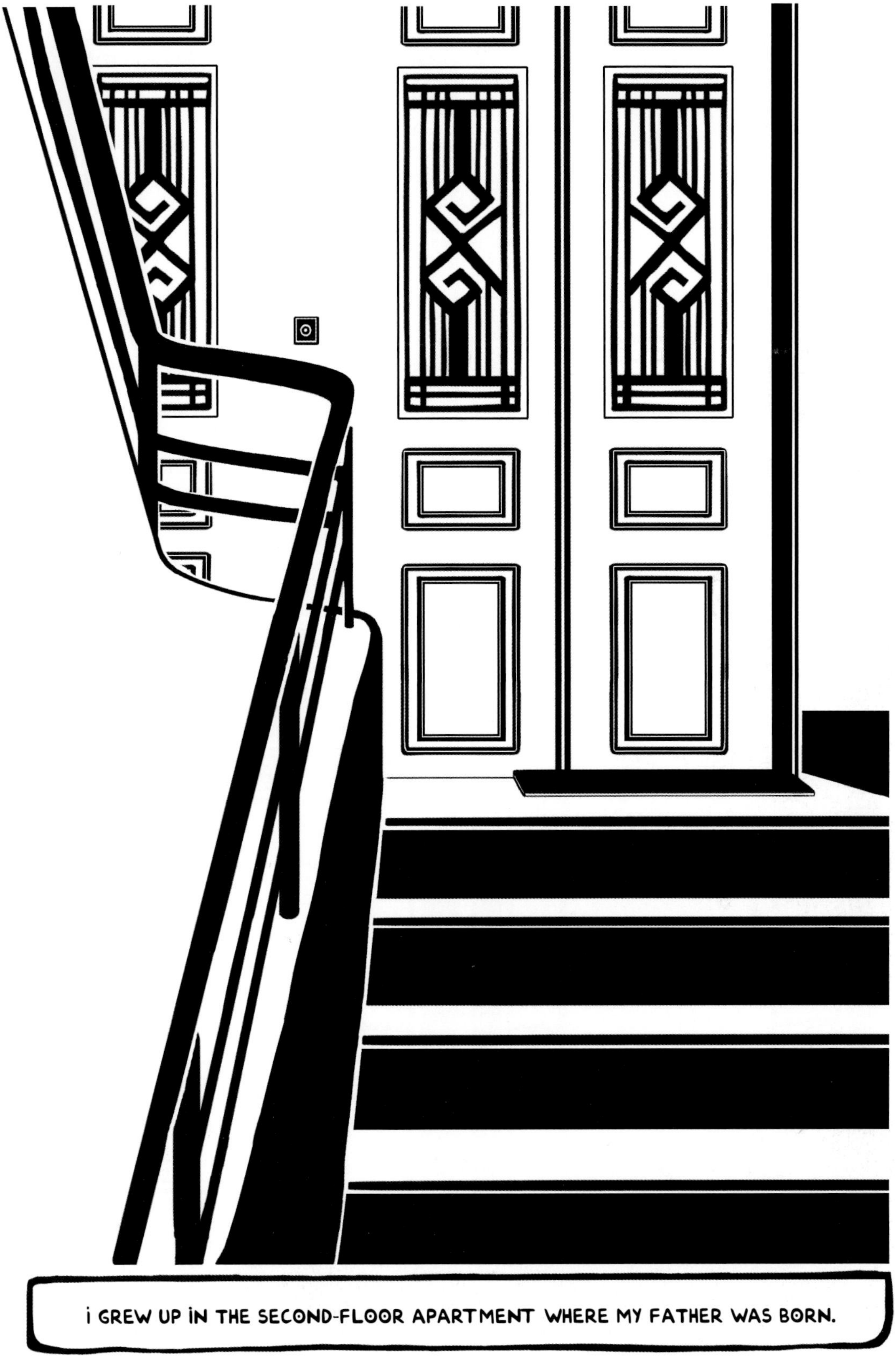
I GREW UP IN THE SECOND-FLOOR APARTMENT WHERE MY FATHER WAS BORN.

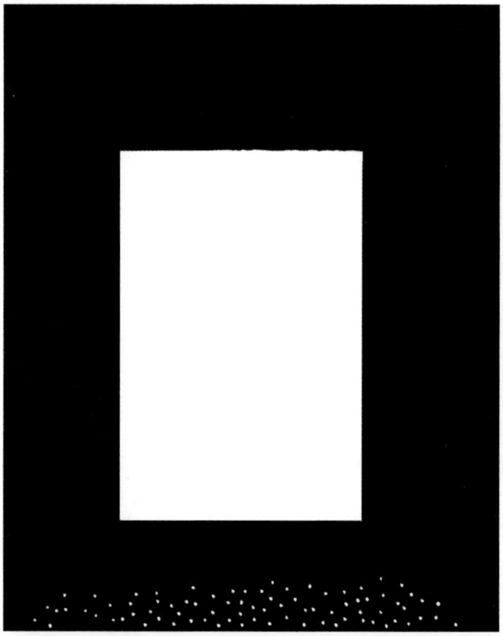

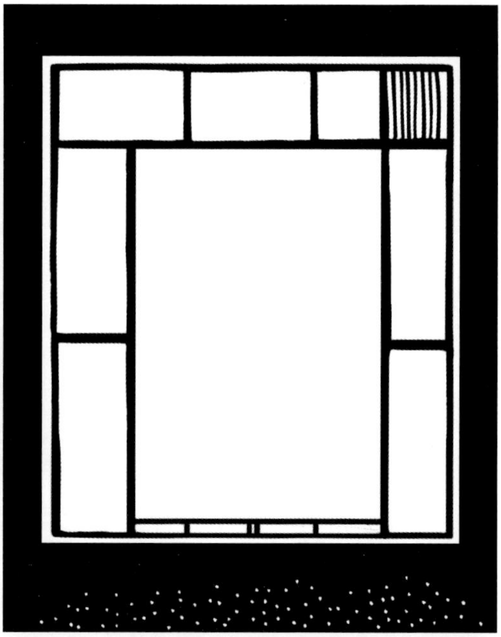

LAID OUT IN THE STYLE OF THE TIME, THE APARTMENT WAS ORGANIZED AROUND THE LIVING ROOM, A LARGE RECTANGLE THAT LINKED THE TWO MAIN PARTS OF OUR HOME.

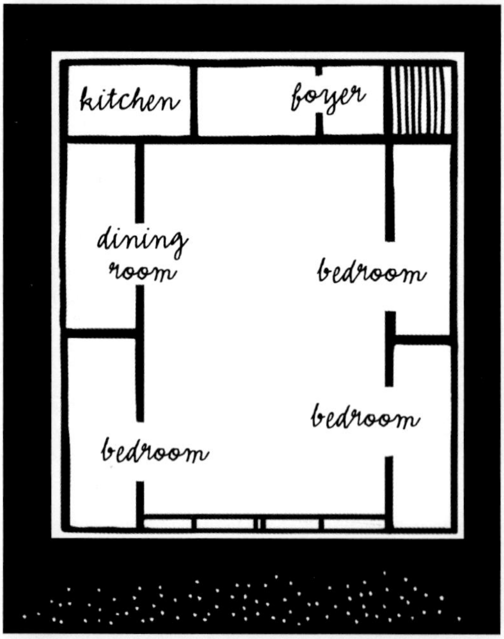
kitchen
foyer
dining room
bedroom
bedroom
bedroom

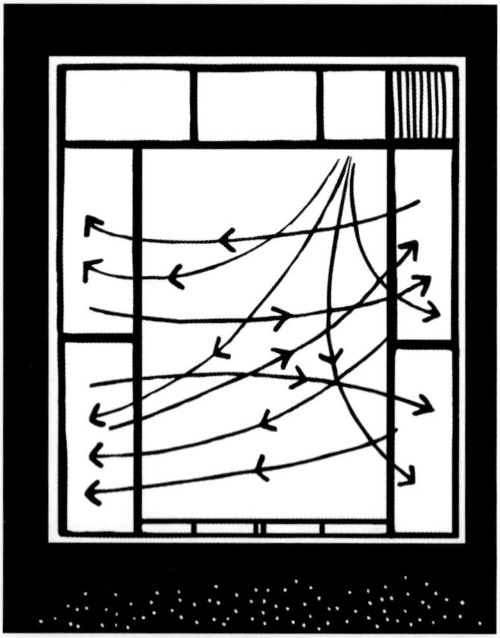

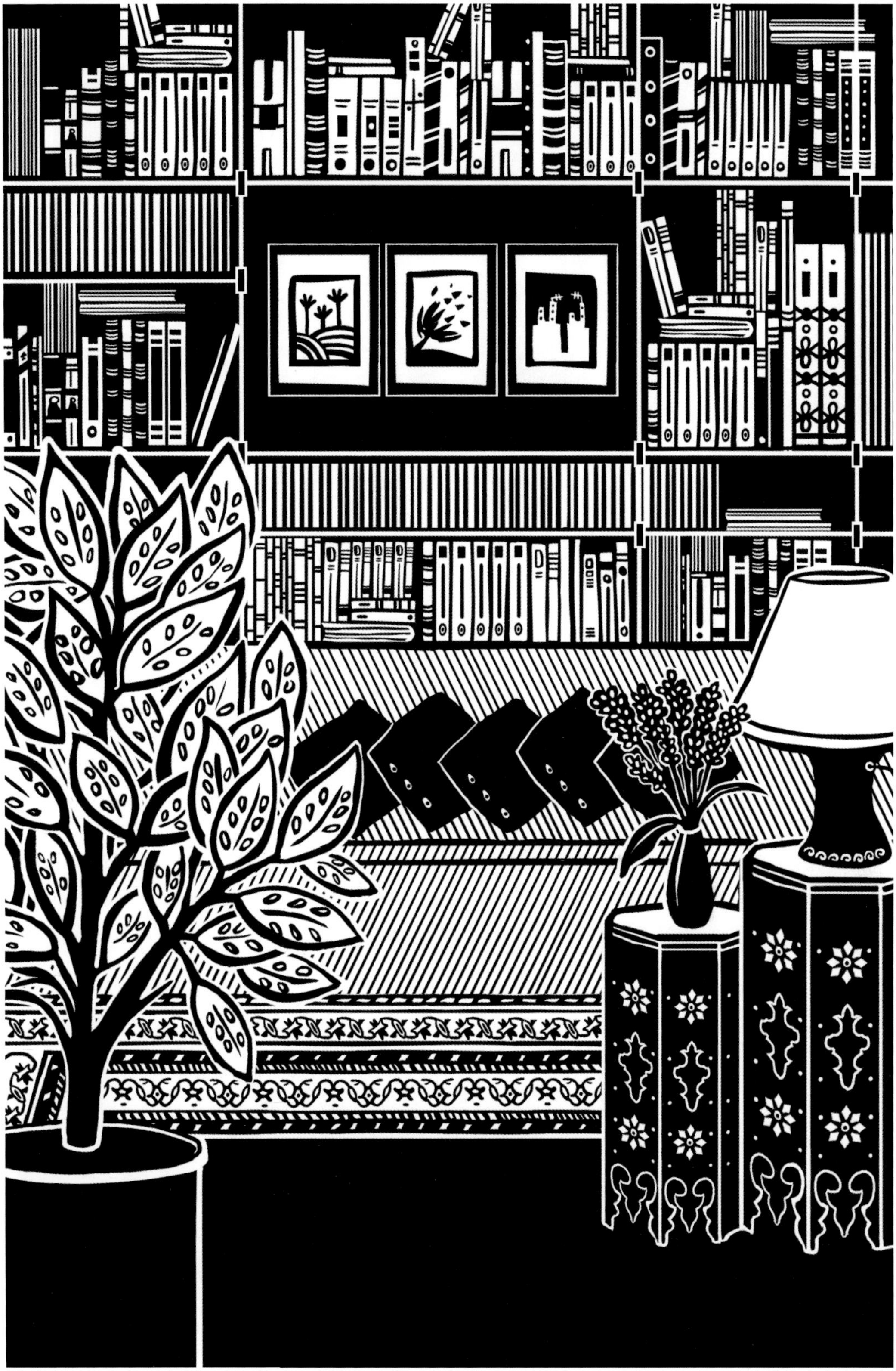

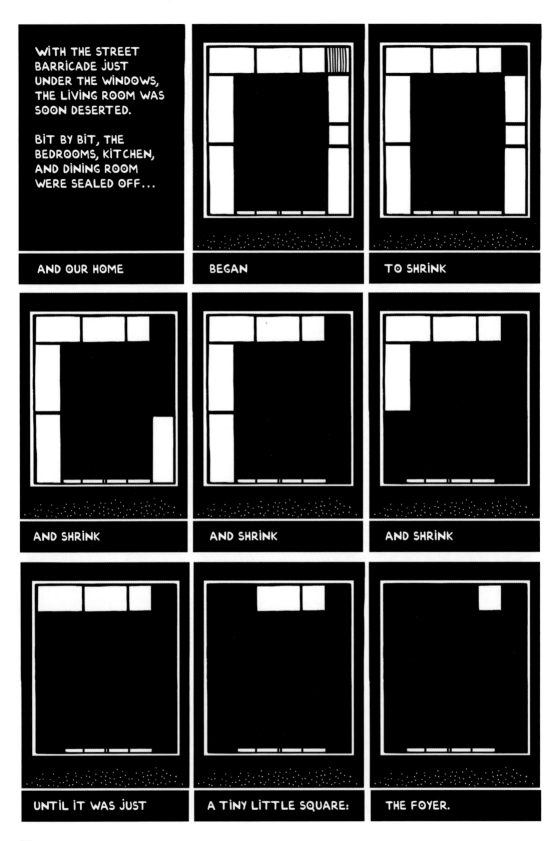

WITH THE STREET BARRICADE JUST UNDER THE WINDOWS, THE LIVING ROOM WAS SOON DESERTED.

BIT BY BIT, THE BEDROOMS, KITCHEN, AND DINING ROOM WERE SEALED OFF...

AND OUR HOME

BEGAN

TO SHRINK

AND SHRINK

AND SHRINK

AND SHRINK

UNTIL IT WAS JUST

A TINY LITTLE SQUARE:

THE FOYER.

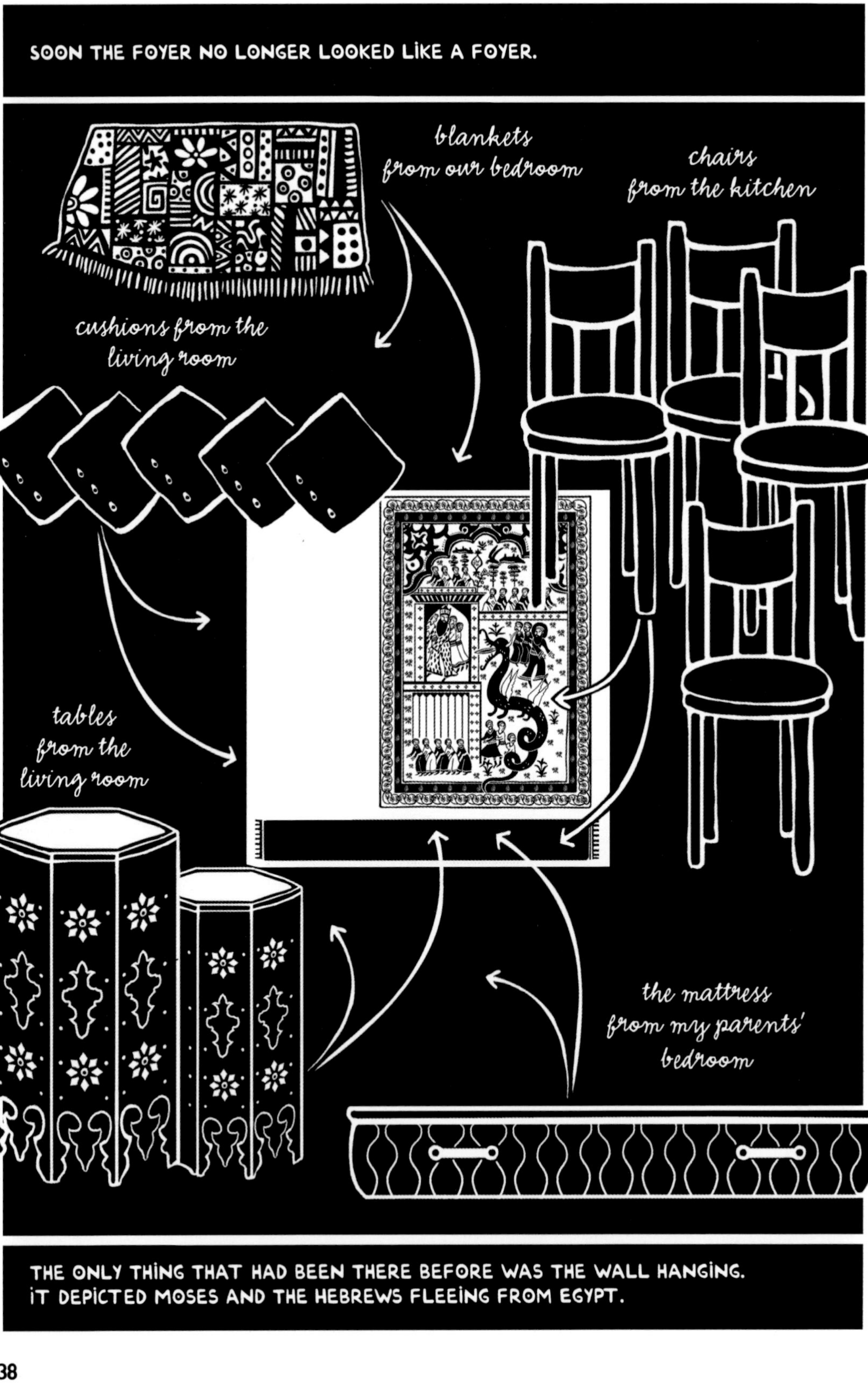
SOON THE FOYER NO LONGER LOOKED LIKE A FOYER.
blankets from our bedroom
chairs from the kitchen
cushions from the living room
tables from the living room
the mattress from my parents' bedroom
THE ONLY THING THAT HAD BEEN THERE BEFORE WAS THE WALL HANGING. IT DEPICTED MOSES AND THE HEBREWS FLEEING FROM EGYPT.

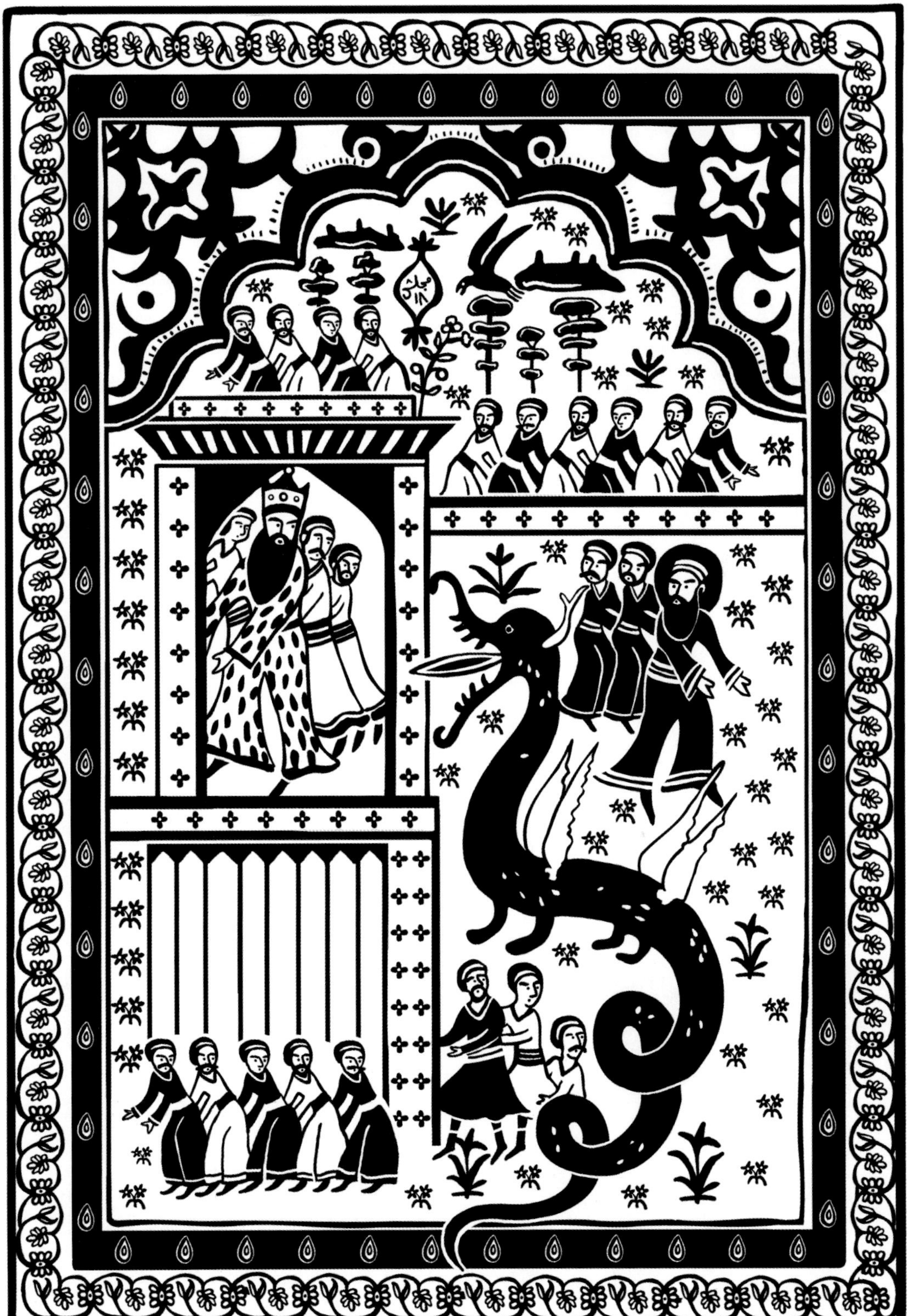

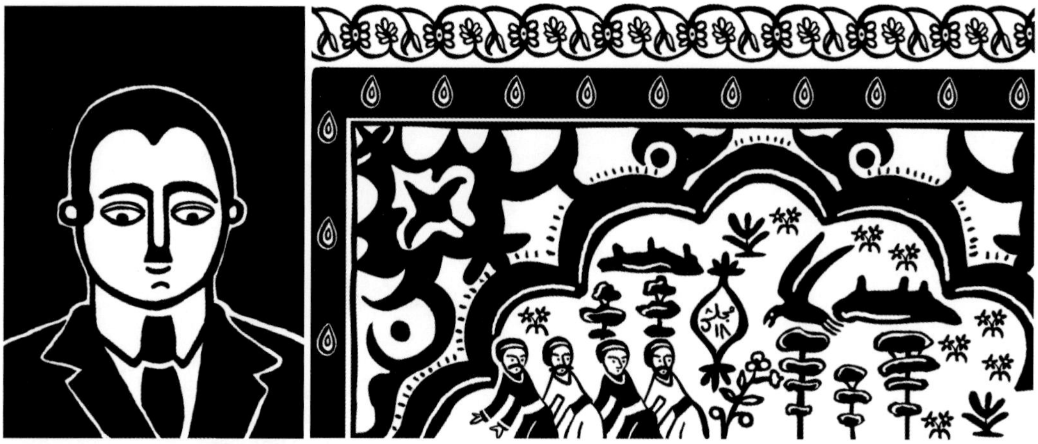

THAT WALL HANGING WAS THE ONLY THING OF MY FATHER'S FATHER LEFT TO US.

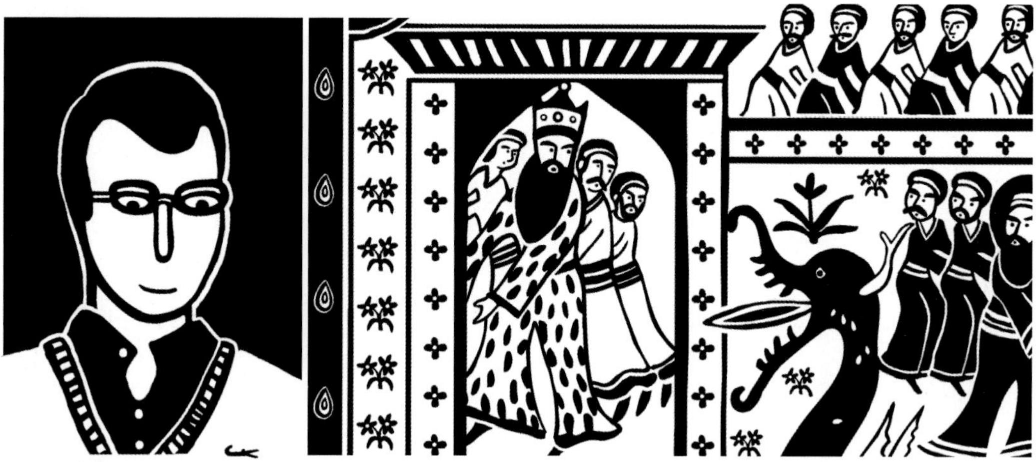

AFTER HIS PARENTS DIED, MY FATHER FOUND IT FOLDED UP IN A BOX IN THE ATTIC.

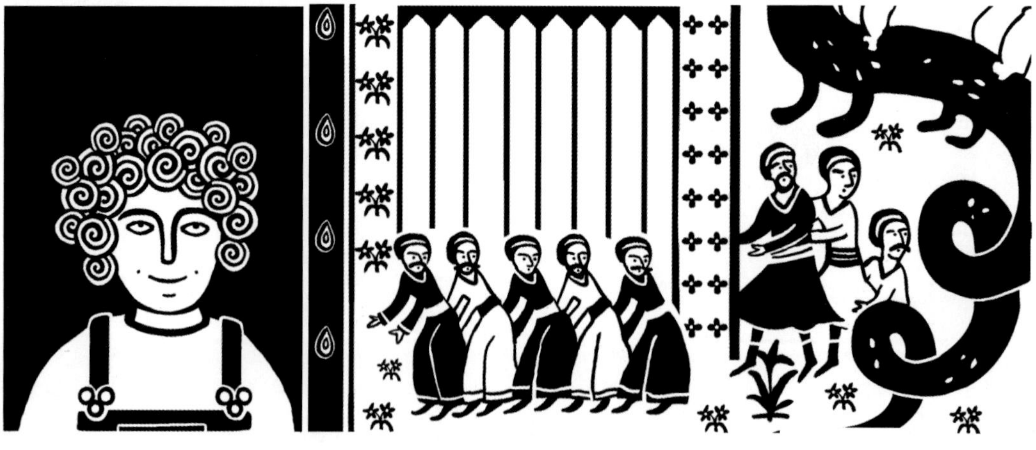

IT WAS ALREADY HANGING IN THE FOYER WHEN I WAS BORN.

I NEVER KNEW MY FATHER'S PARENTS, AND I ALWAYS ASSOCIATED THEM WITH THAT WALL HANGING.
GATHERED TOGETHER IN THE FOYER, WE WERE SAFE.

- HELLO?
- ...
- MOMMMM!
- ...
- YES, EVERYTHING'S FINE. WE'RE TOGETHER, AND ANHALA'S WITH US.
- ...
- NO. NO, I'M NOT AFRAID.
- ...
- ...OF COURSE I'LL WATCH OUT FOR HIM.
- ...
- DO YOU WANT TO TALK TO ANHALA?
- ...
- MOM?
- ...
- WHEN ARE YOU AND POP COMING BACK?

SINCE WE LIVED ON THE SECOND FLOOR, THE FLOOR LEAST EXPOSED TO SHELLING, OUR APARTMENT'S FOYER WAS THE SAFEST ROOM IN THE WHOLE BUILDING... AND OUR NEIGHBORS HAD GOTTEN INTO THE HABIT OF GATHERING THERE EVENINGS WHEN THERE WAS BOMBING.

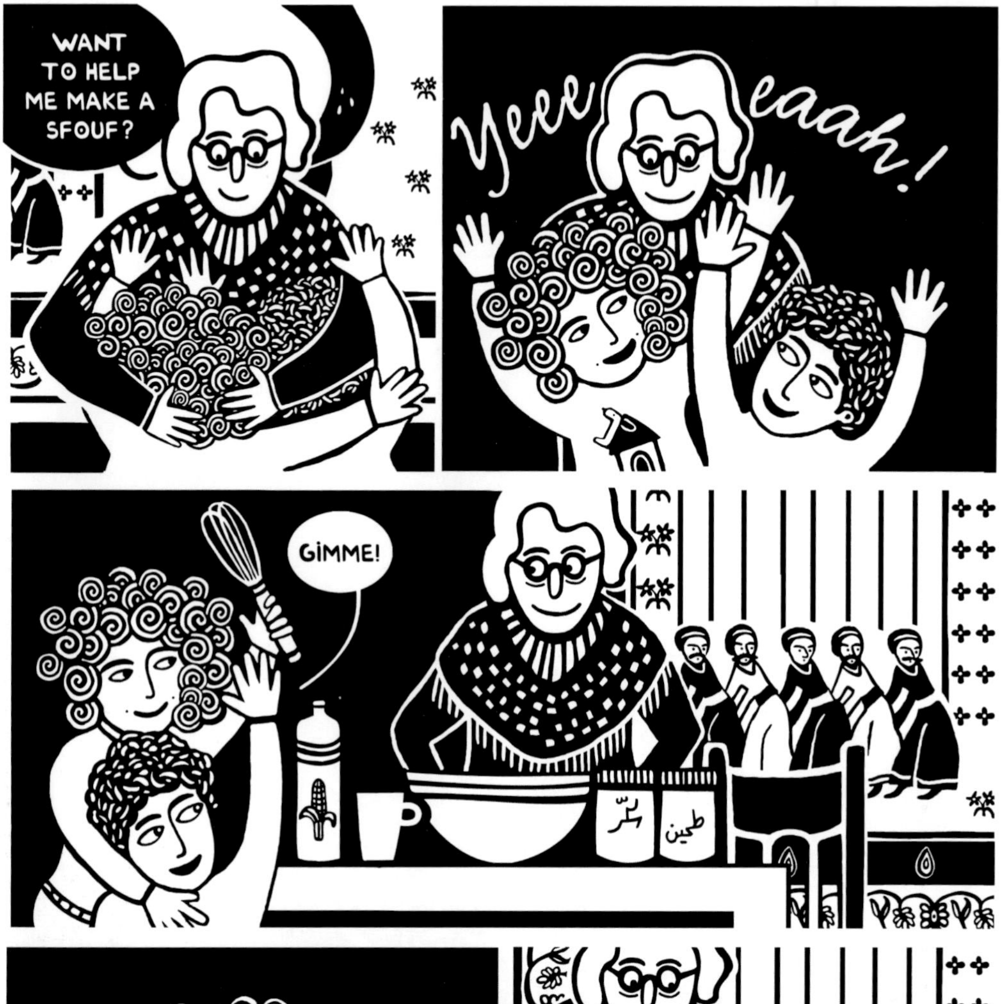
WANT TO HELP ME MAKE A SFOUF?
Yeeeeaah!
GIMME!
طحين
طحين

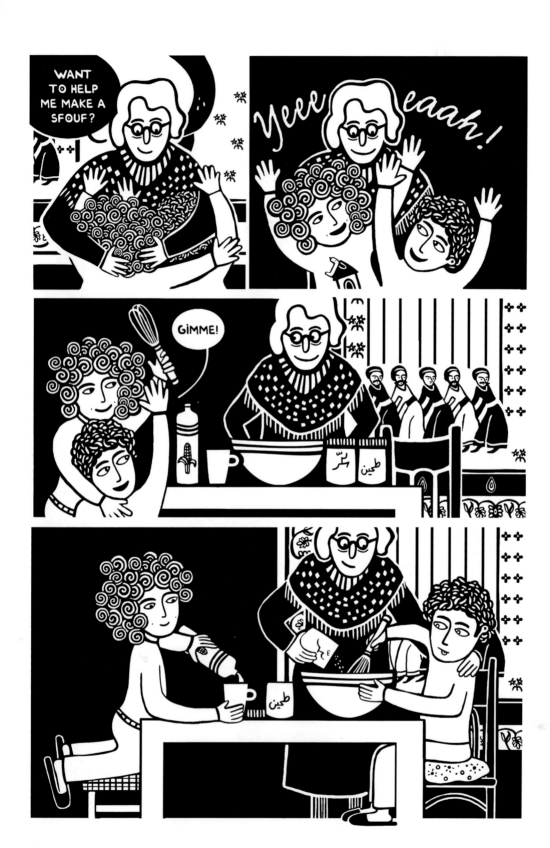

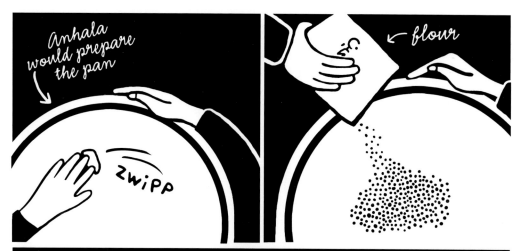

SFOUF WAS ANHALA'S FAVORITE CAKE. IT WAS DEFINITELY THE EASIEST CAKE TO BAKE AT THE TIME. YOU DIDN'T NEED CHOCOLATE OR EGGS. ALL IT TOOK WAS FLOUR, VEGETABLE OIL, SUGAR, AND CURCUMA (TURMERIC), WHICH GAVE IT THAT SPECIAL FLAVOR AND A PRETTY YELLOW COLOR.

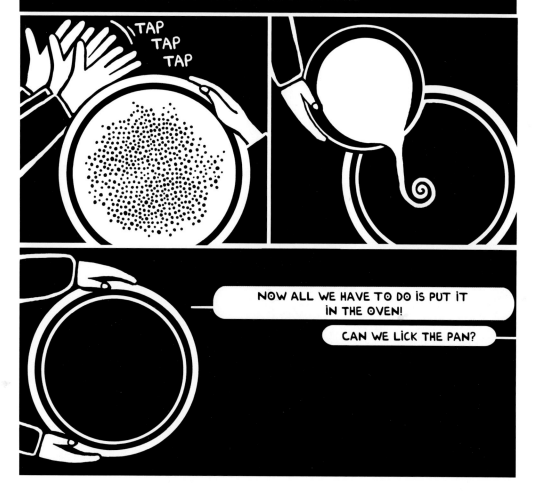

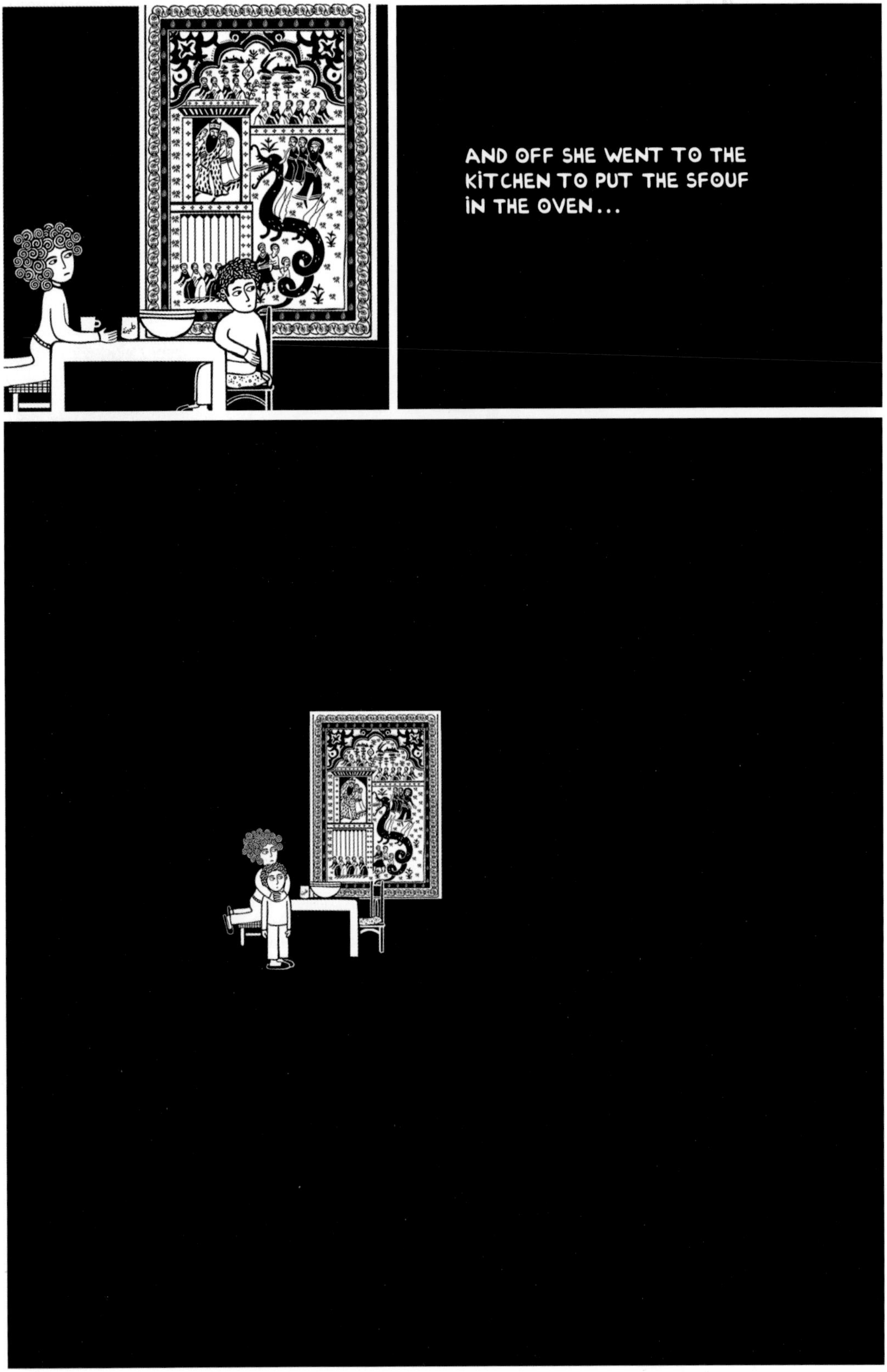
AND OFF SHE WENT TO THE KITCHEN TO PUT THE SFOUF IN THE OVEN...

47

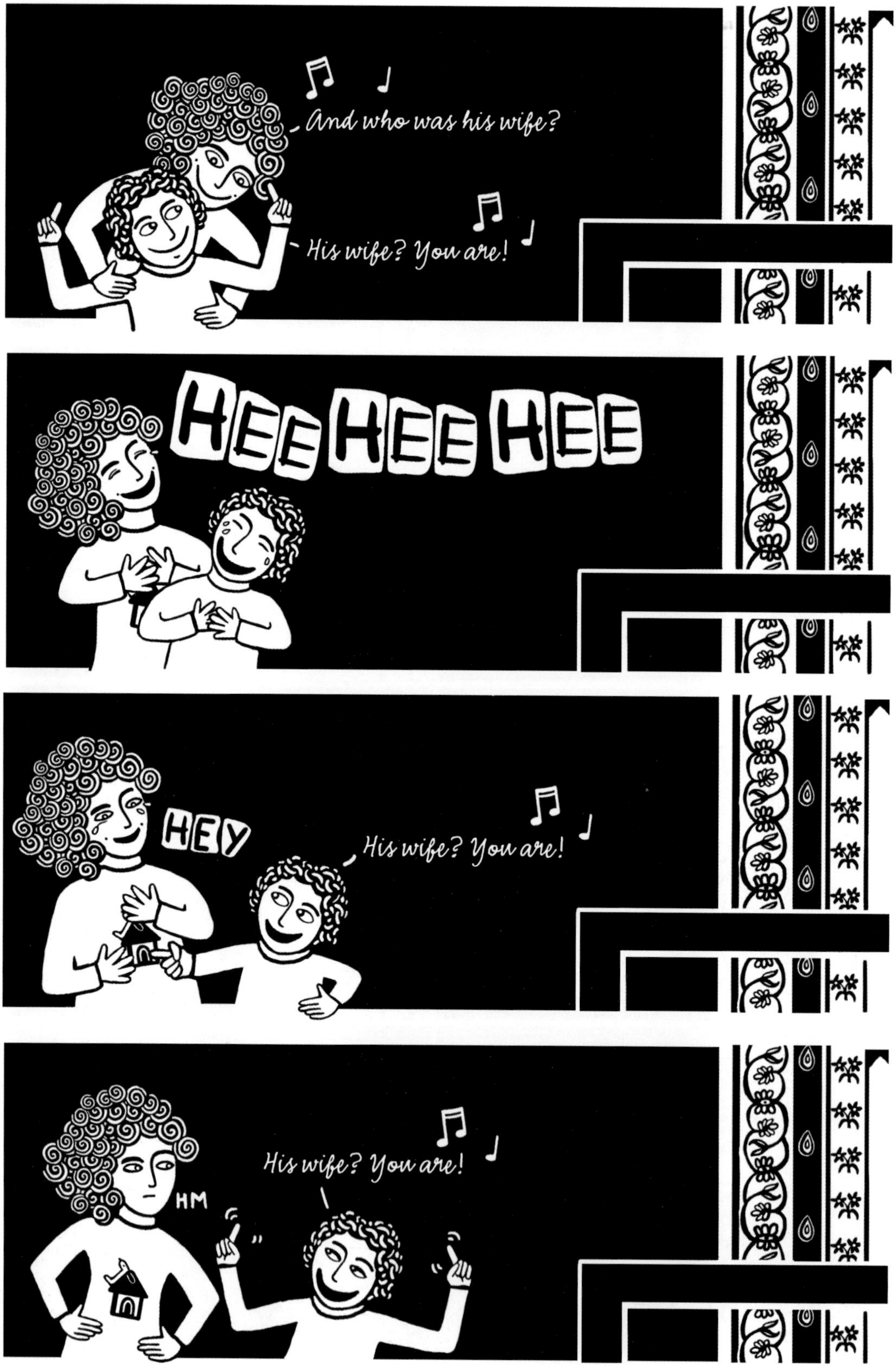
And who was his wife?
His wife? You are!
HEE HEE HEE
HEY
His wife? You are!
HM
His wife? You are!

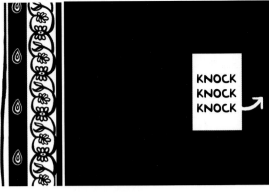

KNOCK
KNOCK
KNOCK

GOOD EVENING, ANHALA. HERE ALREADY?

YES. THE CHILDREN WERE ALL ALONE WHEN IT STARTED.

IT MIGHT BE A LONG NIGHT. I BROUGHT SOME BLANKETS... AND A HEAD OF LETTUCE! FRESHLY WASHED!

WASHED LETTUCE? WHY, THANK YOU, CHUCRI! SET IT OVER THERE AND COME IN!

ROAAAR!

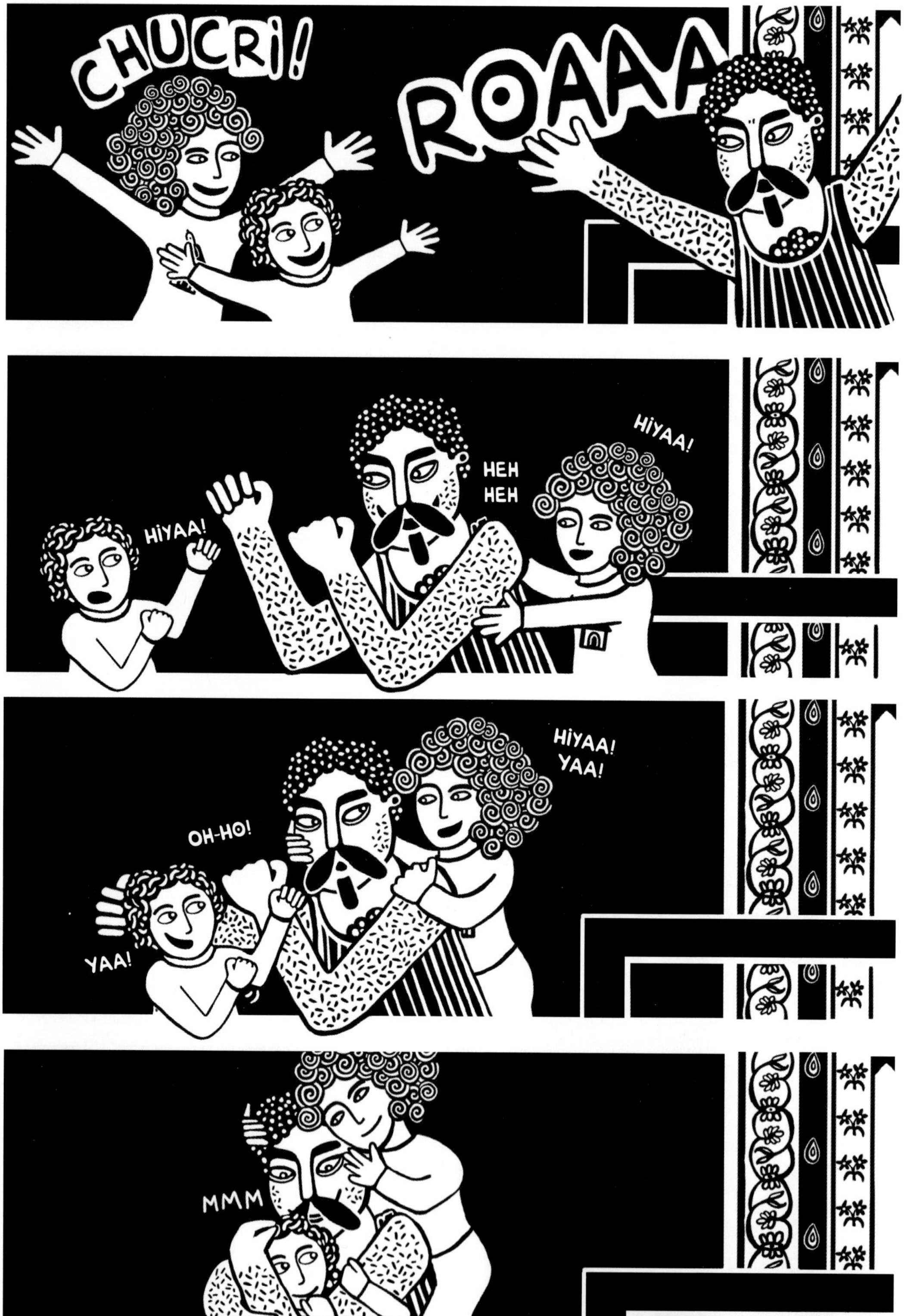
CHUCRI!
ROAAA
HIYAA!
HEH HEH
HIYAA!
HIYAA! YAA!
OH-HO!
YAA!
MMM

I MADE SOME COFFEE.

CHUCRI WAS THE SON OF SALMA, THE BUILDING CARETAKER.

HE WAS 16 WHEN WAR BROKE OUT IN 1975.

A YEAR LATER, HIS FATHER, SAÏD, A TAXI DRIVER, DISAPPEARED.

HE HAD JUST DROPPED A CUSTOMER OFF AT THE CENTRAL BANK, WEST OF THE CITY, AND WAS HEADING HOME.
HE PHONED HIS WIFE TO REASSURE HER BEFORE HITTING THE ROAD. CHUCRI ANSWERED.
"TELL YOUR MOTHER I'M COMING," HIS FATHER SAID.

THE NEXT DAY, SAÏD'S CAR WAS FOUND ABANDONED ON THE SIDE OF THE ROAD, WITHOUT SEATS OR TIRES, ON ONE OF THE ROADS ALLOWING PASSAGE BETWEEN THE EASTERN AND WESTERN PARTS OF THE CITY.
NO ONE EVER FOUND OUT WHAT HAD HAPPENED TO SAÏD.

FROM A YOUNG AGE, CHUCRI HAD TO SCRAMBLE TO SUPPORT HIS MOTHER AND PROVIDE FOR HIS THREE YOUNGER SISTERS.

THE YOUNGEST, JEANETTE, WAS VERY GOOD WITH HER HANDS. TO HELP HIM OUT, SHE DID LITTLE BITS OF SEWING FOR PEOPLE IN THE NEIGHBORHOOD.

CHUCRI STARTED OUT RUNNING LITTLE ERRANDS FOR PEOPLE IN THE BUILDING: CLEARING AWAY BROKEN TILE, PASTING CLEAR PLASTIC SHEETING ON THE WINDOWS, PLUGGING UP SHRAPNEL HOLES IN THE WALLS...

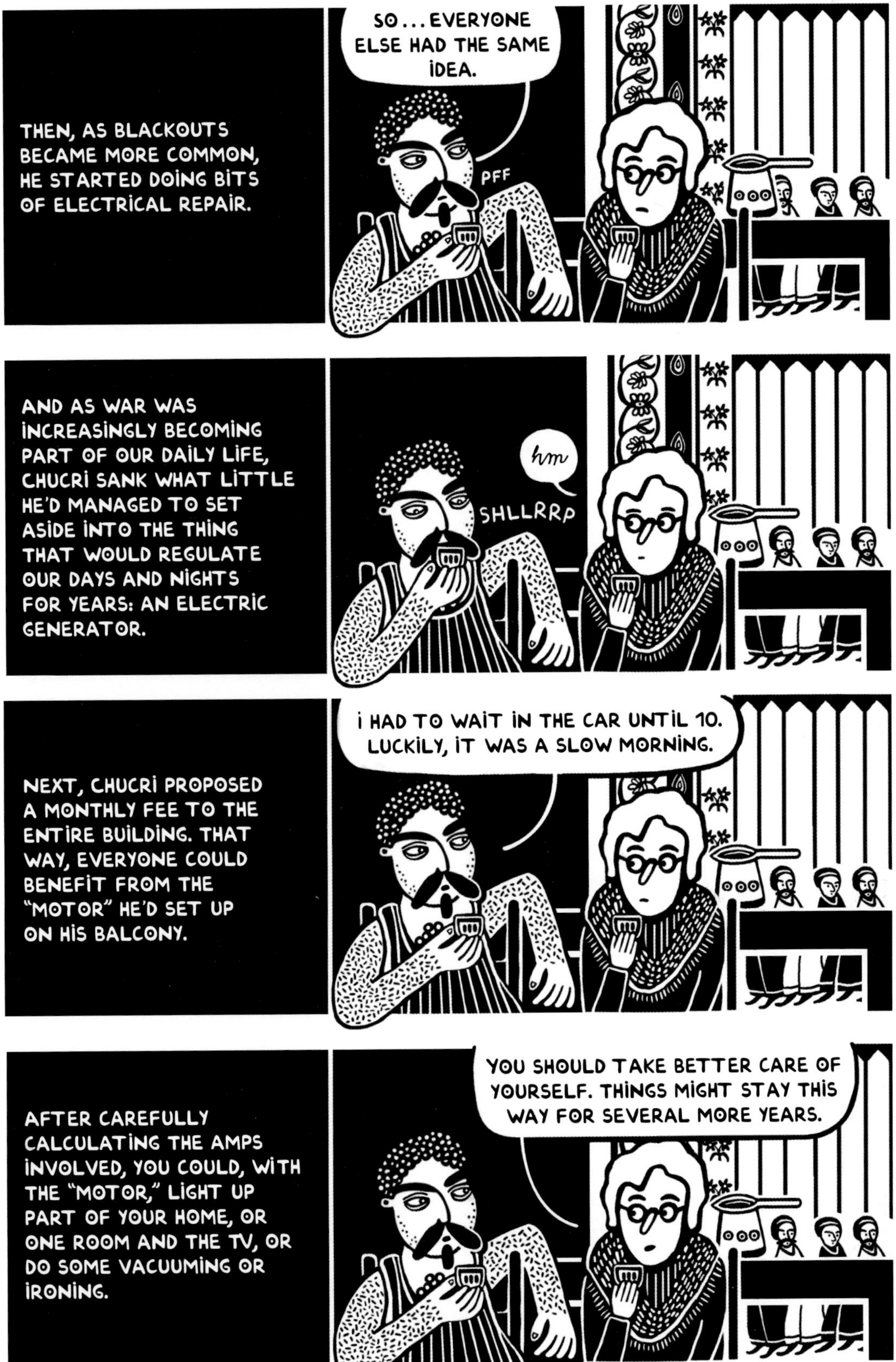
THEN, AS BLACKOUTS BECAME MORE COMMON, HE STARTED DOING BITS OF ELECTRICAL REPAIR.
SO... EVERYONE ELSE HAD THE SAME IDEA.
PFF
AND AS WAR WAS INCREASINGLY BECOMING PART OF OUR DAILY LIFE, CHUCRI SANK WHAT LITTLE HE'D MANAGED TO SET ASIDE INTO THE THING THAT WOULD REGULATE OUR DAYS AND NIGHTS FOR YEARS: AN ELECTRIC GENERATOR.
hm
SHLLRRP
NEXT, CHUCRI PROPOSED A MONTHLY FEE TO THE ENTIRE BUILDING. THAT WAY, EVERYONE COULD BENEFIT FROM THE "MOTOR" HE'D SET UP ON HIS BALCONY.
I HAD TO WAIT IN THE CAR UNTIL 10. LUCKILY, IT WAS A SLOW MORNING.
AFTER CAREFULLY CALCULATING THE AMPS INVOLVED, YOU COULD, WITH THE "MOTOR," LIGHT UP PART OF YOUR HOME, OR ONE ROOM AND THE TV, OR DO SOME VACUUMING OR IRONING.
YOU SHOULD TAKE BETTER CARE OF YOURSELF. THINGS MIGHT STAY THIS WAY FOR SEVERAL MORE YEARS.

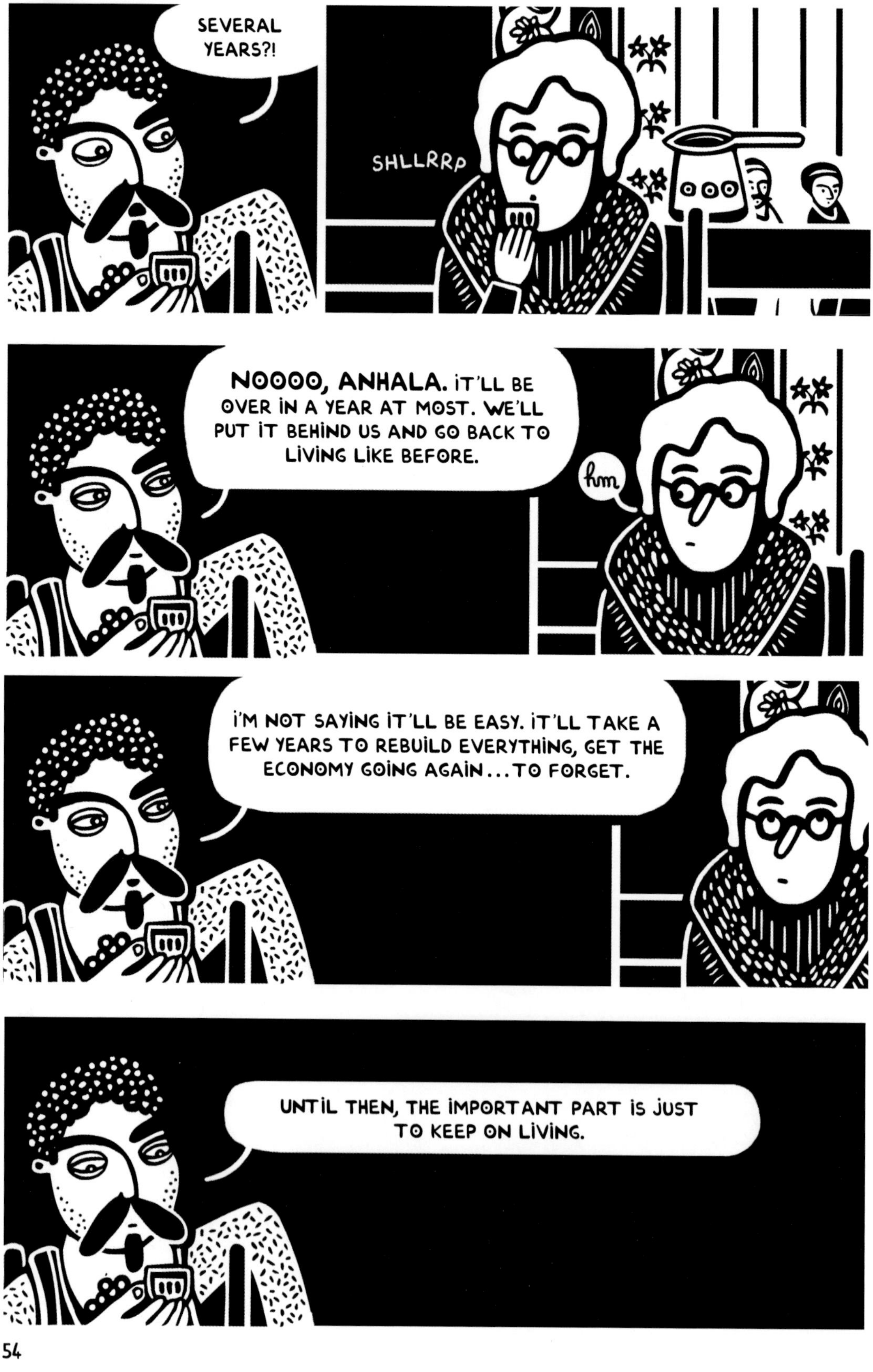
SEVERAL YEARS?!
SHLLRRP
NOOOO, ANHALA. IT'LL BE OVER IN A YEAR AT MOST. WE'LL PUT IT BEHIND US AND GO BACK TO LIVING LIKE BEFORE.
hm
I'M NOT SAYING IT'LL BE EASY. IT'LL TAKE A FEW YEARS TO REBUILD EVERYTHING, GET THE ECONOMY GOING AGAIN... TO FORGET.
UNTIL THEN, THE IMPORTANT PART IS JUST TO KEEP ON LIVING.

BUT IT WON'T BE LONG NOW, THAT'S FOR SURE!

SHLLRRP

OTHERWISE, DO YOU THINK I'D HAVE GONE TO ALL THIS TROUBLE? **NOT AT ALL!** I'D HAVE LEFT THE COUNTRY TOO!

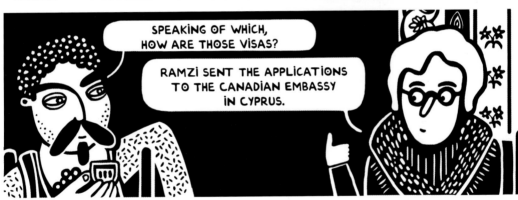

SPEAKING OF WHICH, HOW ARE THOSE VISAS?

RAMZI SENT THE APPLICATIONS TO THE CANADIAN EMBASSY IN CYPRUS.

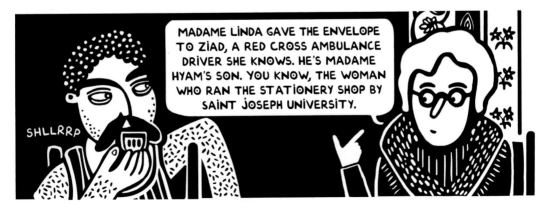

MADAME LINDA GAVE THE ENVELOPE TO ZIAD, A RED CROSS AMBULANCE DRIVER SHE KNOWS. HE'S MADAME HYAM'S SON. YOU KNOW, THE WOMAN WHO RAN THE STATIONERY SHOP BY SAINT JOSEPH UNIVERSITY.

SHLLRRP

55

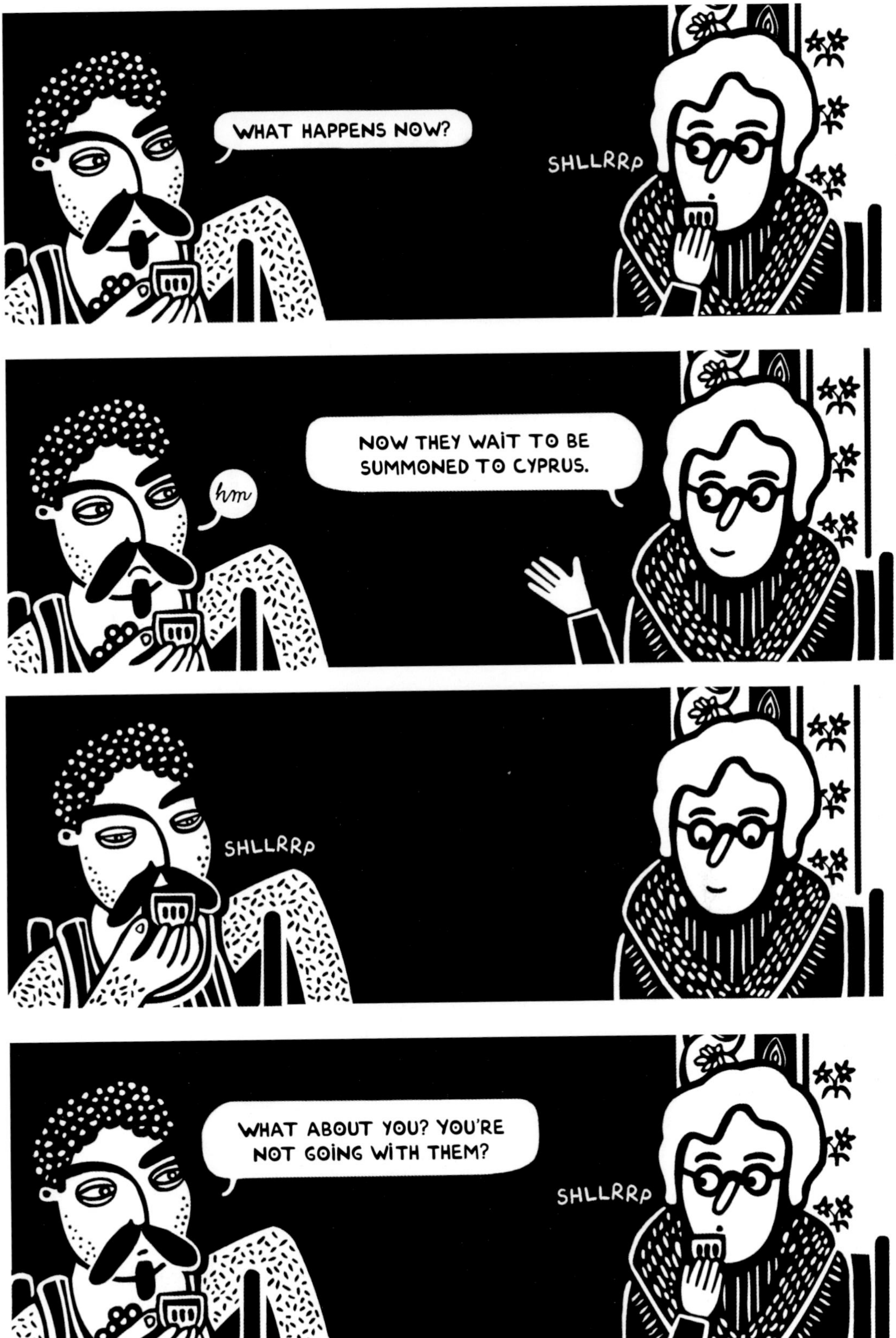
WHAT HAPPENS NOW?
SHLLRRP
NOW THEY WAIT TO BE SUMMONED TO CYPRUS.
hm
SHLLRRP
WHAT ABOUT YOU? YOU'RE NOT GOING WITH THEM?
SHLLRRP

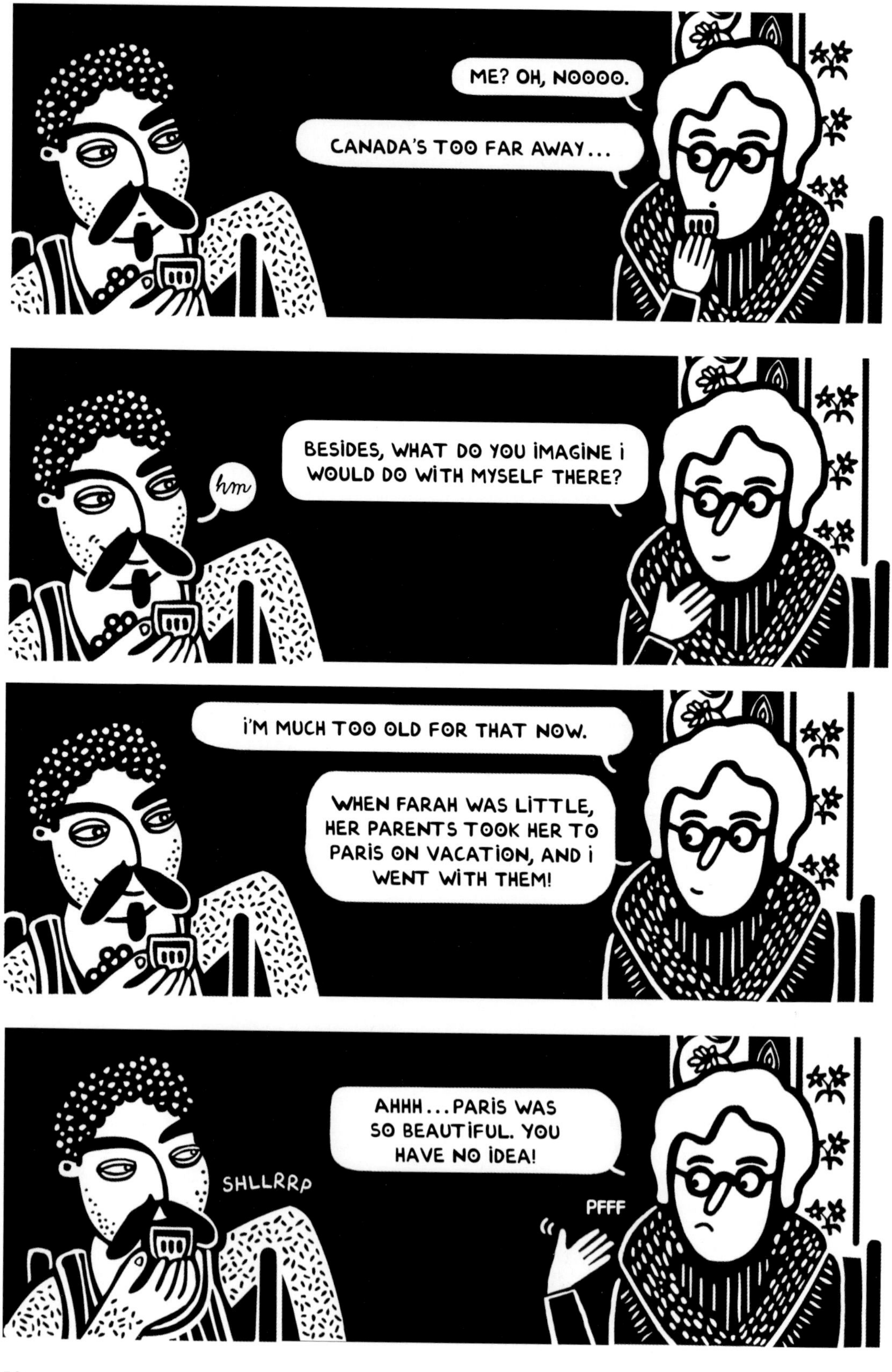

ME? OH, NOOOO.
CANADA'S TOO FAR AWAY...
hm
BESIDES, WHAT DO YOU IMAGINE I WOULD DO WITH MYSELF THERE?
I'M MUCH TOO OLD FOR THAT NOW.
WHEN FARAH WAS LITTLE, HER PARENTS TOOK HER TO PARIS ON VACATION, AND I WENT WITH THEM!
AHHH...PARIS WAS SO BEAUTIFUL. YOU HAVE NO IDEA!
SHLLRRP
PFFF

ANHALA HAD BEEN WITH FARAH'S FAMILY FOR SIXTY-FIVE YEARS.

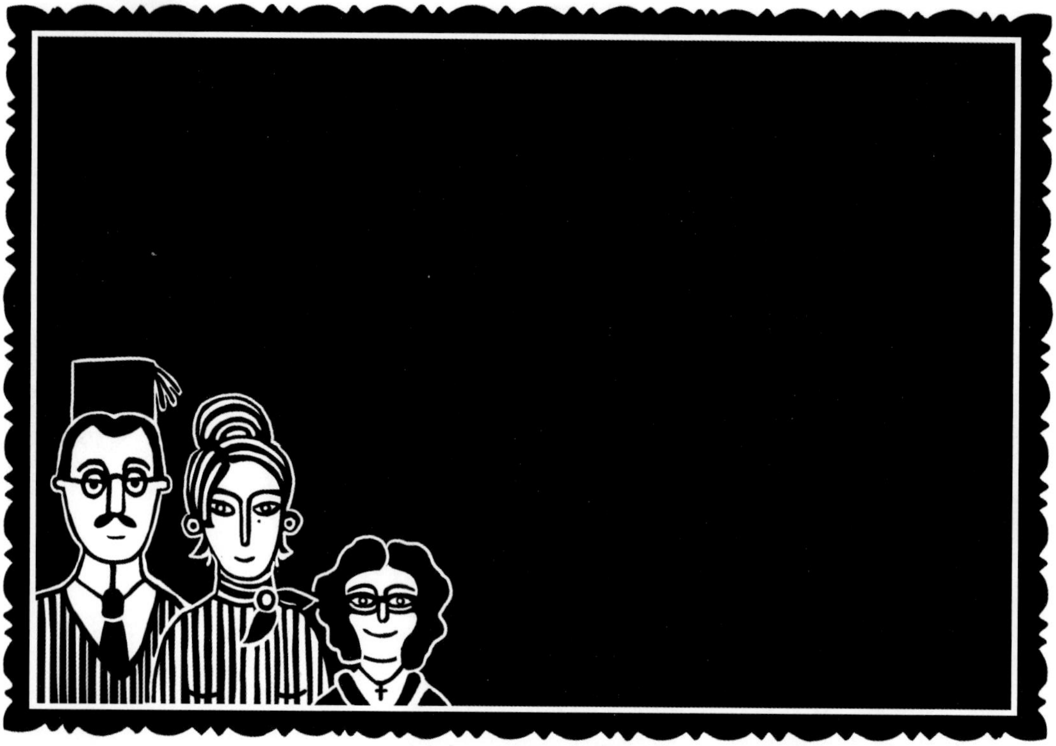

SHE STARTED WORKING AT THE AGE OF 10 FOR FARAH'S GREAT-GRANDPARENTS.

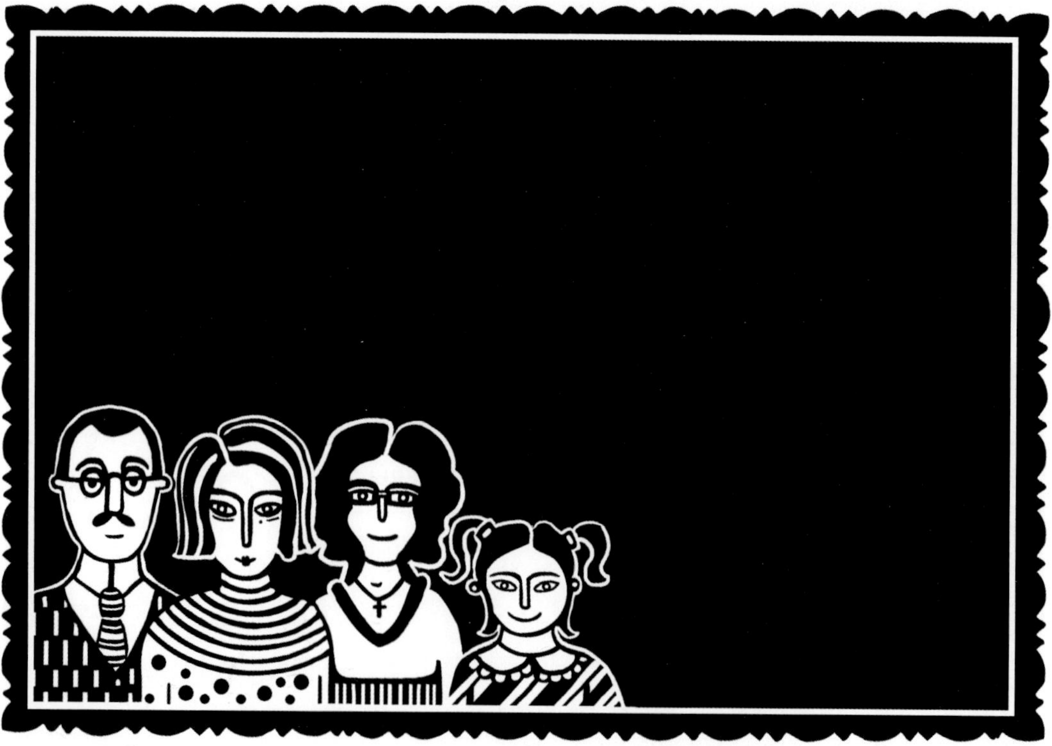

SHE WAS THERE WHEN SONIA, FARAH'S GRANDMOTHER, WAS BORN.

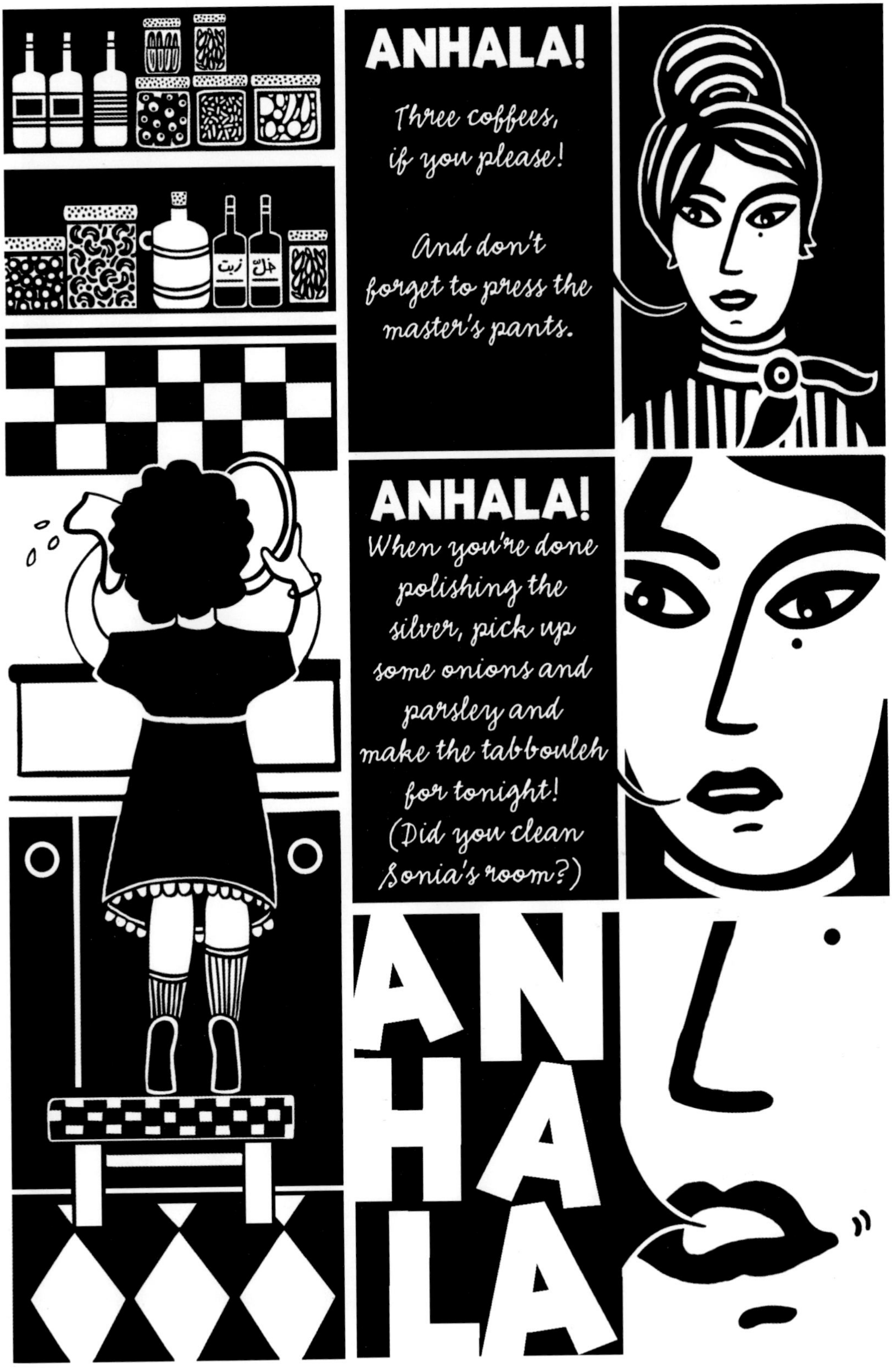

زيت
خل
ANHALA!
Three coffees, if you please!
And don't forget to press the master's pants.
ANHALA!
When you're done polishing the silver, pick up some onions and parsley and make the tabbouleh for tonight! (Did you clean Sonia's room?)
ANHALAHALA

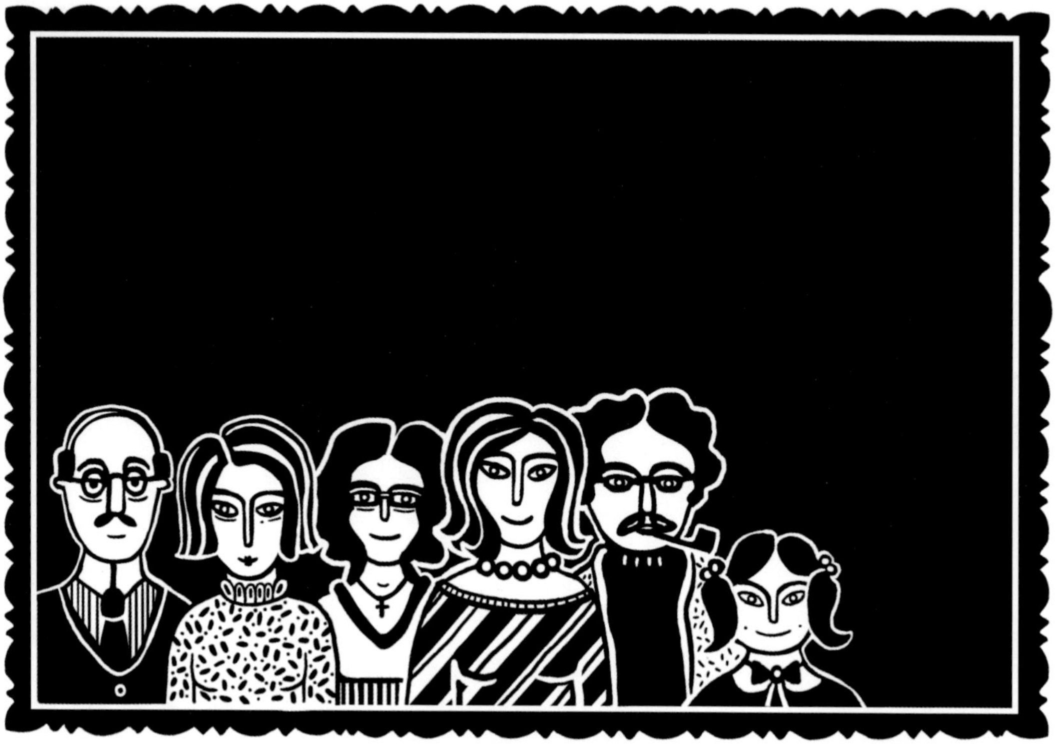

SHE WAS THERE WHEN LENA, FARAH'S MOTHER, WAS BORN.

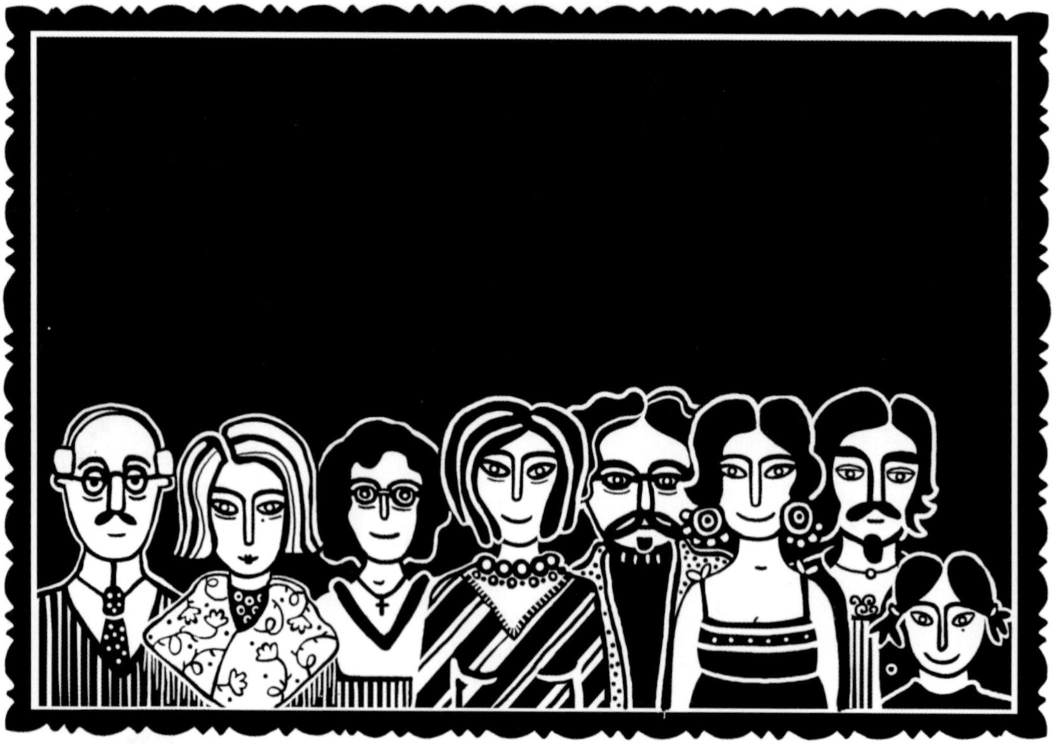

AND WHEN FARAH WAS BORN.

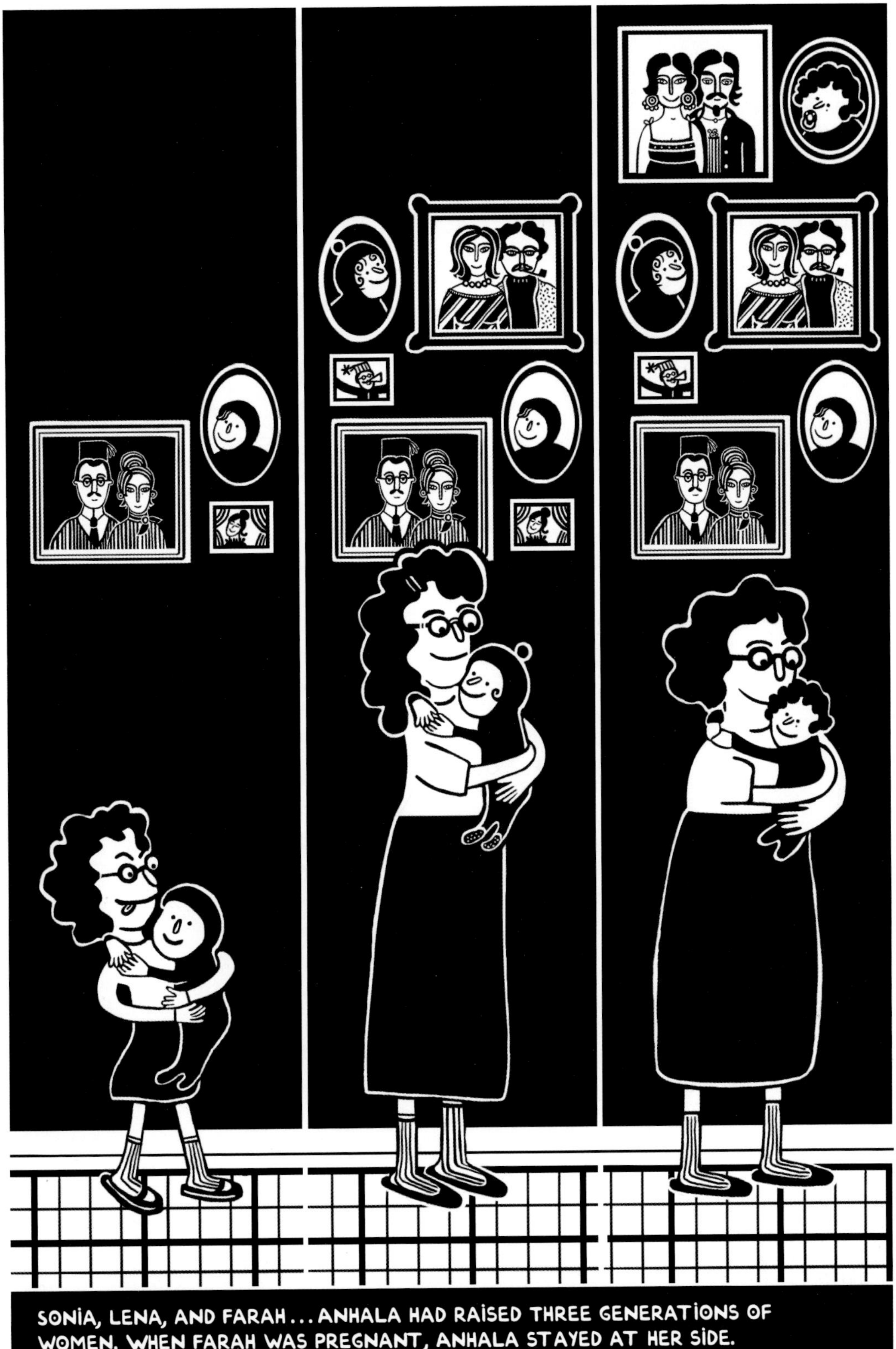
SONIA, LENA, AND FARAH... ANHALA HAD RAISED THREE GENERATIONS OF WOMEN. WHEN FARAH WAS PREGNANT, ANHALA STAYED AT HER SIDE.

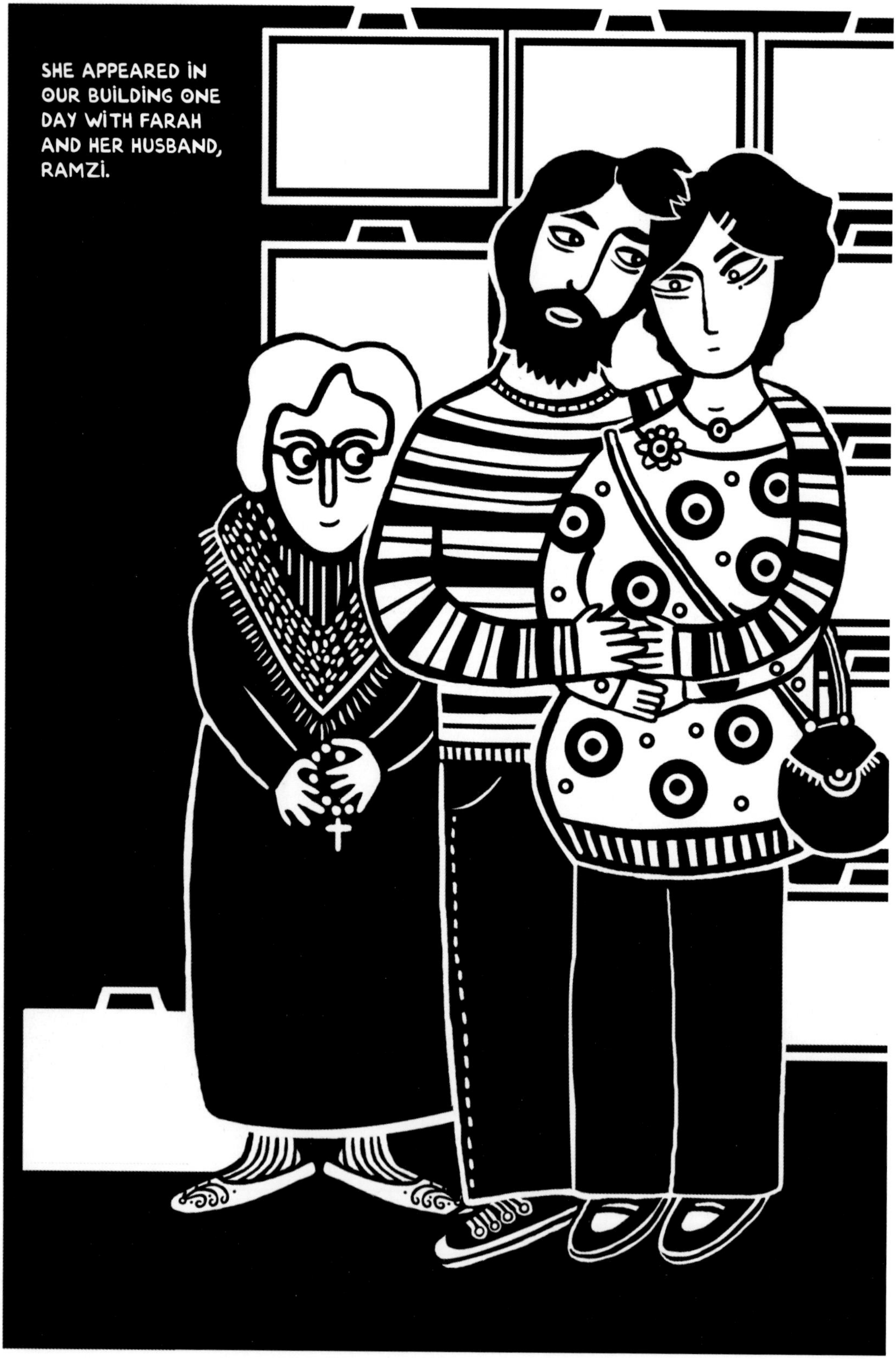
SHE APPEARED IN OUR BUILDING ONE DAY WITH FARAH AND HER HUSBAND, RAMZI.

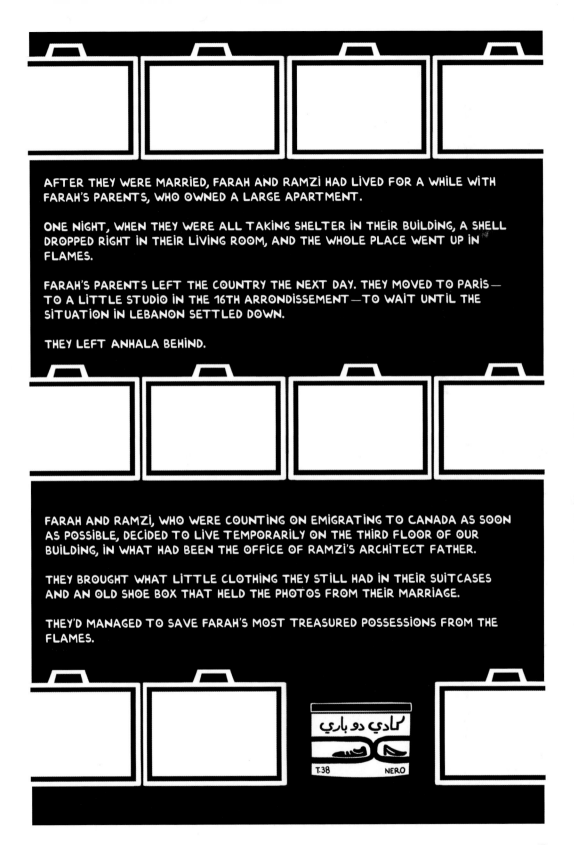

AFTER THEY WERE MARRIED, FARAH AND RAMZI HAD LIVED FOR A WHILE WITH
FARAH'S PARENTS, WHO OWNED A LARGE APARTMENT.

ONE NIGHT, WHEN THEY WERE ALL TAKING SHELTER IN THEIR BUILDING, A SHELL
DROPPED RIGHT IN THEIR LIVING ROOM, AND THE WHOLE PLACE WENT UP IN
FLAMES.

FARAH'S PARENTS LEFT THE COUNTRY THE NEXT DAY. THEY MOVED TO PARIS—
TO A LITTLE STUDIO IN THE 16TH ARRONDISSEMENT—TO WAIT UNTIL THE
SITUATION IN LEBANON SETTLED DOWN.

THEY LEFT ANHALA BEHIND.

FARAH AND RAMZI, WHO WERE COUNTING ON EMIGRATING TO CANADA AS SOON
AS POSSIBLE, DECIDED TO LIVE TEMPORARILY ON THE THIRD FLOOR OF OUR
BUILDING, IN WHAT HAD BEEN THE OFFICE OF RAMZI'S ARCHITECT FATHER.

THEY BROUGHT WHAT LITTLE CLOTHING THEY STILL HAD IN THEIR SUITCASES
AND AN OLD SHOE BOX THAT HELD THE PHOTOS FROM THEIR MARRIAGE.

THEY'D MANAGED TO SAVE FARAH'S MOST TREASURED POSSESSIONS FROM THE
FLAMES.

كادي دو باري

T-38   NERO

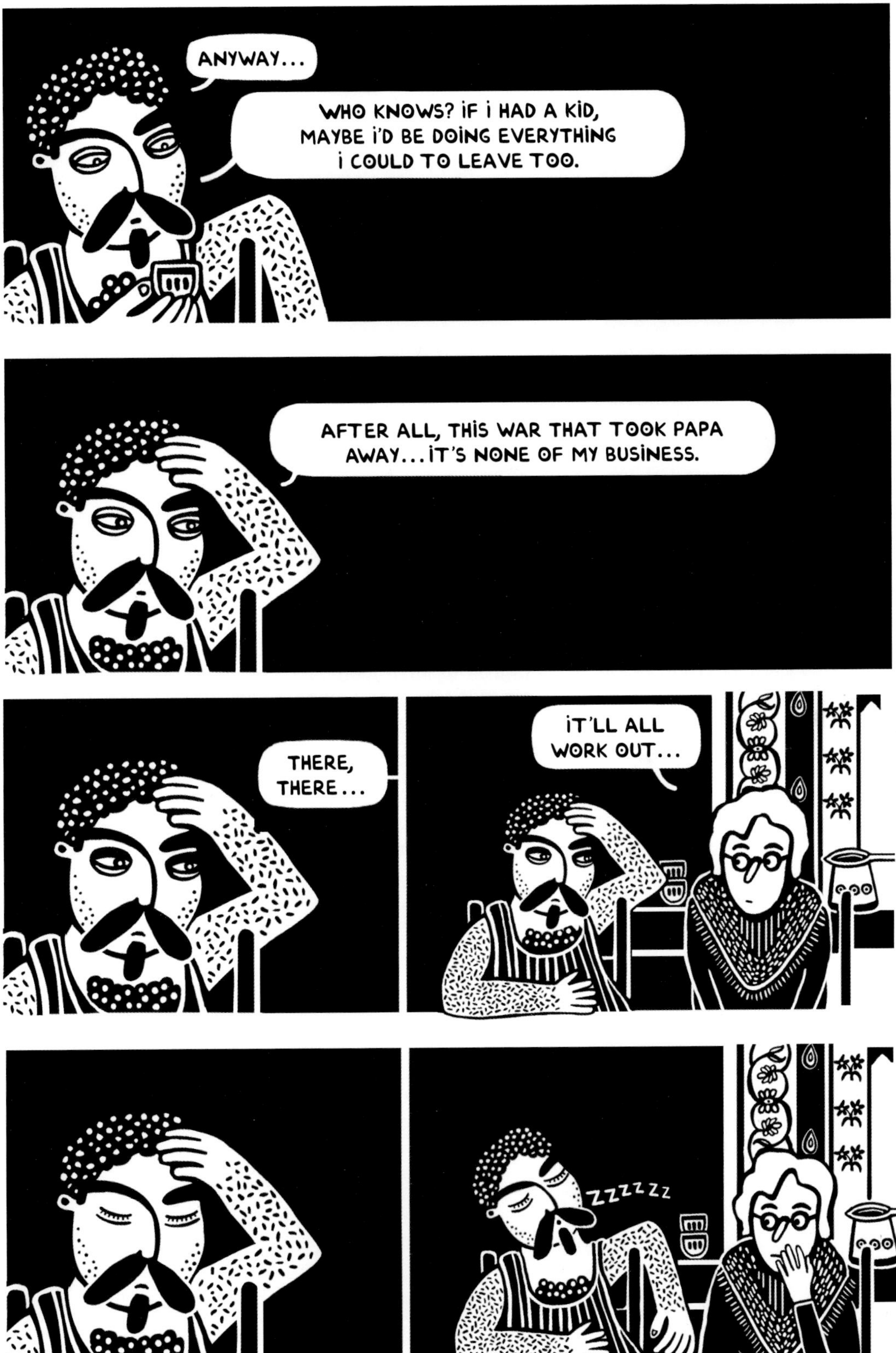
ANYWAY...
WHO KNOWS? IF I HAD A KID, MAYBE I'D BE DOING EVERYTHING I COULD TO LEAVE TOO.
AFTER ALL, THIS WAR THAT TOOK PAPA AWAY... IT'S NONE OF MY BUSINESS.
THERE, THERE...
IT'LL ALL WORK OUT...
ZZZZZZ

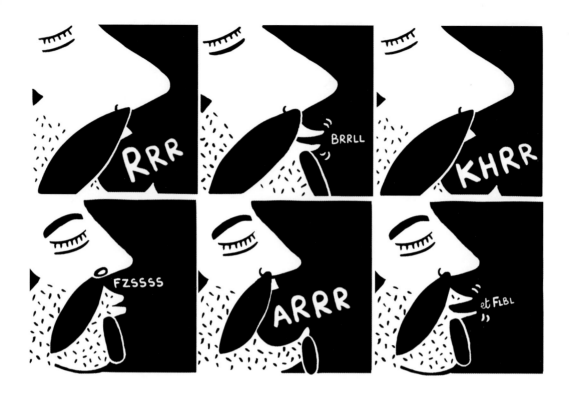

WHEN HIS MOTHER DECIDED TO LEAVE BEIRUT AND TAKE HIS SISTERS TO LIVE WHERE IT WAS CALMER—BACK TO THE VILLAGE WHERE SHE'D GROWN UP ON THE NORTHERN COAST OF LEBANON—CHUCRI GOT HIS FATHER'S CAR OUT OF THE BUILDING'S GARAGE. HE PATCHED IT UP, CLEANED IT OUT, AND PUT A DRIVER'S SEAT BACK IN.

THE LITTLE APARTMENT ON THE GROUND FLOOR WAS MUCH MORE COMFORTABLE NOW WITH ONLY ONE PERSON IN IT, BUT CHUCRI SPENT MORE TIME IN HIS CAR THAN AT HOME.

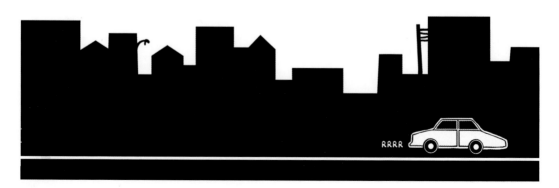

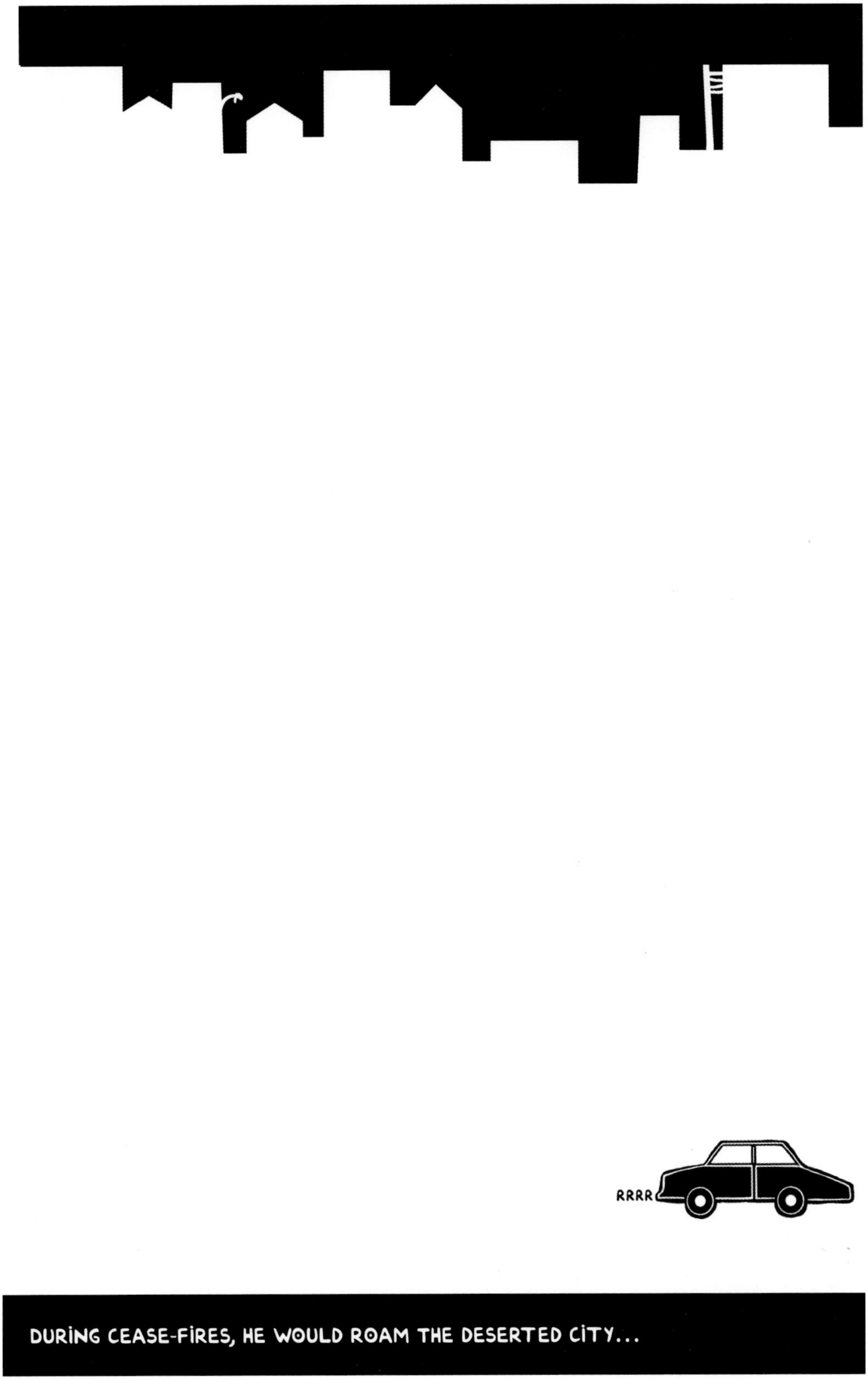
RRRR
DURING CEASE-FIRES, HE WOULD ROAM THE DESERTED CITY...

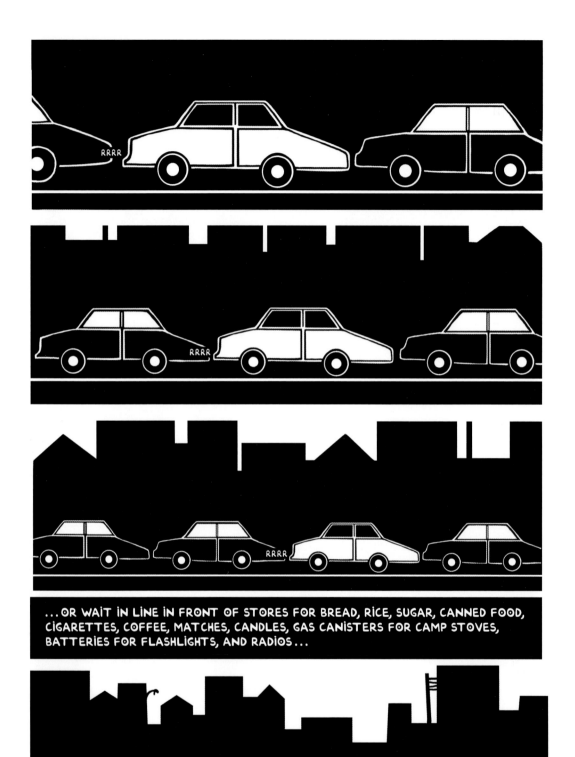

...OR WAIT IN LINE IN FRONT OF STORES FOR BREAD, RICE, SUGAR, CANNED FOOD, CIGARETTES, COFFEE, MATCHES, CANDLES, GAS CANISTERS FOR CAMP STOVES, BATTERIES FOR FLASHLIGHTS, AND RADIOS...

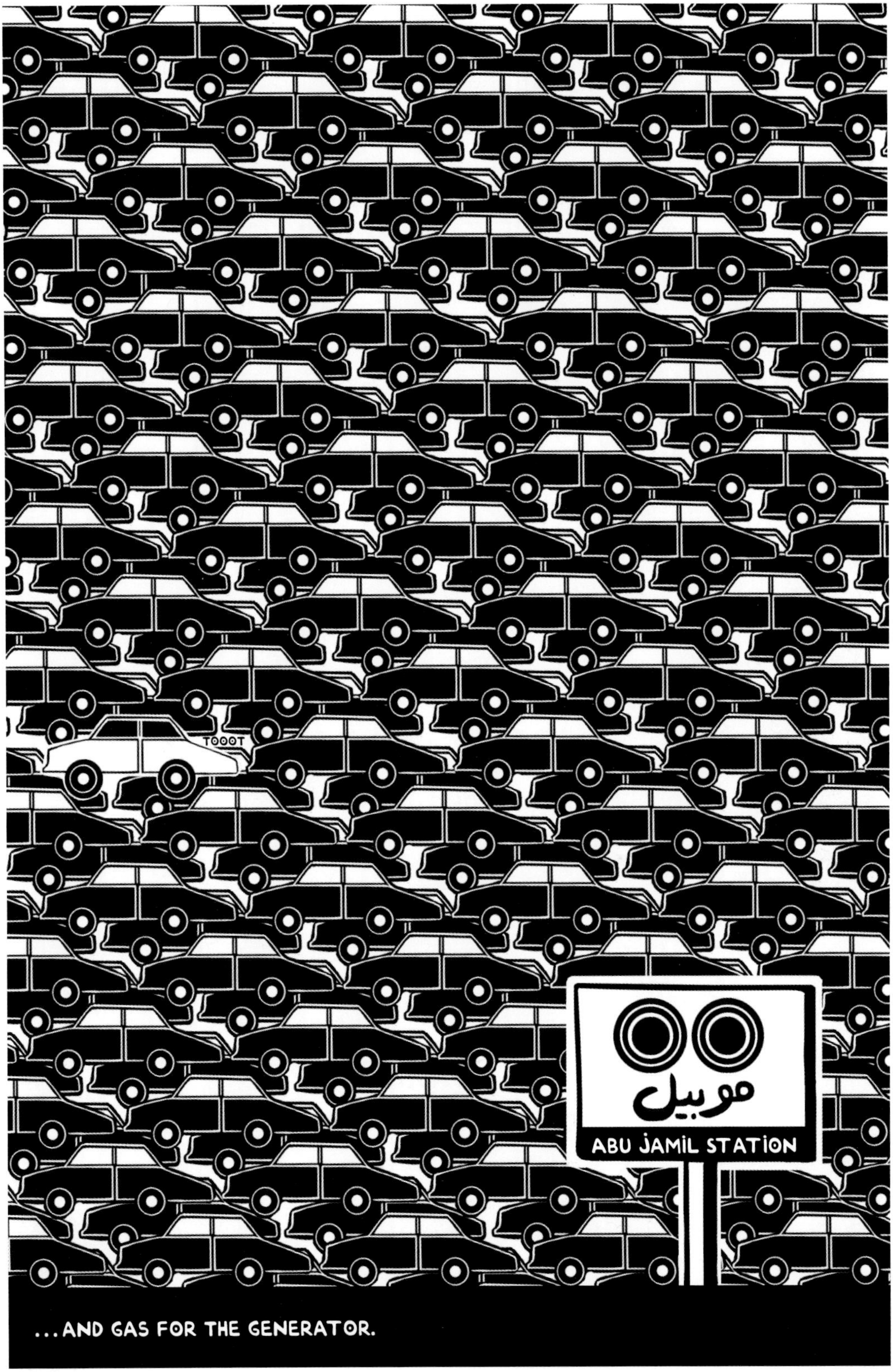
TOOOT
موبيل
ABU JAMIL STATION
...AND GAS FOR THE GENERATOR.

TA-DAA!

AAAH!

ARRR

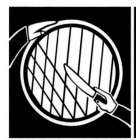

slap

AFTER TAKING THE SFOUF OUT OF THE OVEN, ANHALA CUT IT INTO LITTLE DIAMOND-SHAPED PIECES, AND THE WHOLE FOYER SMELLED LIKE CURCUMA.

WAIT FOR IT TO COOL DOWN A BIT! YOU'LL GIVE YOURSELVES A TUMMY ACHE!

BRRLL?

I'LL START THE MOTOR RUNNING.

YUM!

mmm!

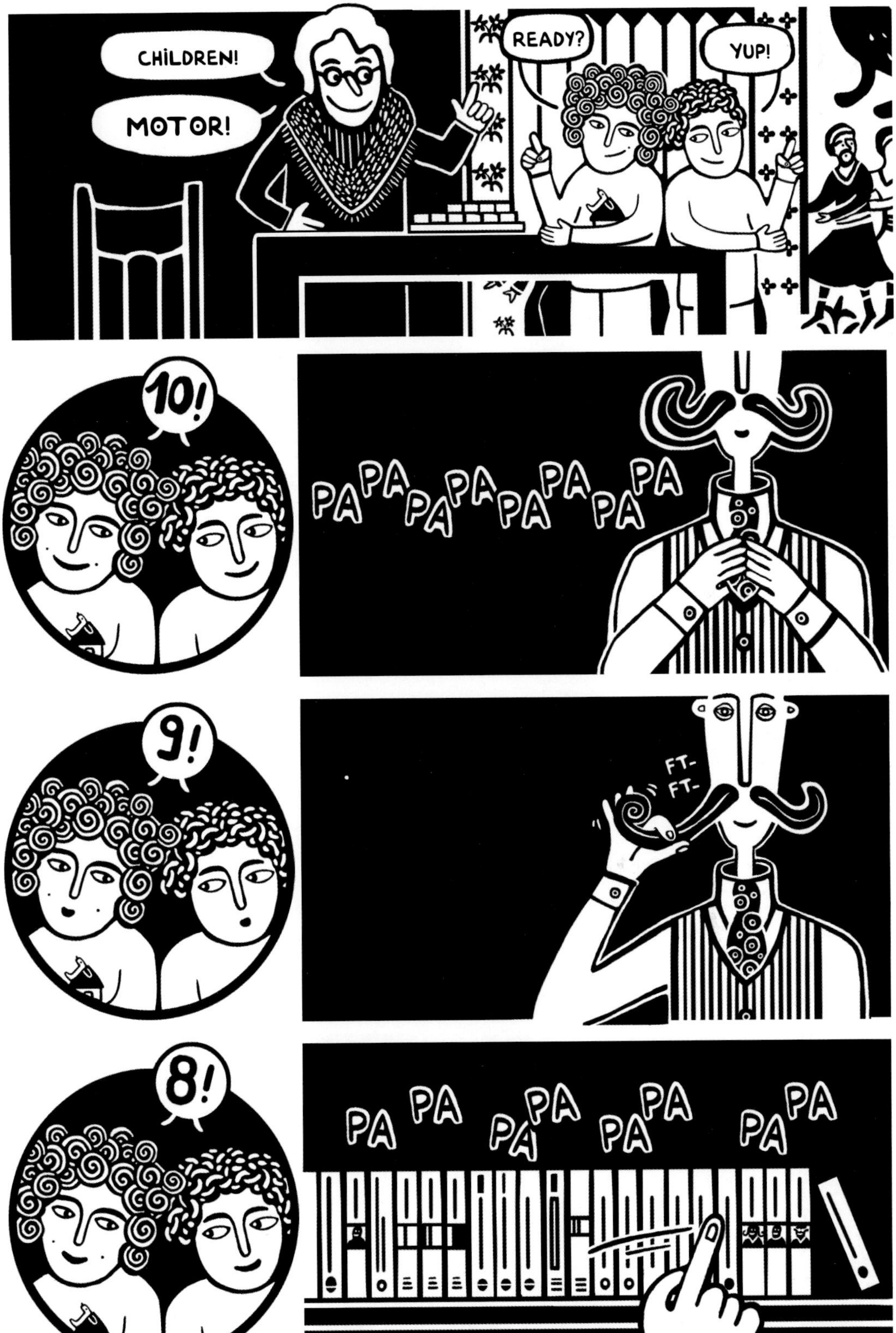
CHILDREN!
MOTOR!
READY?
YUP!
10!
PA PA PA PA PA PA PA PA PA PA
9!
FT-
FT-
8!
PA PA PA PA PA PA PA PA

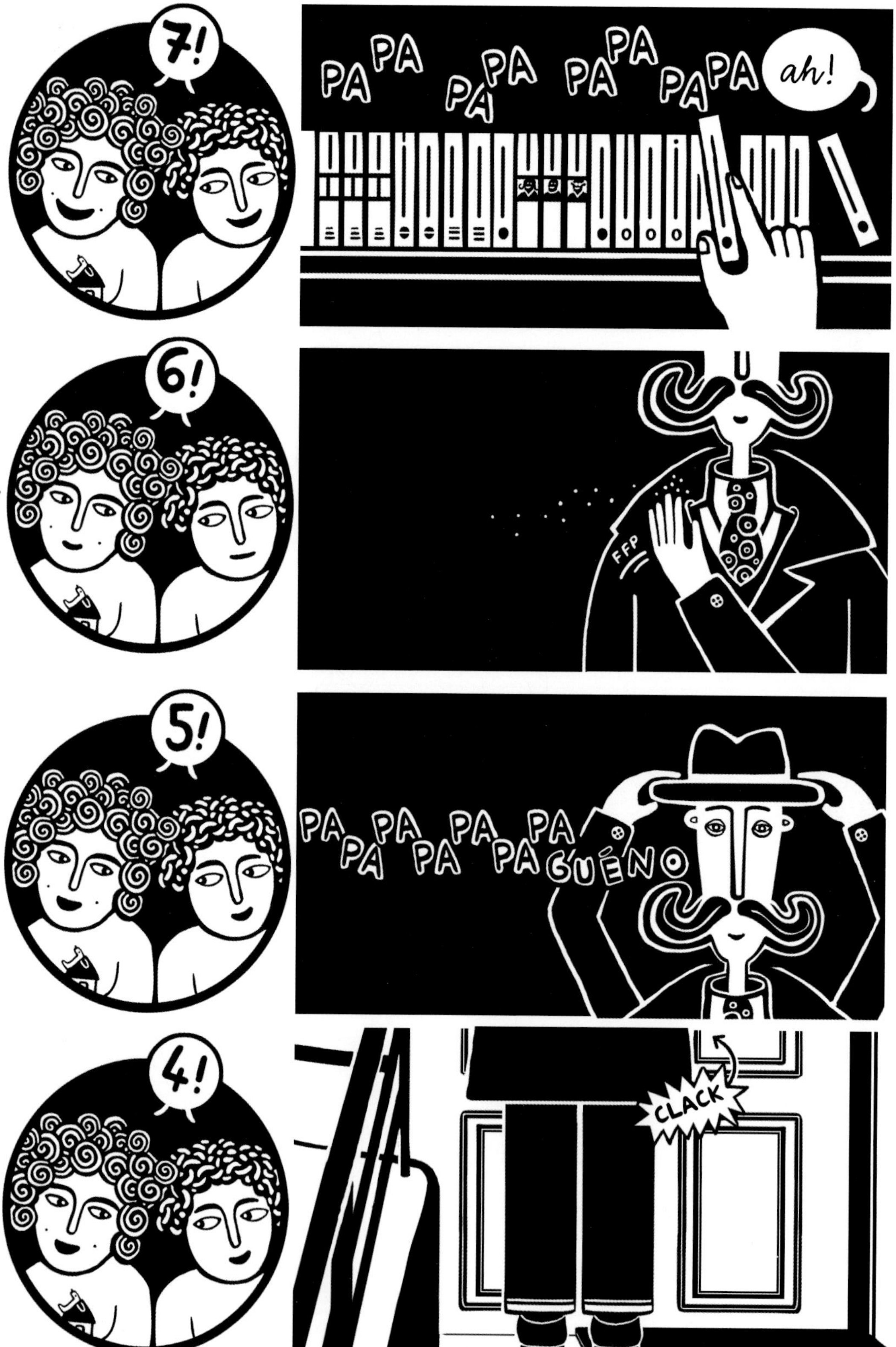
7!
PA PA PA PA PA PA PA PA
ah!
6!
FFP
5!
PA PA PA PA PA PA PA PA PA PA GUÉNO
4!
CLACK

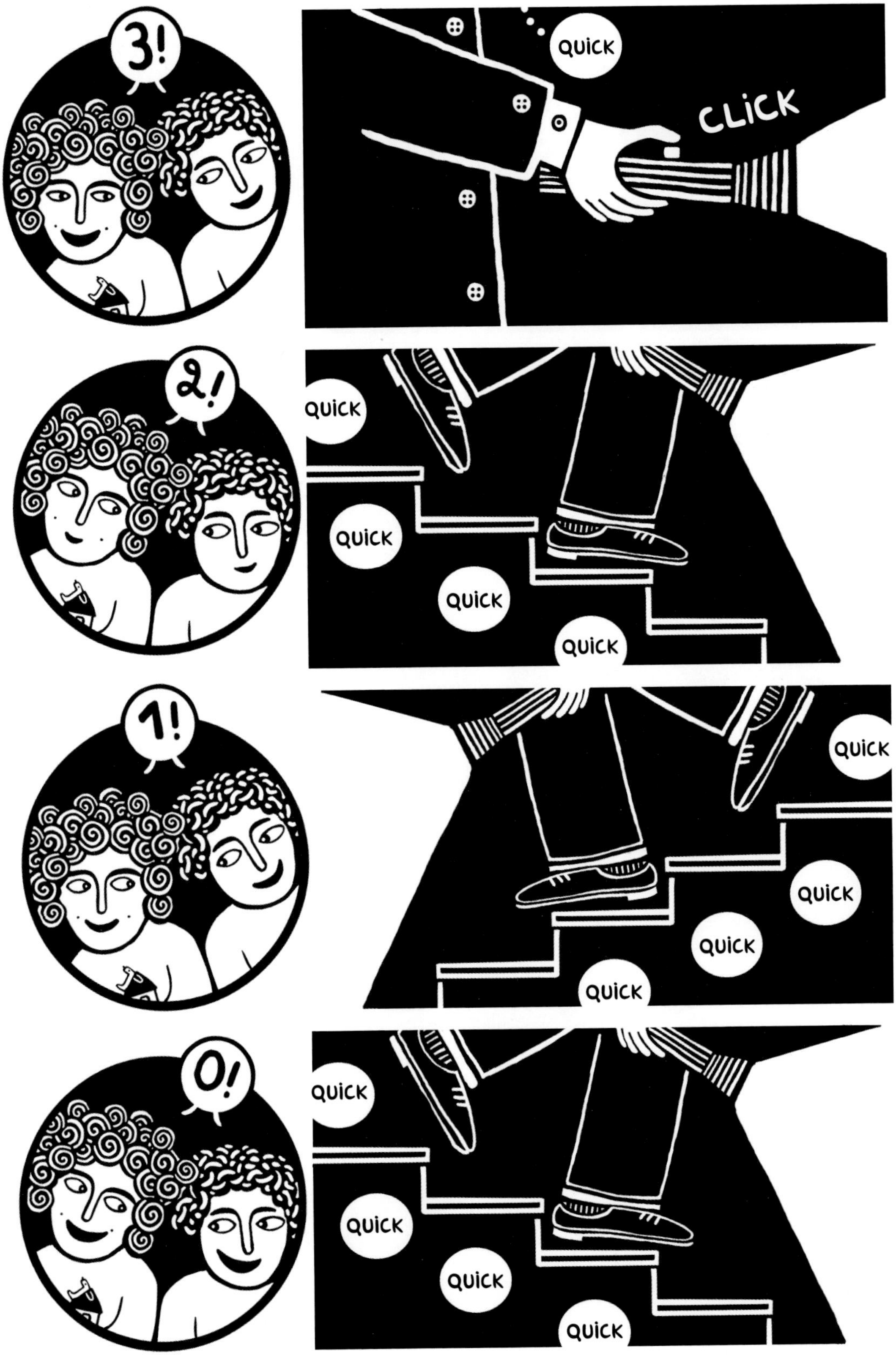
3!
QUICK
CLICK
2!
QUICK
QUICK
QUICK
QUICK
1!
QUICK
QUICK
QUICK
QUICK
0!
QUICK
QUICK
QUICK
QUICK

EVERY NIGHT, EXACTLY 10 SECONDS AFTER THE MOTOR STARTED WITH A VROOOOOOM, ERNEST CHALLITA WOULD TAP ON THE GLASS OF OUR DOOR WITH HIS KEY.

THERE HE IS!

GOOD EVENING, CHILDREN.

GOOD EVENING, ANHALA.

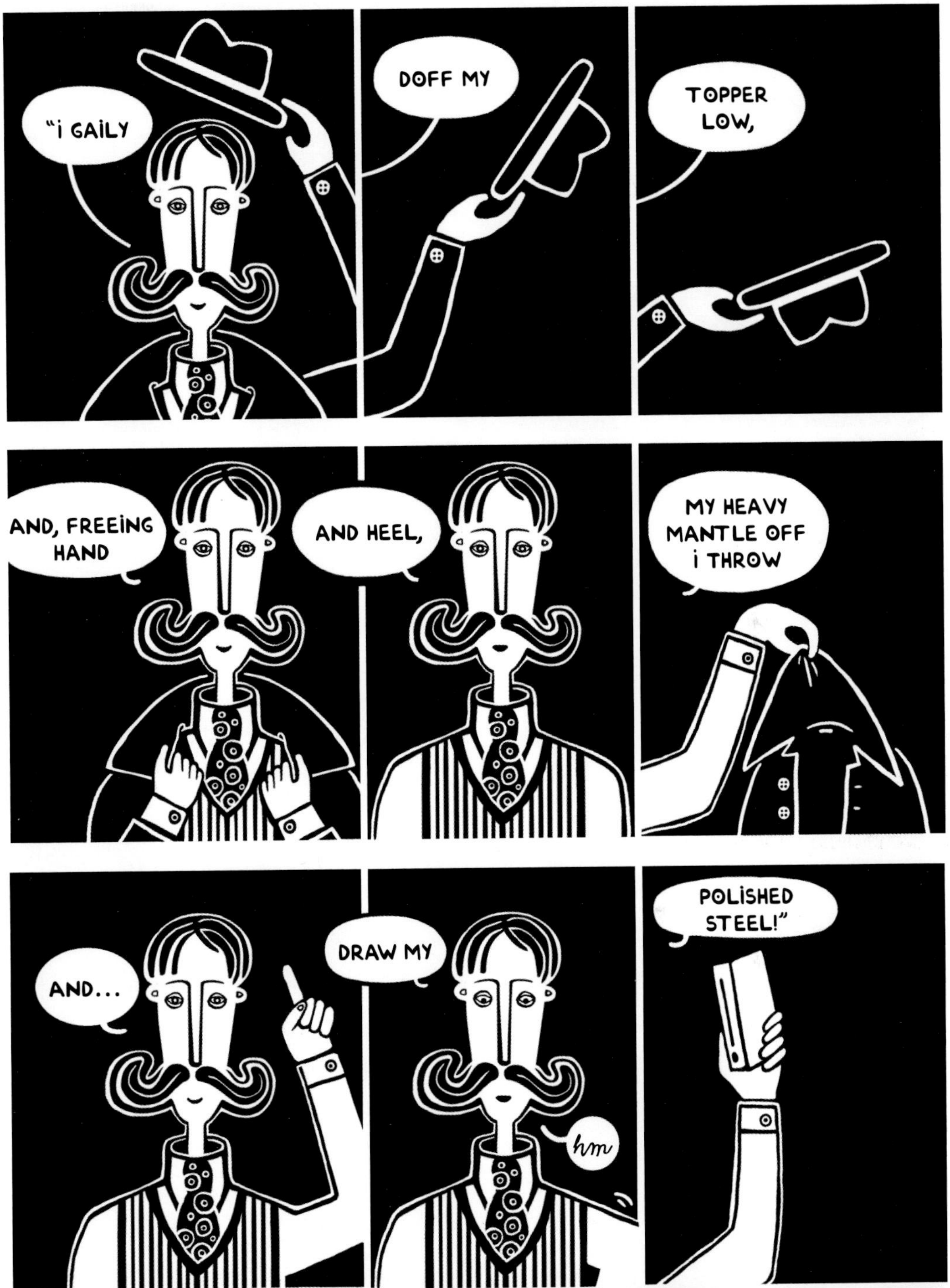
"i GAILY
DOFF MY
TOPPER LOW,
AND, FREEING HAND
AND HEEL,
MY HEAVY MANTLE OFF i THROW
AND...
DRAW MY
hm
POLISHED STEEL!"

ERNEST CHALLITA WAS OUR FOURTH-FLOOR NEIGHBOR. BEFORE THE WAR, HE TAUGHT FRENCH AT THE HIGH SCHOOL ON BAYDOUN STREET.

"COME, YOUNG HEROES!

ERNEST KNEW WHOLE SECTIONS OF *CYRANO DE BERGERAC* BY HEART.

EVERY NIGHT, IN THE FOYER, HE'D PERFORM A SCENE FOR US. (HE WAS AFRAID OF MEMORY LAPSES, SO HE ALWAYS BROUGHT THE BOOK WITH HIM, BUT HE NEVER NEEDED IT.)

EACH IN HIS TURN! I'M TAKING NUMBERS.

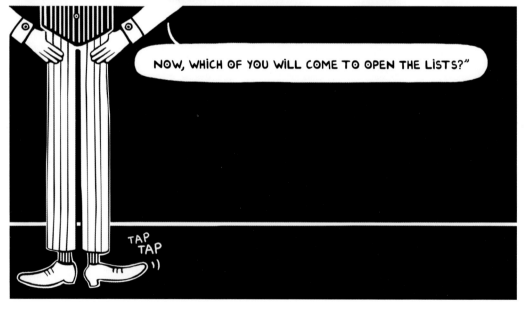

NOW, WHICH OF YOU WILL COME TO OPEN THE LISTS?"

TAP TAP

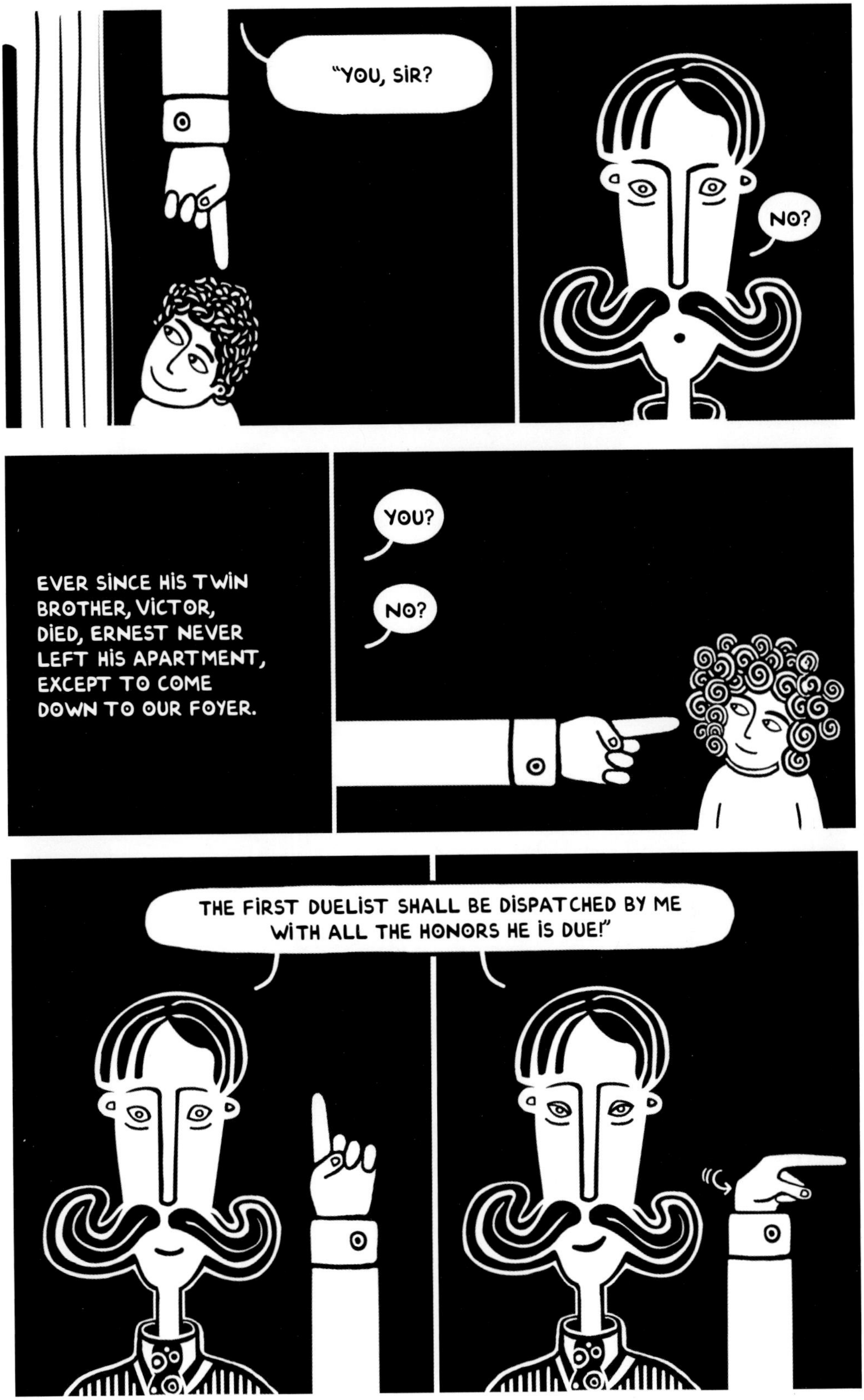
"YOU, SIR?
NO?
EVER SINCE HIS TWIN BROTHER, VICTOR, DIED, ERNEST NEVER LEFT HIS APARTMENT, EXCEPT TO COME DOWN TO OUR FOYER.
YOU?
NO?
THE FIRST DUELIST SHALL BE DISPATCHED BY ME WITH ALL THE HONORS HE IS DUE!"

ERNEST AND VICTOR HAD BEEN THE IDOLS OF THE NEIGHBORHOOD.

BEFORE THE WAR, THEY WOULD COMPETE WITH EACH OTHER AT TRICTRAC EVERY SATURDAY MORNING ON THE SIDEWALK IN FRONT OF OUR BUILDING.

names and numbers in Turkish (from the time of the Ottoman Empire)

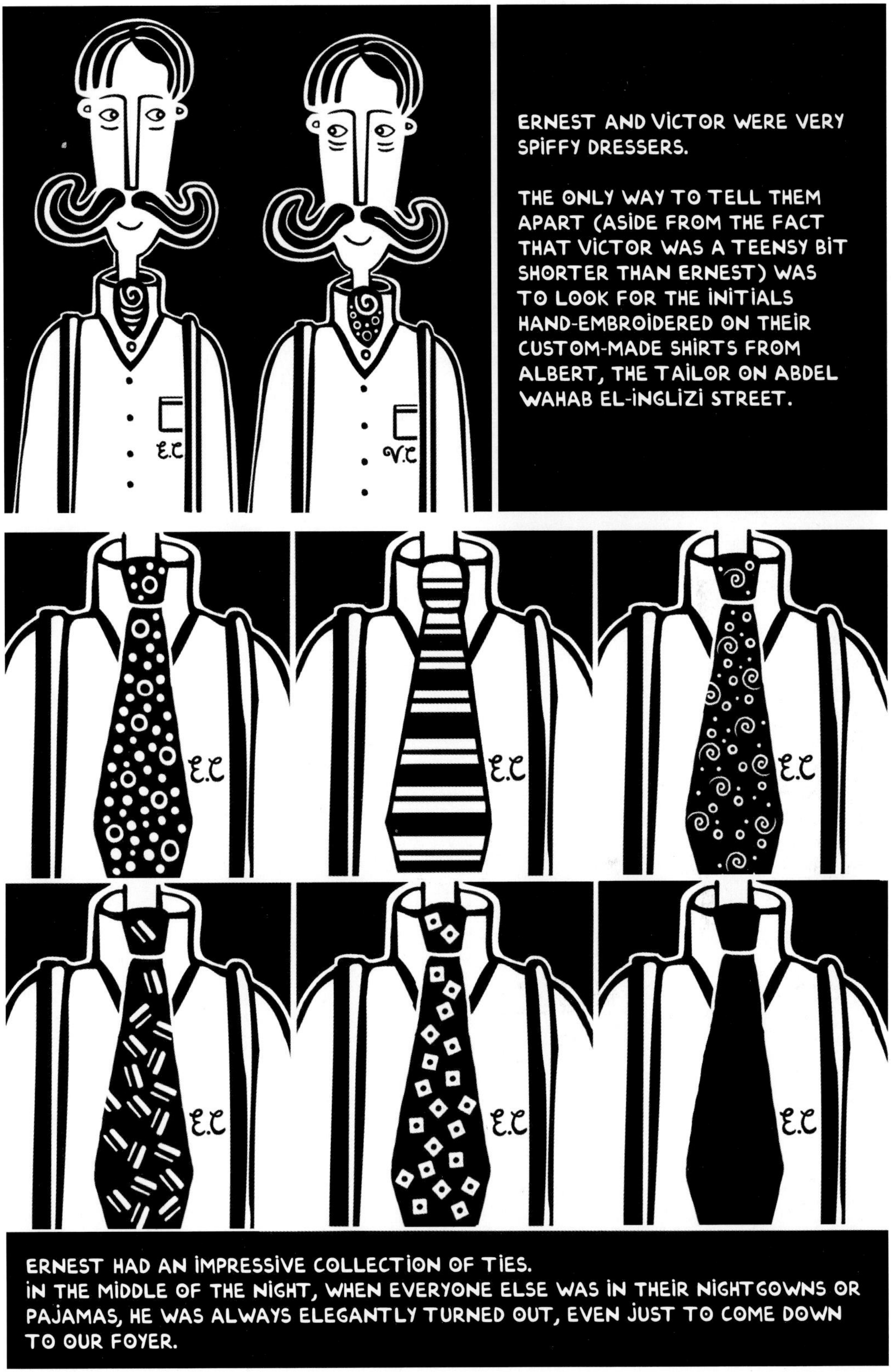
ERNEST AND VICTOR WERE VERY SPIFFY DRESSERS.
THE ONLY WAY TO TELL THEM APART (ASIDE FROM THE FACT THAT VICTOR WAS A TEENSY BIT SHORTER THAN ERNEST) WAS TO LOOK FOR THE INITIALS HAND-EMBROIDERED ON THEIR CUSTOM-MADE SHIRTS FROM ALBERT, THE TAILOR ON ABDEL WAHAB EL-INGLIZI STREET.
E.C
V.C
E.C
E.C
E.C
E.C
E.C
E.C
ERNEST HAD AN IMPRESSIVE COLLECTION OF TIES.
IN THE MIDDLE OF THE NIGHT, WHEN EVERYONE ELSE WAS IN THEIR NIGHTGOWNS OR PAJAMAS, HE WAS ALWAYS ELEGANTLY TURNED OUT, EVEN JUST TO COME DOWN TO OUR FOYER.

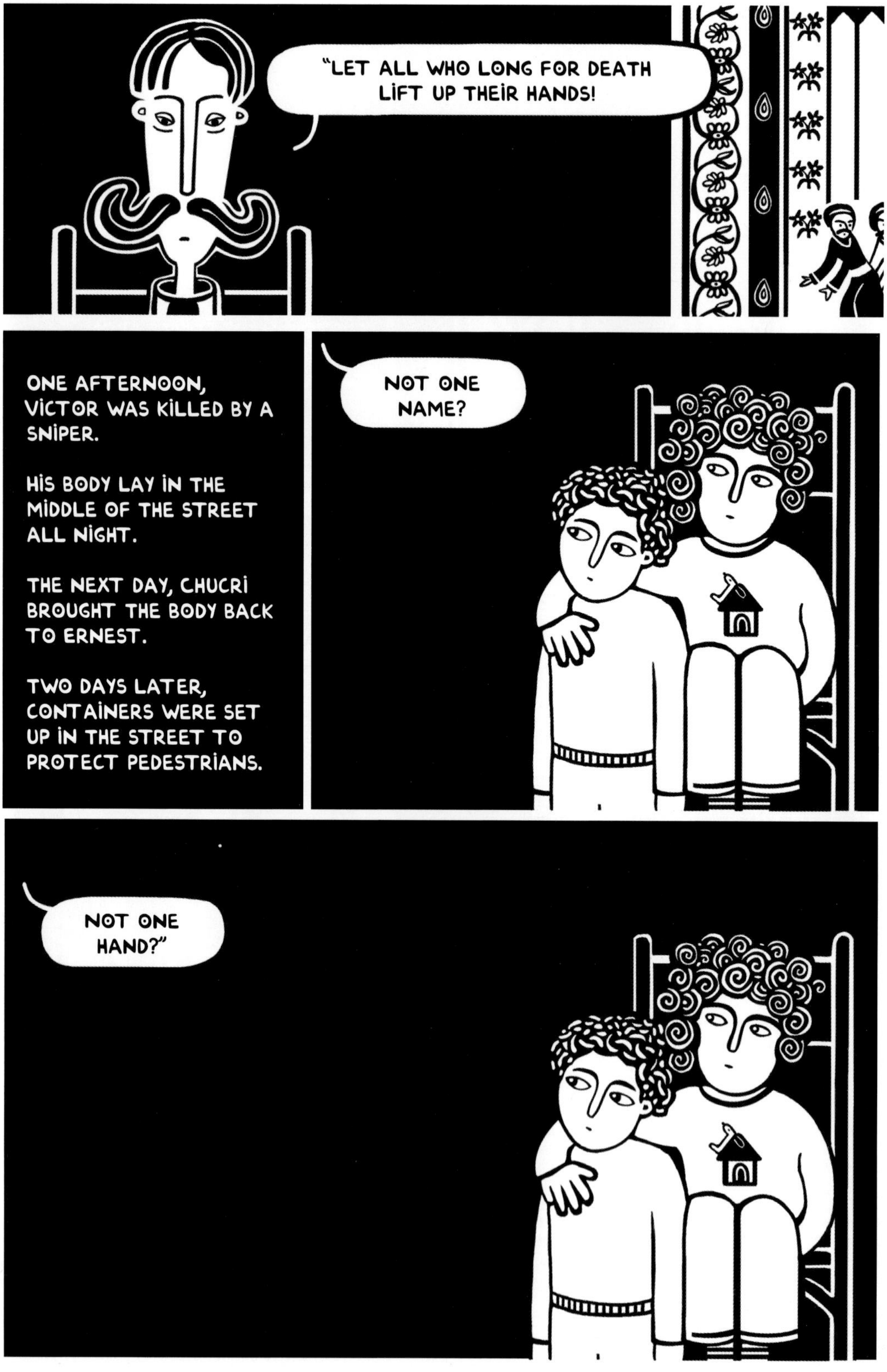
"LET ALL WHO LONG FOR DEATH LIFT UP THEIR HANDS!
ONE AFTERNOON, VICTOR WAS KILLED BY A SNIPER.
HIS BODY LAY IN THE MIDDLE OF THE STREET ALL NIGHT.
THE NEXT DAY, CHUCRI BROUGHT THE BODY BACK TO ERNEST.
TWO DAYS LATER, CONTAINERS WERE SET UP IN THE STREET TO PROTECT PEDESTRIANS.
NOT ONE NAME?
NOT ONE HAND?"

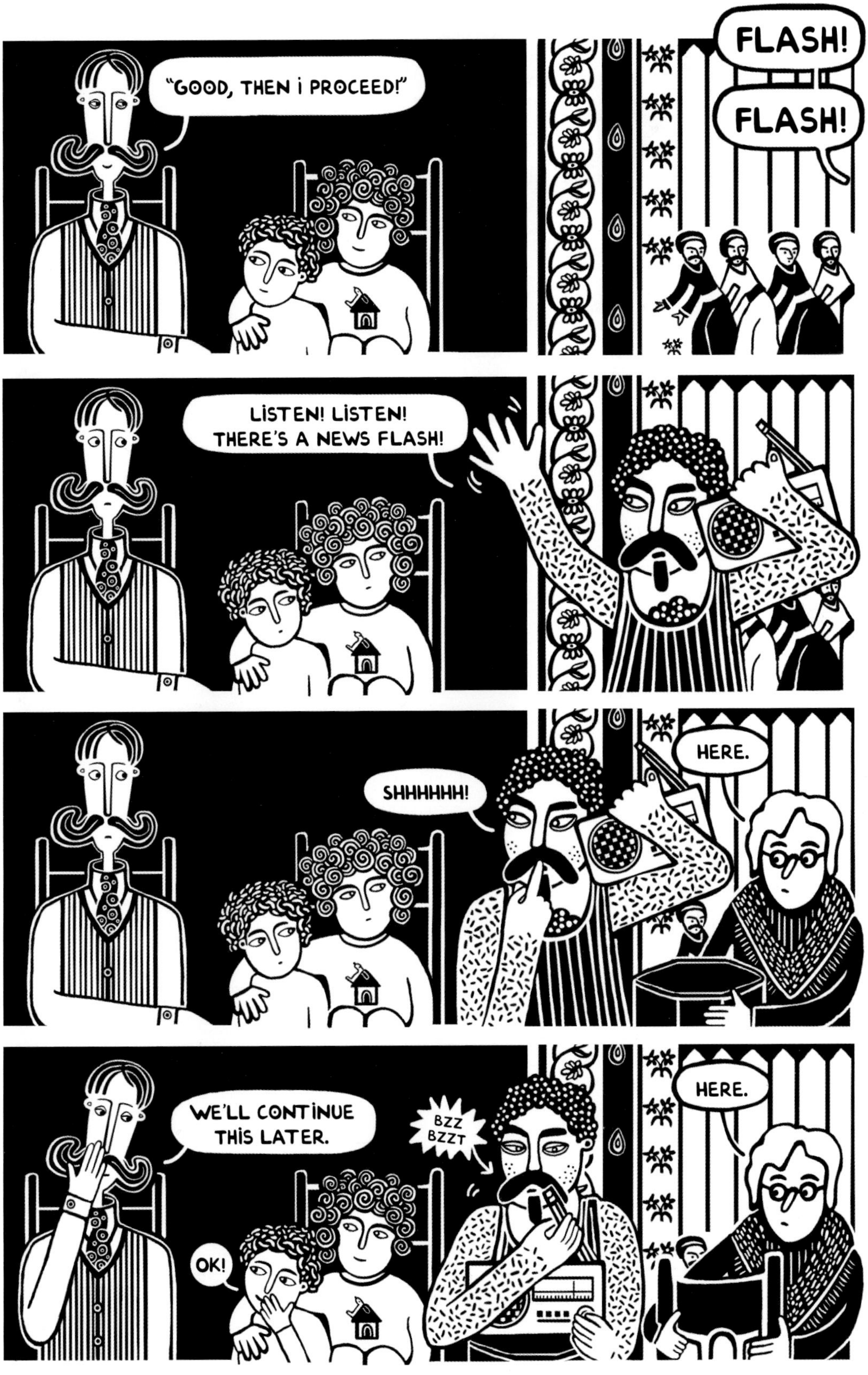
"GOOD, THEN I PROCEED!"
FLASH!
FLASH!
LISTEN! LISTEN! THERE'S A NEWS FLASH!
SHHHHHH!
HERE.
WE'LL CONTINUE THIS LATER.
BZZ BZZT
HERE.
OK!

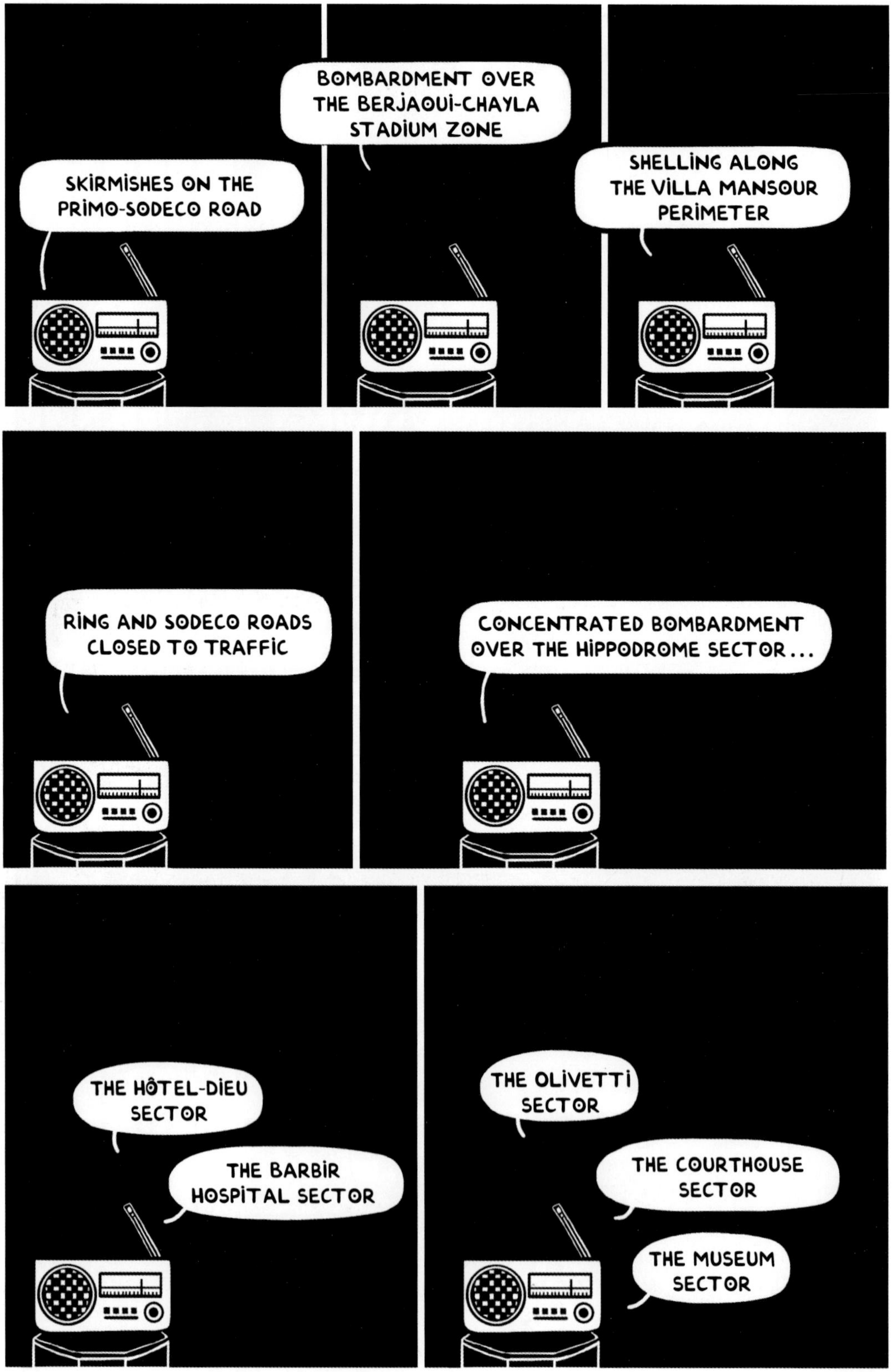
SKIRMISHES ON THE PRIMO-SODECO ROAD
BOMBARDMENT OVER THE BERJAOUI-CHAYLA STADIUM ZONE
SHELLING ALONG THE VILLA MANSOUR PERIMETER
RING AND SODECO ROADS CLOSED TO TRAFFIC
CONCENTRATED BOMBARDMENT OVER THE HIPPODROME SECTOR...
THE HÔTEL-DIEU SECTOR
THE BARBIR HOSPITAL SECTOR
THE OLIVETTI SECTOR
THE COURTHOUSE SECTOR
THE MUSEUM SECTOR

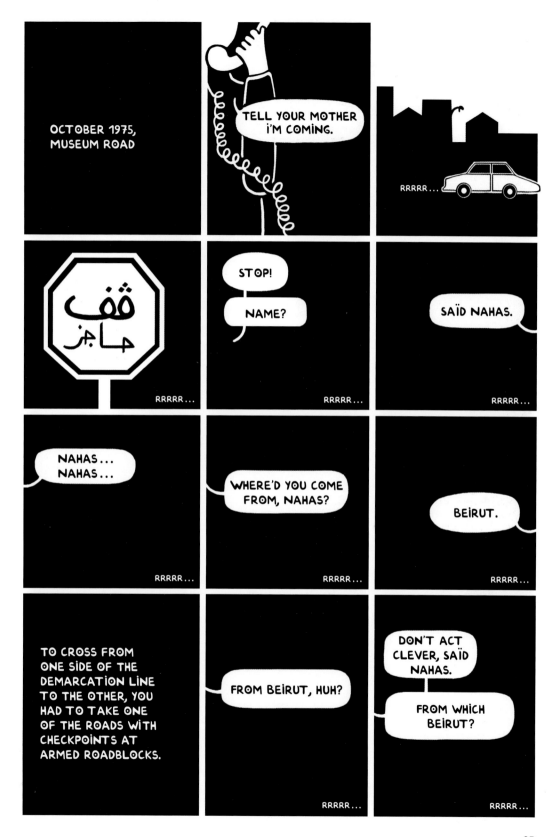

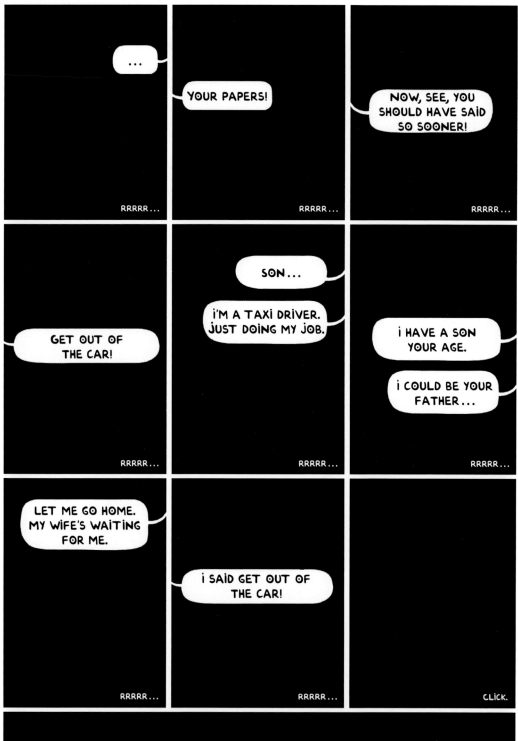

AT THE CHECKPOINTS, YOU COULD BE ARRESTED, KIDNAPPED, OR KILLED JUST ON THE BASIS OF WHAT RELIGION WAS LISTED ON YOUR IDENTITY CARD.

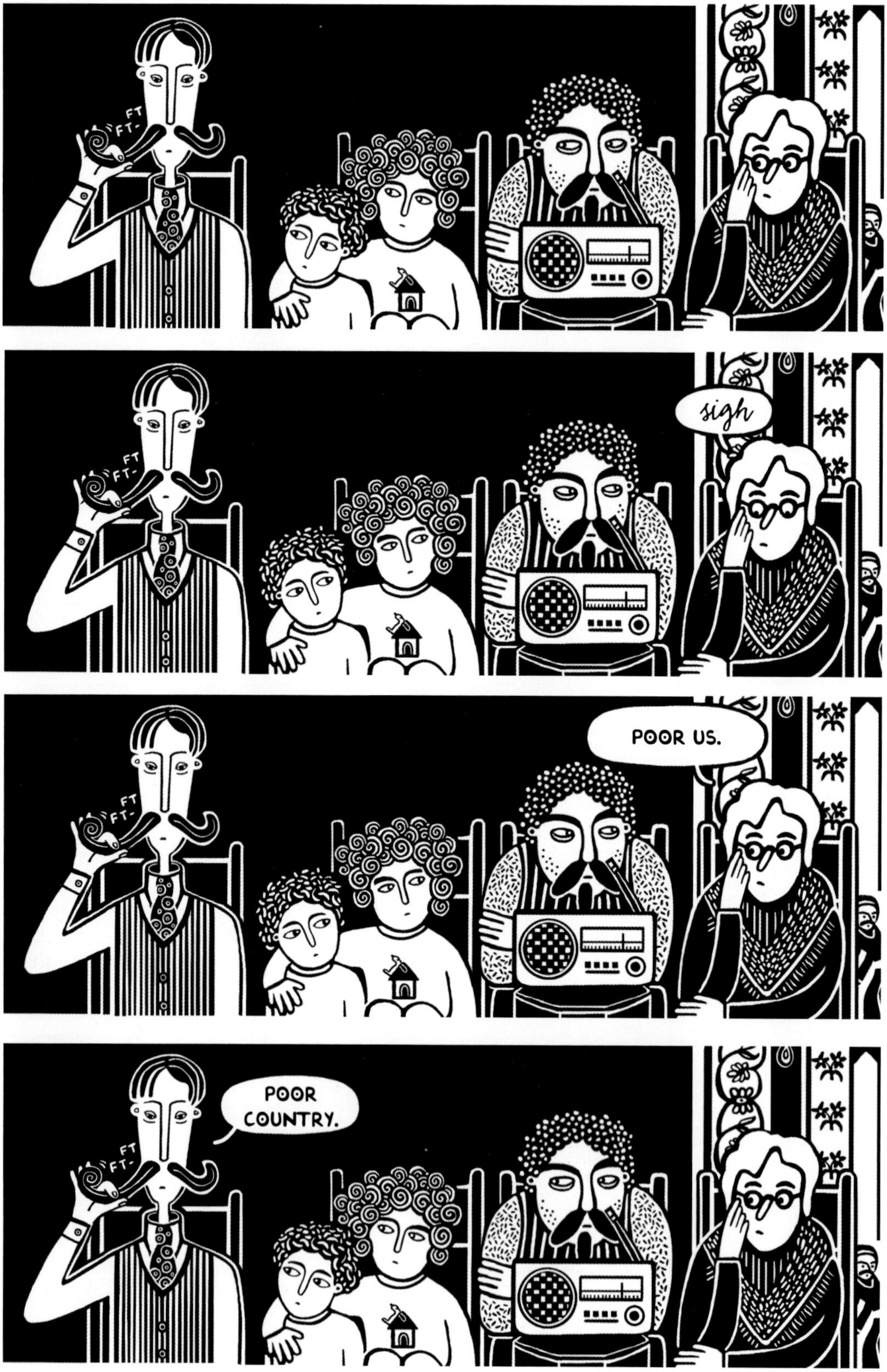
FT
FT-
FT
FT-
sigh
FT
FT-
POOR US.
FT
FT-
POOR COUNTRY.

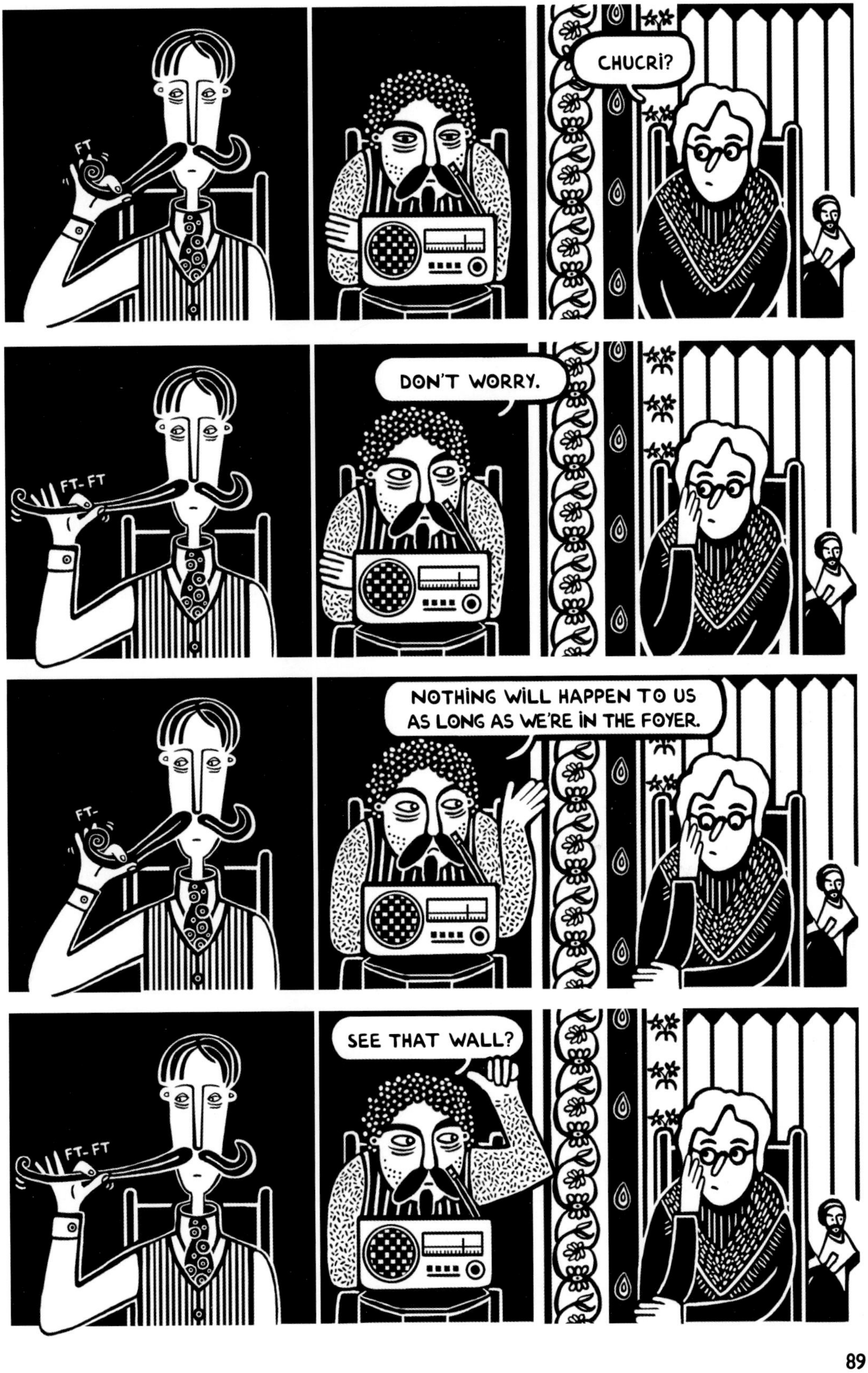
FT
CHUCRI?
FT- FT
DON'T WORRY.
FT-
NOTHING WILL HAPPEN TO US AS LONG AS WE'RE IN THE FOYER.
FT- FT
SEE THAT WALL?

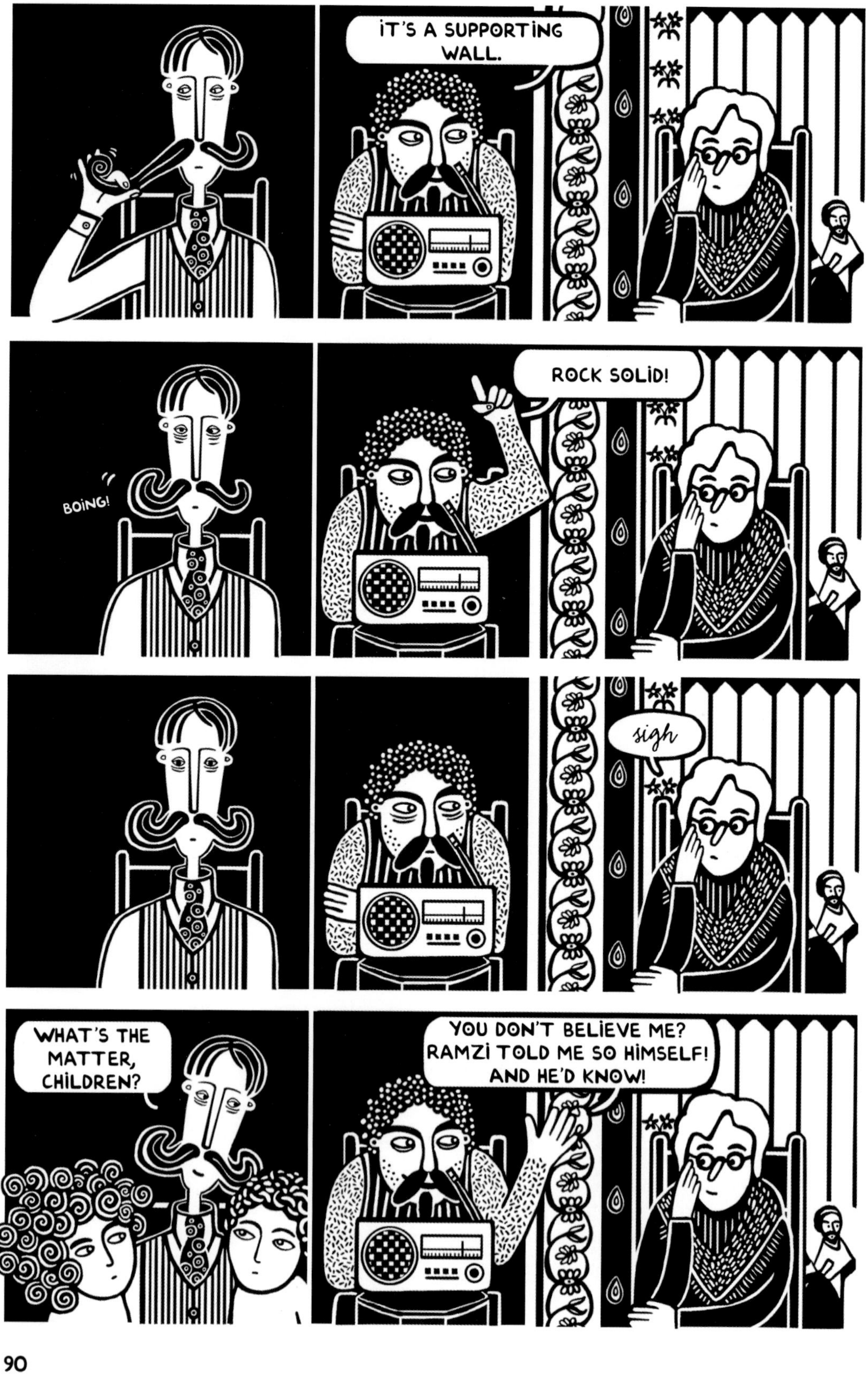
IT'S A SUPPORTING WALL.
BOING!
ROCK SOLID!
sigh
WHAT'S THE MATTER, CHILDREN?
YOU DON'T BELIEVE ME? RAMZI TOLD ME SO HIMSELF! AND HE'D KNOW!

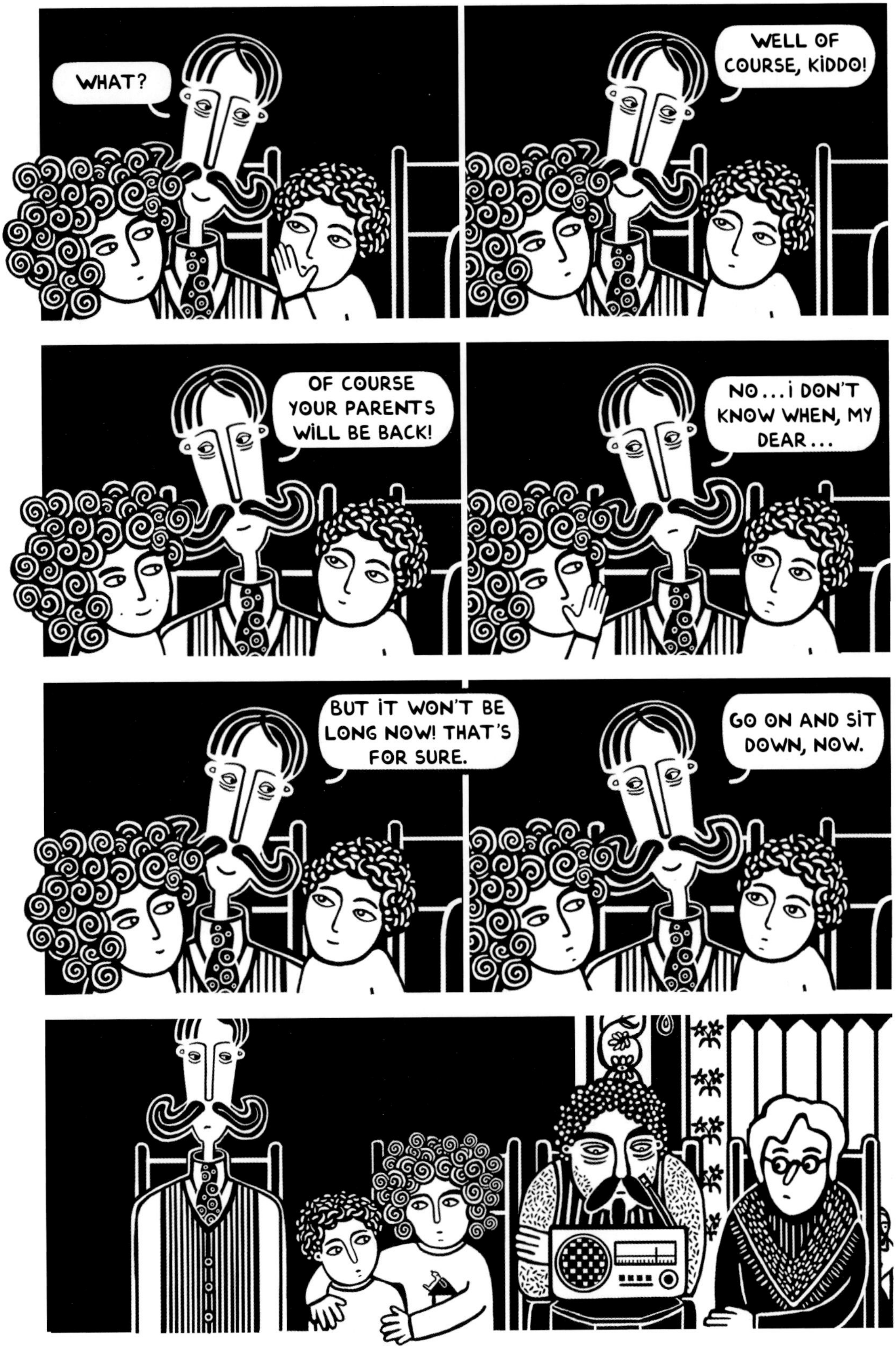
WHAT?
WELL OF COURSE, KIDDO!
OF COURSE YOUR PARENTS WILL BE BACK!
NO... I DON'T KNOW WHEN, MY DEAR...
BUT IT WON'T BE LONG NOW! THAT'S FOR SURE.
GO ON AND SIT DOWN, NOW.

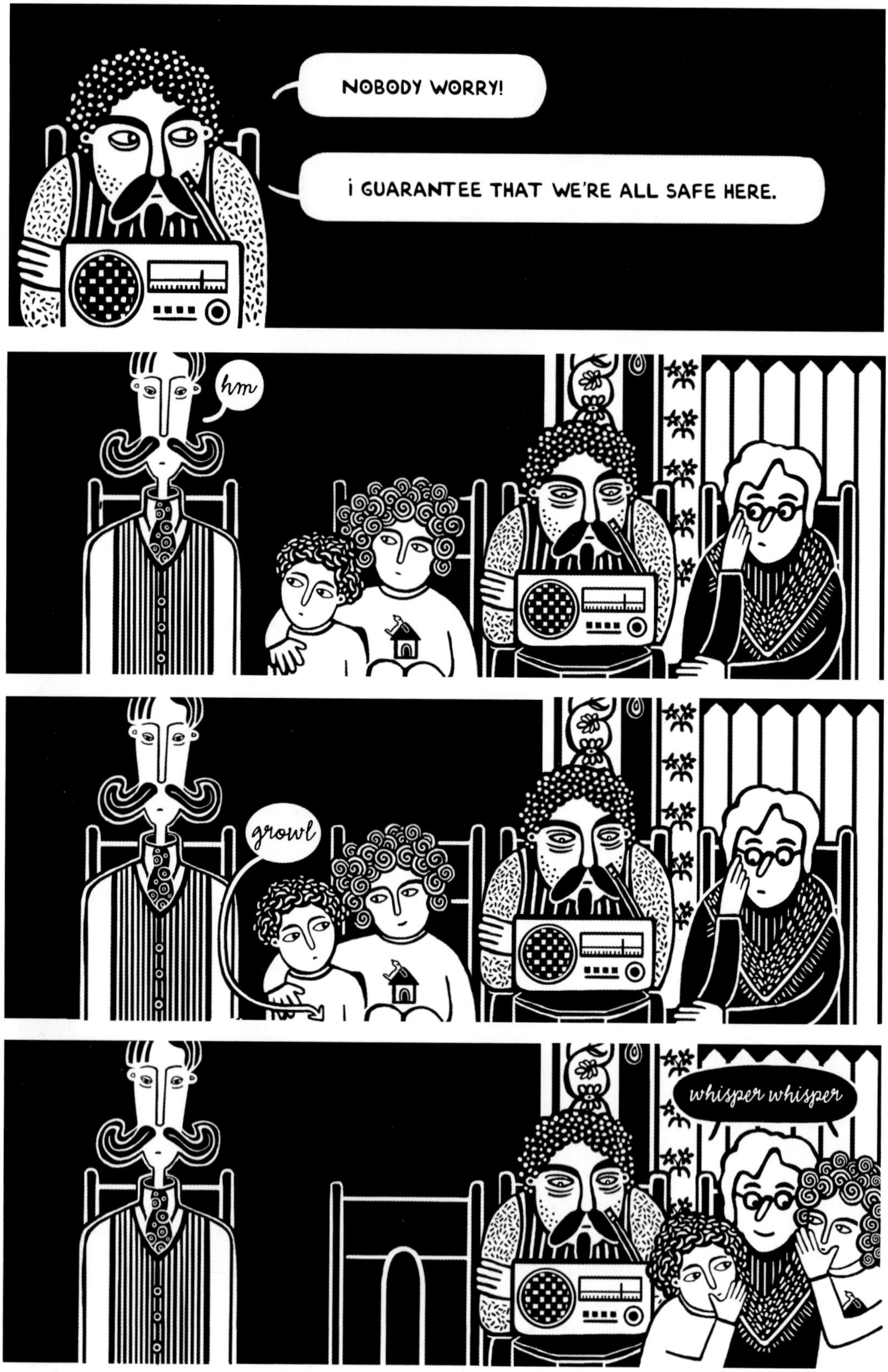
NOBODY WORRY!
I GUARANTEE THAT WE'RE ALL SAFE HERE.
hm
growl
whisper whisper

93

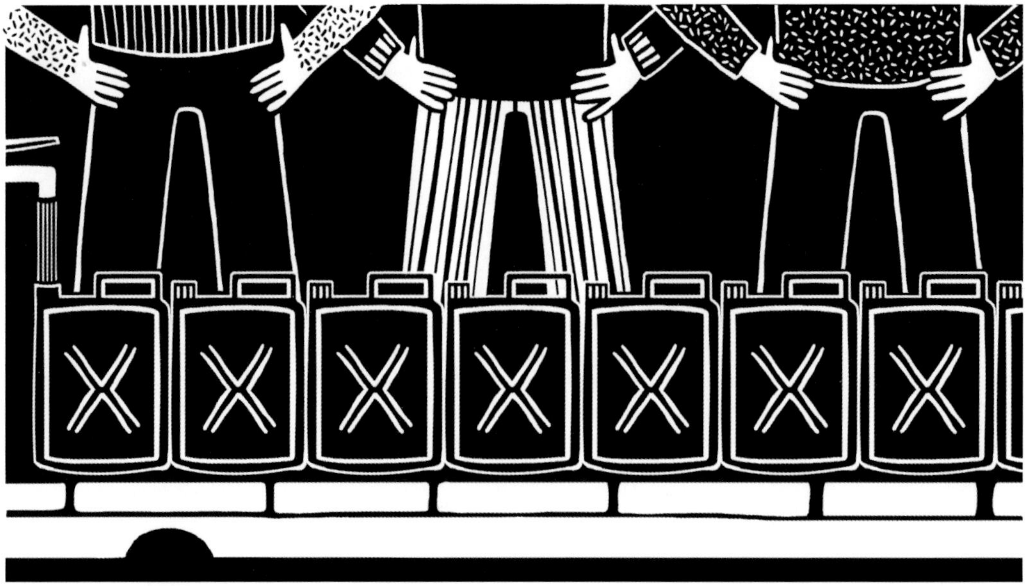

DURING THE WAR, FRUITS AND VEGETABLES WERE IN THEMSELVES A NICE GIFT FOR YOUR NEIGHBOR. AND IF YOU WENT TO THE TROUBLE OF WASHING THEM, WELL, THEY WERE BEYOND VALUE!
CHUCRI WAS THE ONE IN CHARGE OF SUPPLYING US WITH WATER.
HE'D FILL THE TRUNK OF HIS CAR WITH EMPTY JERRY CANS. THEN HE, MY FATHER, AND THE OTHER MEN IN THE NEIGHBORHOOD WOULD GO TO SEE VERA, THE SISTER OF OUR FIFTH-FLOOR NEIGHBOR, MADAME LINDA. VERA LIVED IN A BUILDING WITH AN ARTESIAN WELL.

AFTER FILLING THE BLUE JERRY CANS (THE GREEN WERE RESERVED FOR GASOLINE), THEY POURED THE WATER INTO GLASS AND PLASTIC BOTTLES (THE GLASS ONES WERE WHISKEY BOTTLES MY MOTHER HAD KEPT AND WASHED).

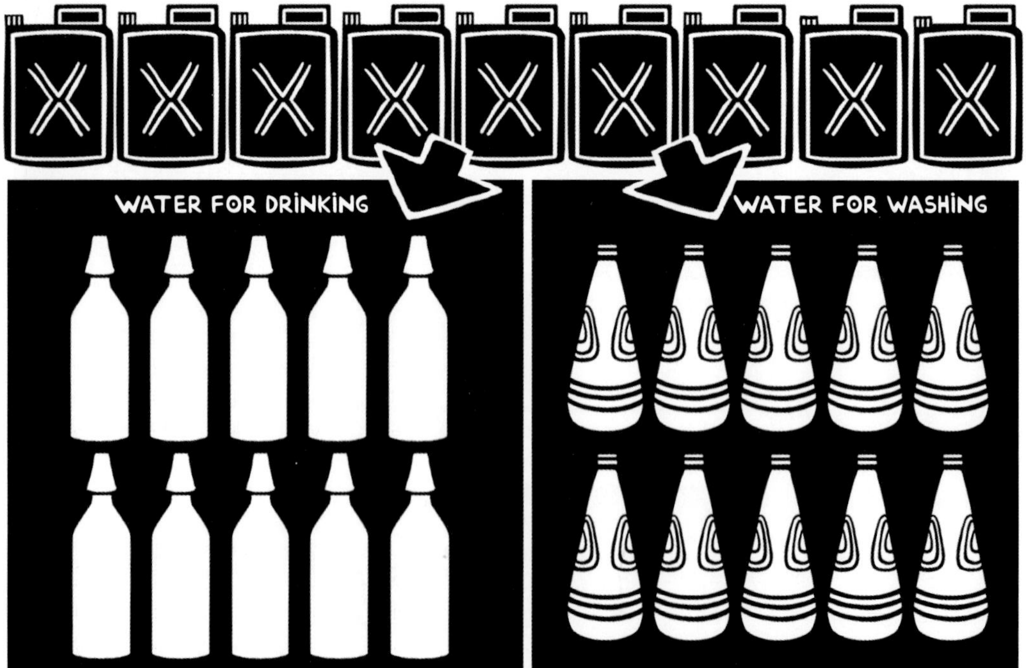
WATER FOR DRINKING
WATER FOR WASHING

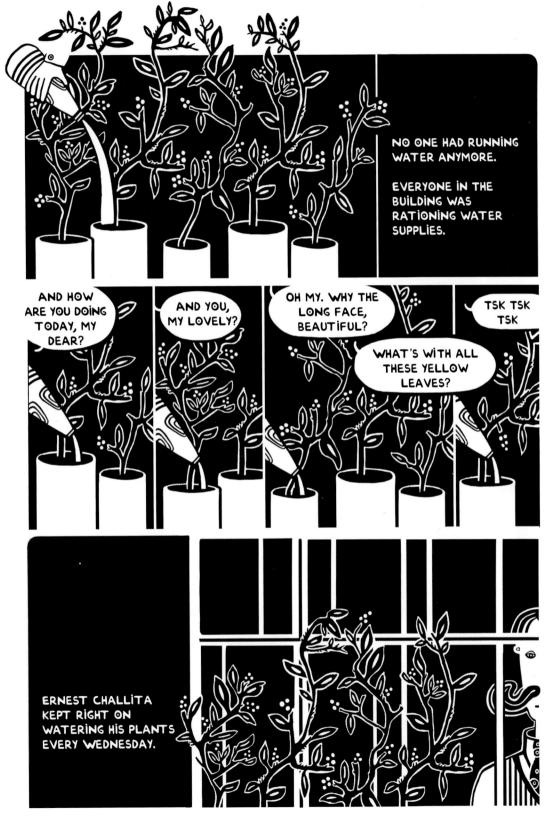

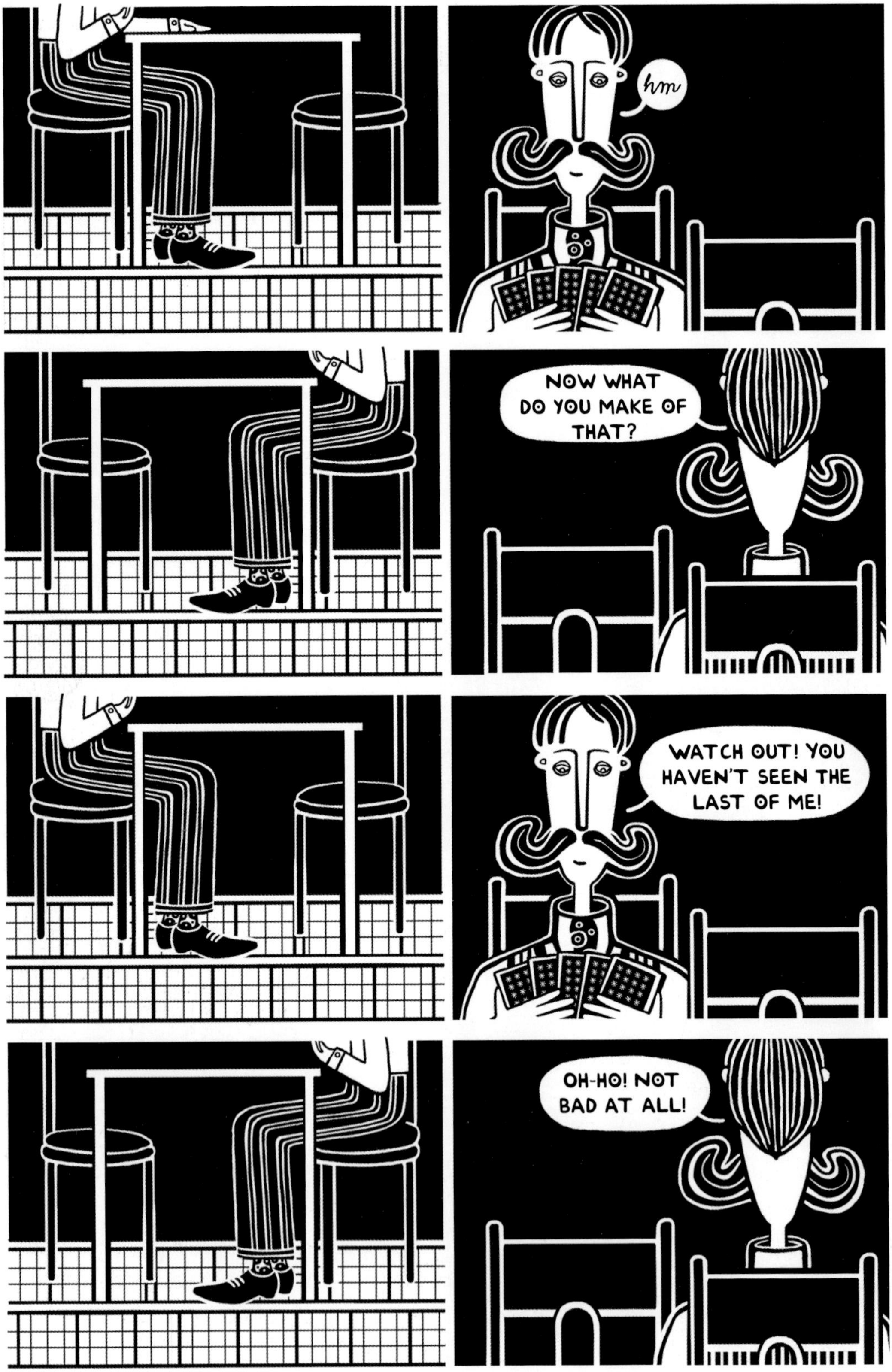
hm
NOW WHAT DO YOU MAKE OF THAT?
WATCH OUT! YOU HAVEN'T SEEN THE LAST OF ME!
OH-HO! NOT BAD AT ALL!

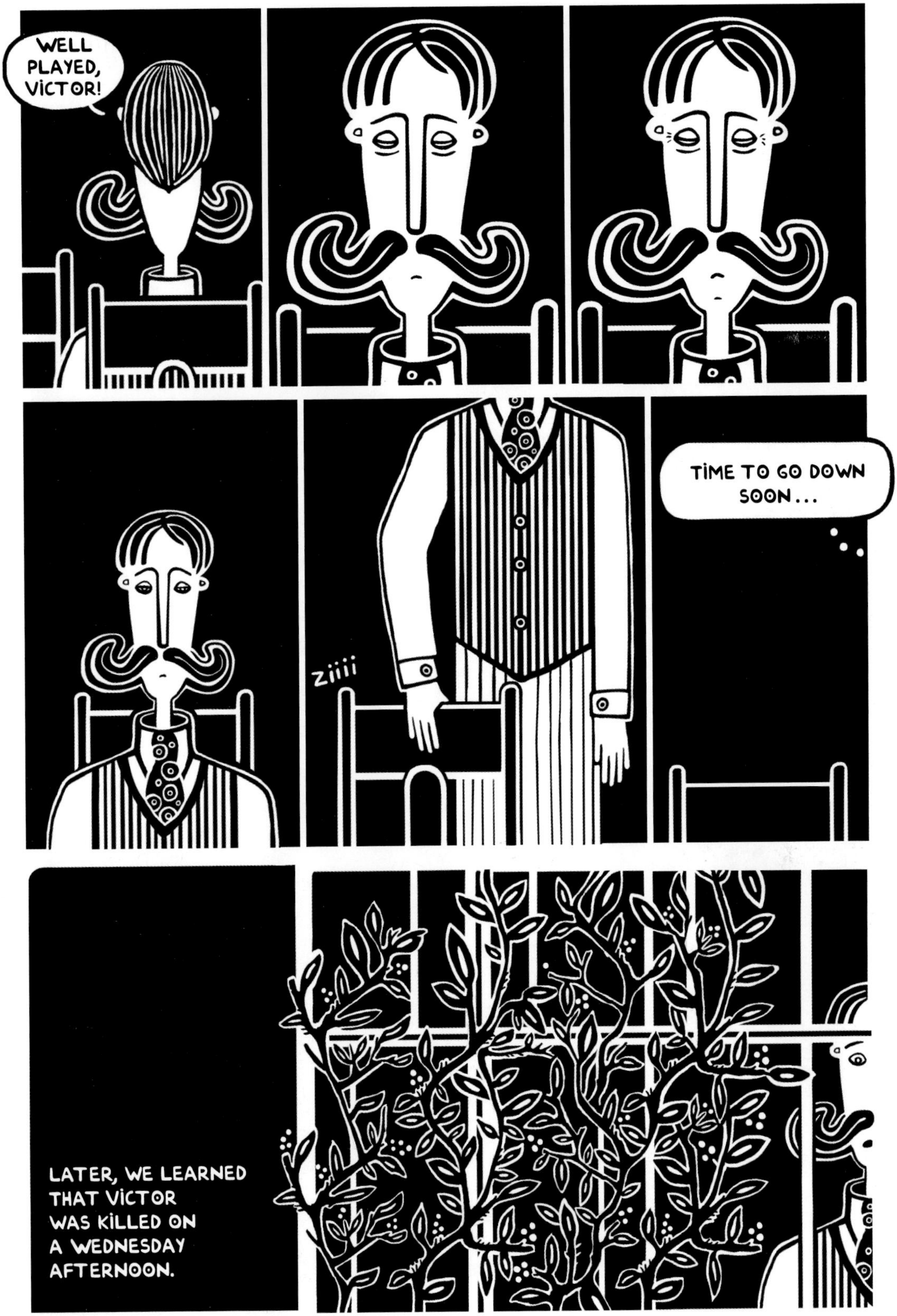
WELL PLAYED, VICTOR!
TIME TO GO DOWN SOON...
ZIIII
LATER, WE LEARNED THAT VICTOR WAS KILLED ON A WEDNESDAY AFTERNOON.

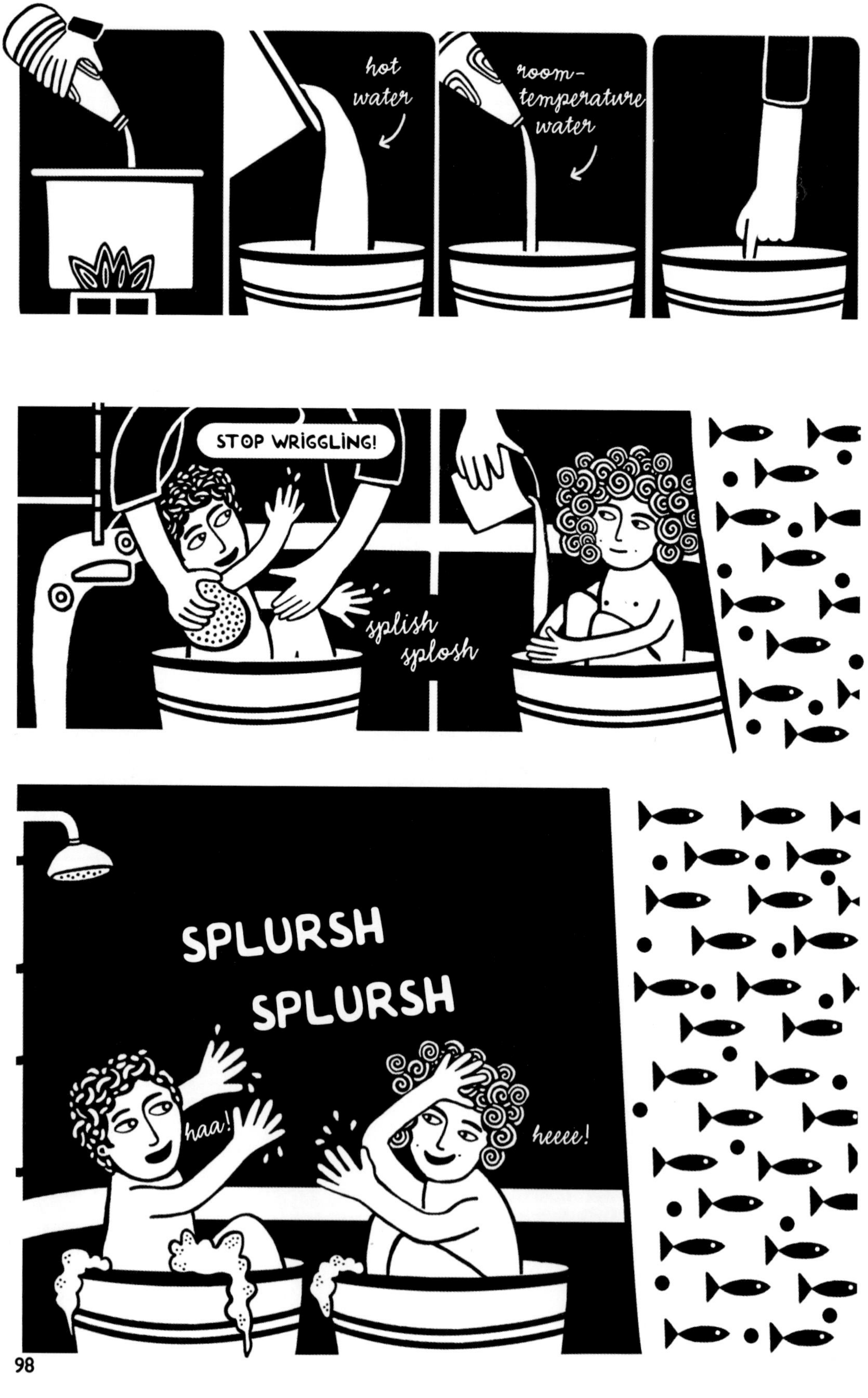
hot water
room-temperature water
STOP WRIGGLING!
splish splosh
SPLURSH
SPLURSH
haa!
heeee!

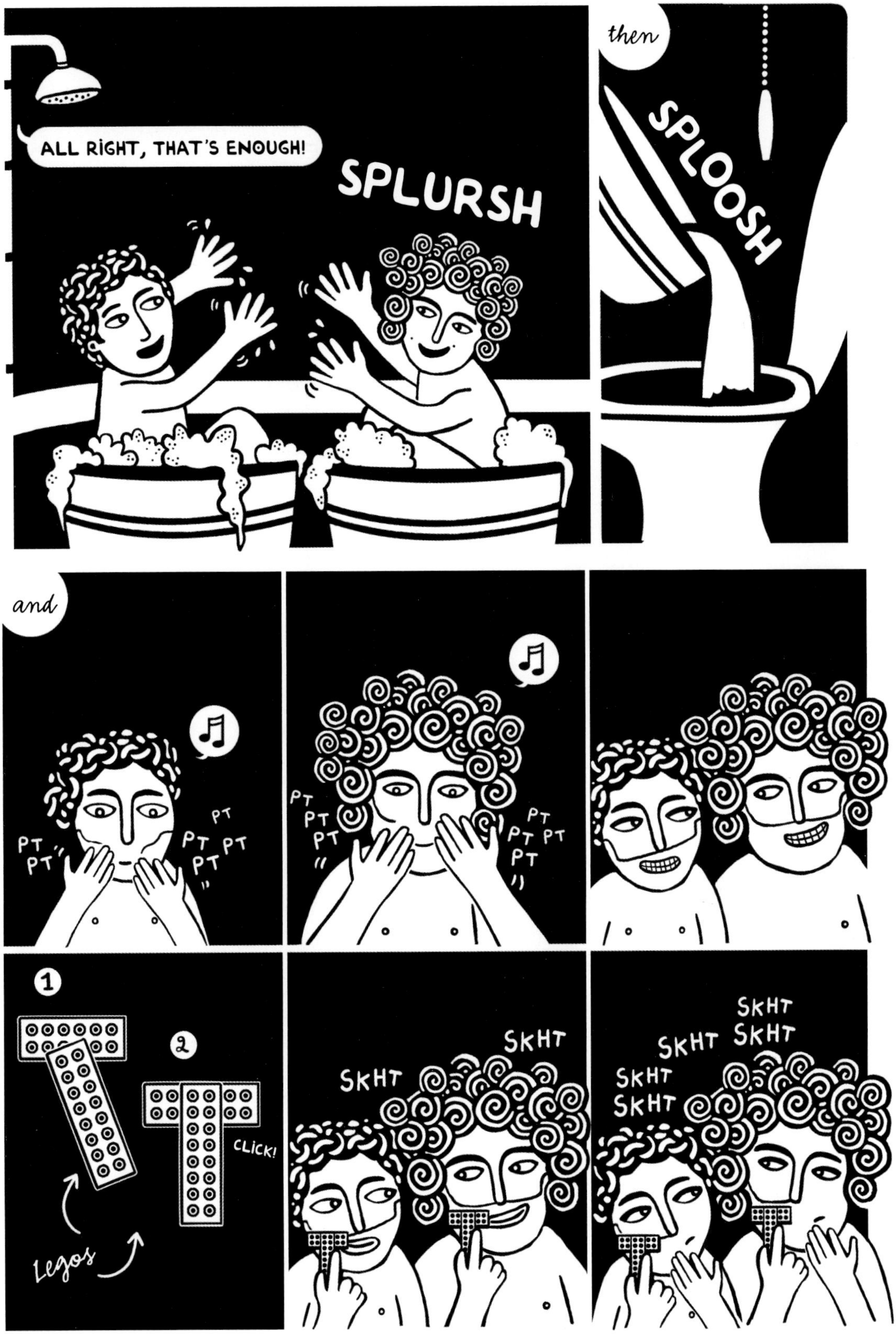
ALL RIGHT, THAT'S ENOUGH!
SPLURSH
then
SPLOOSH
and
PT PT
PT PT PT PT
PT PT PT
PT PT PT PT
1
2
CLICK!
Legos
SKHT
SKHT
SKHT SKHT
SKHT SKHT
SKHT

THERE'S A LEBANESE EXPRESSION THAT MEANS "A VERY MESSY PLACE." THEY SAY IT'S LIKE "A BATHROOM WITH THE WATER CUT OFF!"

MONSIEUR KHALED LIVED ON THE FIFTH FLOOR WITH HIS WIFE, MADAME LINDA.

BEFORE THE WAR, MONSIEUR KHALED HAD OPENED VENI VIDI VICI, A RESTAURANT AND NIGHTCLUB THAT SOON BECAME ONE OF THE HOT SPOTS FOR BEIRUT'S RICH KIDS IN THE 1960s.

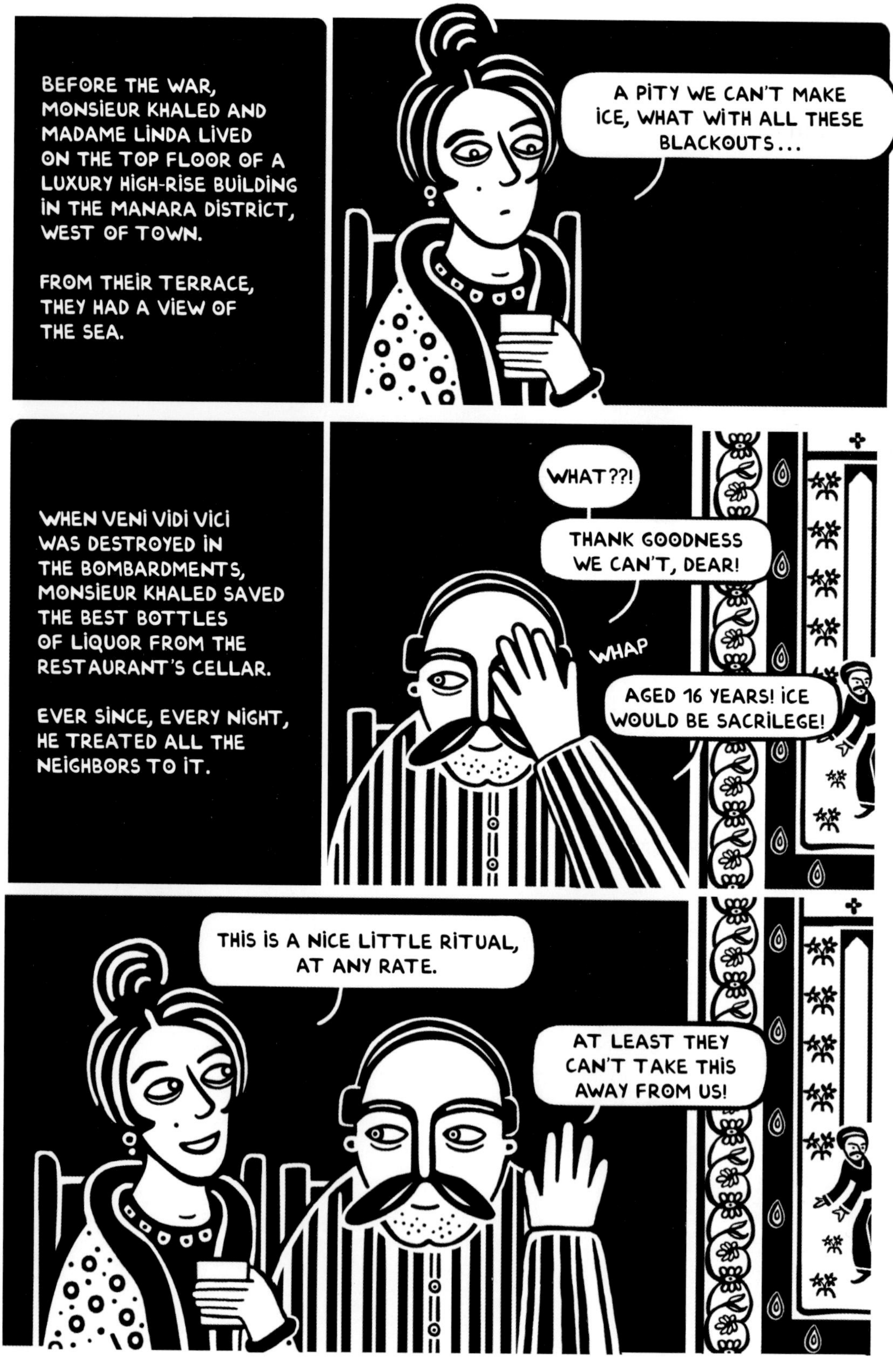
BEFORE THE WAR, MONSIEUR KHALED AND MADAME LINDA LIVED ON THE TOP FLOOR OF A LUXURY HIGH-RISE BUILDING IN THE MANARA DISTRICT, WEST OF TOWN.
FROM THEIR TERRACE, THEY HAD A VIEW OF THE SEA.
A PITY WE CAN'T MAKE ICE, WHAT WITH ALL THESE BLACKOUTS...
WHEN VENI VIDI VICI WAS DESTROYED IN THE BOMBARDMENTS, MONSIEUR KHALED SAVED THE BEST BOTTLES OF LIQUOR FROM THE RESTAURANT'S CELLAR.
EVER SINCE, EVERY NIGHT, HE TREATED ALL THE NEIGHBORS TO IT.
WHAT??!
THANK GOODNESS WE CAN'T, DEAR!
WHAP
AGED 16 YEARS! ICE WOULD BE SACRILEGE!
THIS IS A NICE LITTLE RITUAL, AT ANY RATE.
AT LEAST THEY CAN'T TAKE THIS AWAY FROM US!

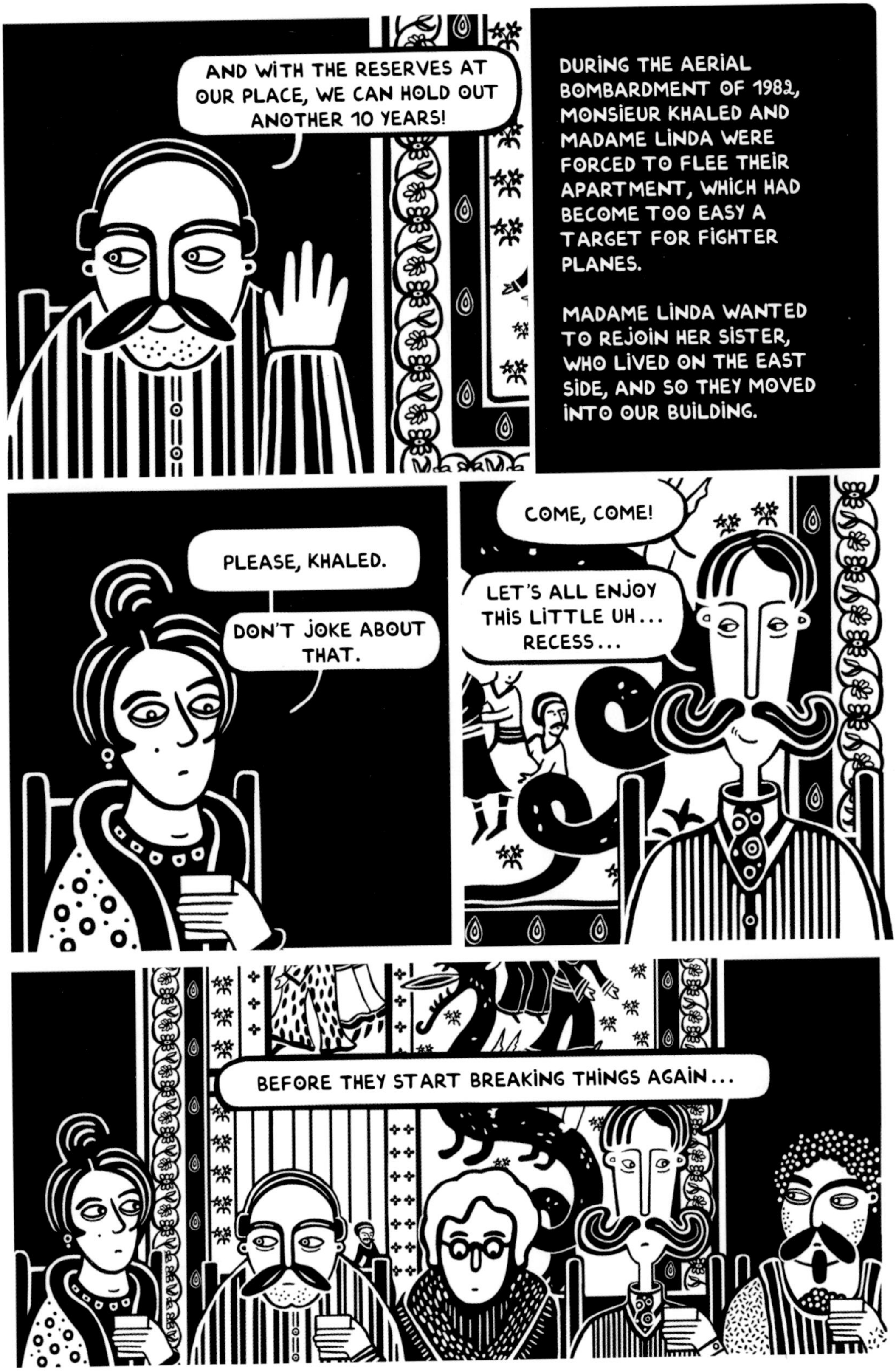
AND WITH THE RESERVES AT OUR PLACE, WE CAN HOLD OUT ANOTHER 10 YEARS!
DURING THE AERIAL BOMBARDMENT OF 1982, MONSIEUR KHALED AND MADAME LINDA WERE FORCED TO FLEE THEIR APARTMENT, WHICH HAD BECOME TOO EASY A TARGET FOR FIGHTER PLANES.
MADAME LINDA WANTED TO REJOIN HER SISTER, WHO LIVED ON THE EAST SIDE, AND SO THEY MOVED INTO OUR BUILDING.
PLEASE, KHALED.
DON'T JOKE ABOUT THAT.
COME, COME!
LET'S ALL ENJOY THIS LITTLE UH... RECESS...
BEFORE THEY START BREAKING THINGS AGAIN...

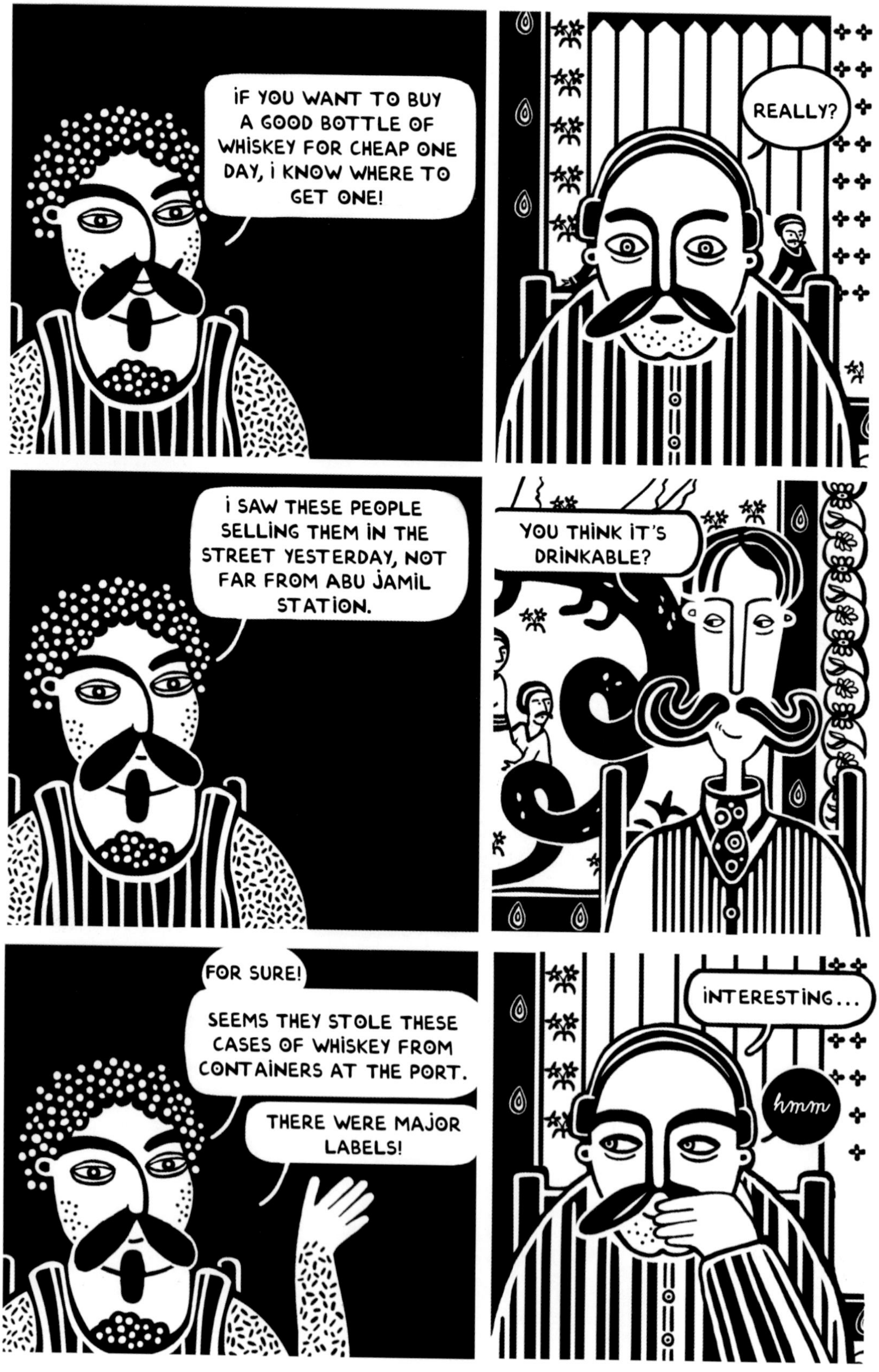
IF YOU WANT TO BUY A GOOD BOTTLE OF WHISKEY FOR CHEAP ONE DAY, I KNOW WHERE TO GET ONE!
REALLY?
I SAW THESE PEOPLE SELLING THEM IN THE STREET YESTERDAY, NOT FAR FROM ABU JAMIL STATION.
YOU THINK IT'S DRINKABLE?
FOR SURE!
SEEMS THEY STOLE THESE CASES OF WHISKEY FROM CONTAINERS AT THE PORT.
THERE WERE MAJOR LABELS!
INTERESTING...
hmm

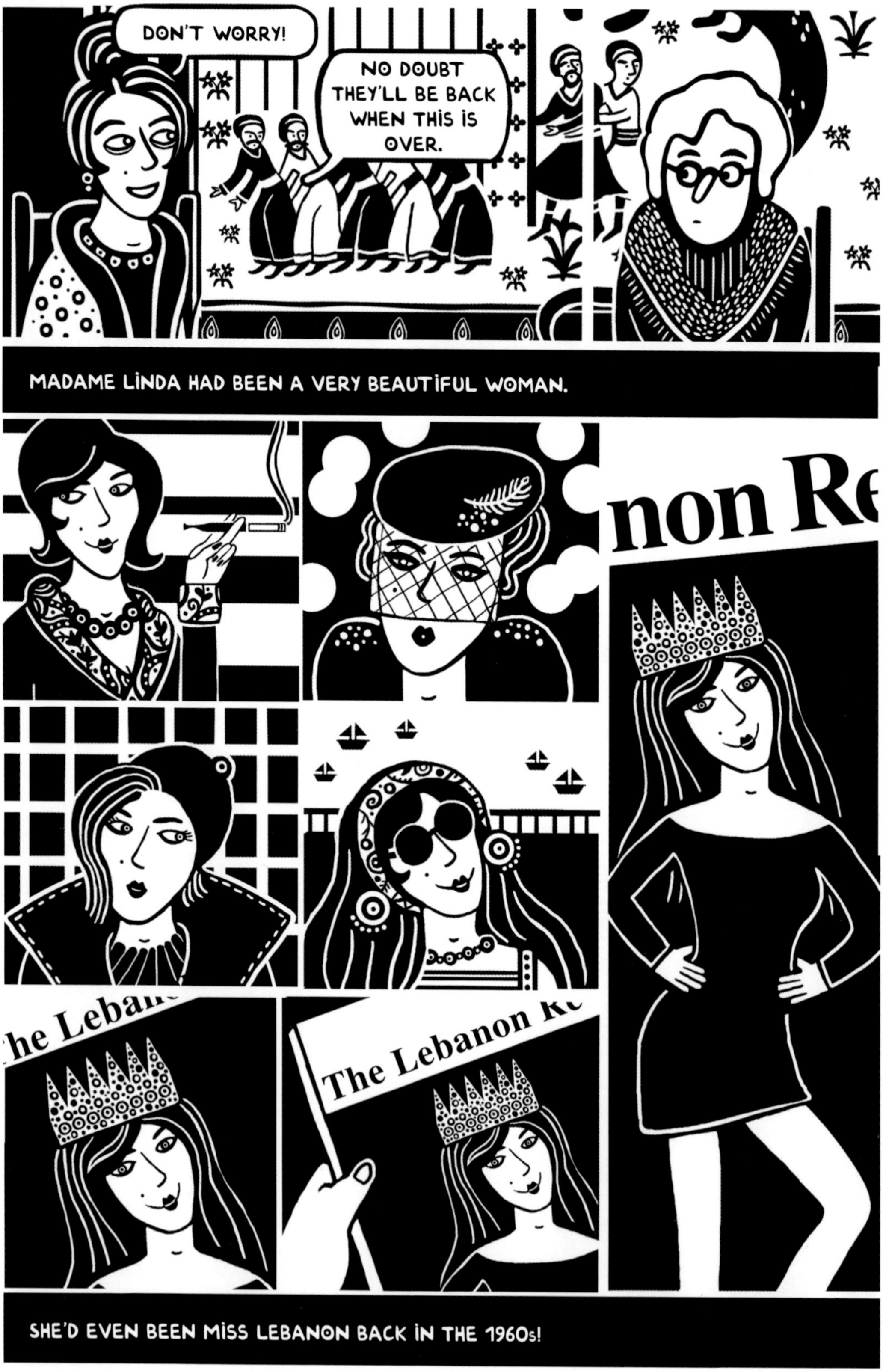

DON'T WORRY!
NO DOUBT THEY'LL BE BACK WHEN THIS IS OVER.
MADAME LINDA HAD BEEN A VERY BEAUTIFUL WOMAN.
non Re
The Leban
The Lebanon Re
SHE'D EVEN BEEN MISS LEBANON BACK IN THE 1960s!

THE DAY AFTER SHE WON THE TITLE, THE PHOTO OF HER IN A MINISKIRT ON THE COVER OF THE *LEBANON REVIEW* WAS HER FATHER'S MISERY AND HER MOTHER'S JOY...

AND THEIR NEIGHBORS' DELIGHT.

RESTAURANT
veni vidi vici

ONE NIGHT, MADAME LINDA CAME TO DINE AT VENI VIDI VICI...

KHALED SAID HE WAS BORN IN TEXAS.
BUT FOR LINDA'S BEAUTIFUL EYES, HE AGREED TO LIVE HERE.

HE TOLD HER THAT OVER
THERE, THEY HAD A VERY
BEAUTIFUL LIGHTHOUSE,

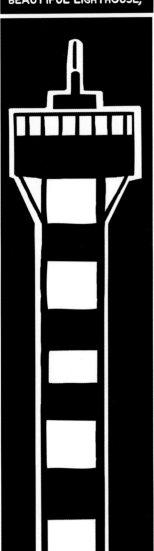

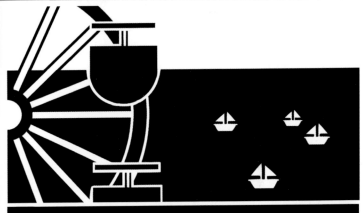

A FERRIS WHEEL, A CLIFF ROAD ALONG THE SEA,
RESTAURANTS, STORES ALL LIT UP,

STREET MERCHANTS, SIDEWALK CAFÉS

AND, ABOVE ALL, THE BEST "MERRY CREAMS" IN THE WORLD.

TEXAS, THE FARTHEST PLACE KHALED COULD THINK OF, WAS HOW HE REFERRED TO THE WEST BEIRUT DISTRICT WHERE HE'D LIVED, WHICH THE WAR HAD DRIVEN HIM FROM.

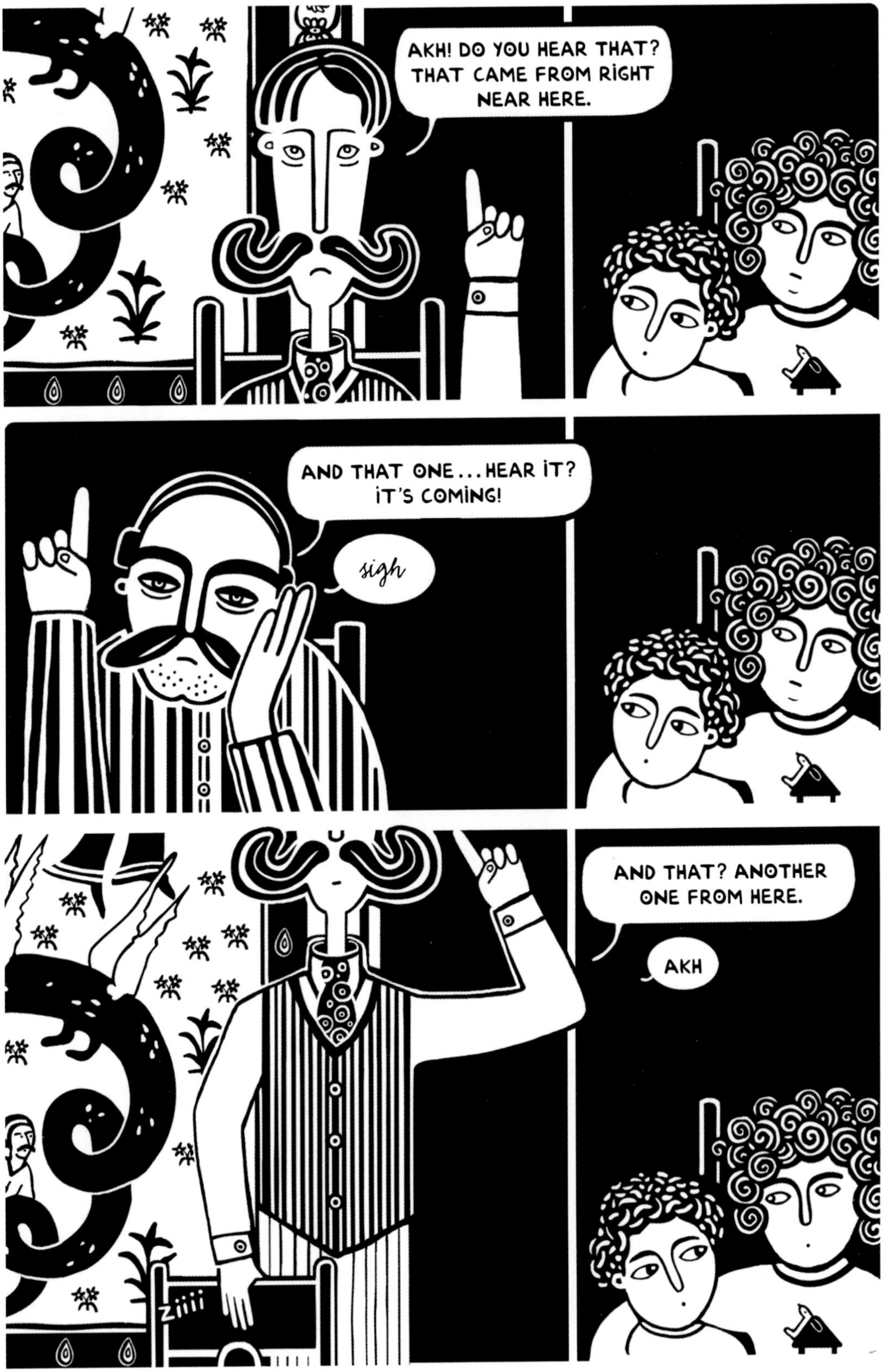
AKH! DO YOU HEAR THAT? THAT CAME FROM RIGHT NEAR HERE.
AND THAT ONE... HEAR IT? IT'S COMING!
sigh
AND THAT? ANOTHER ONE FROM HERE.
AKH
ziiii

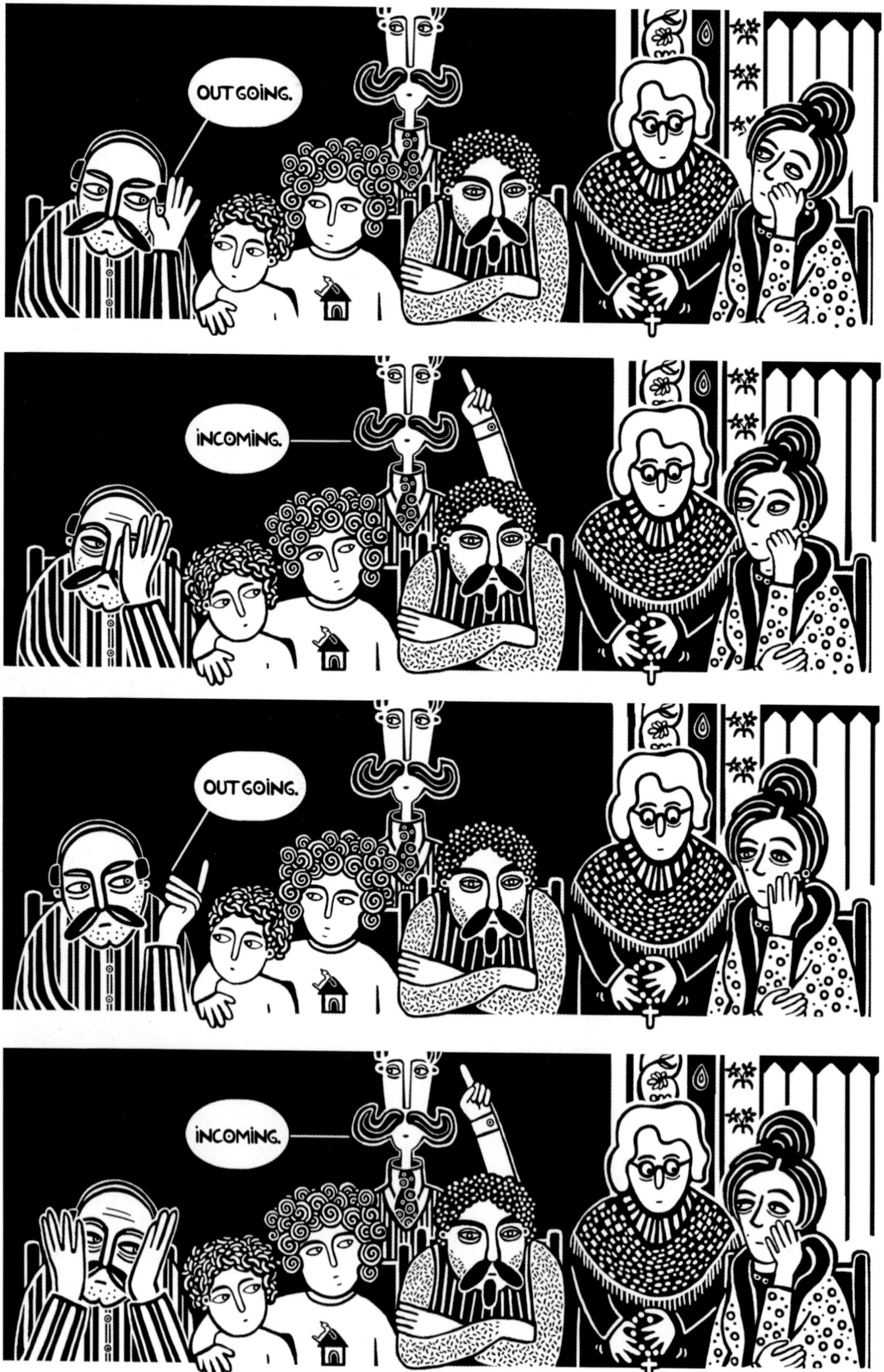
OUTGOING.
INCOMING.
OUTGOING.
INCOMING.

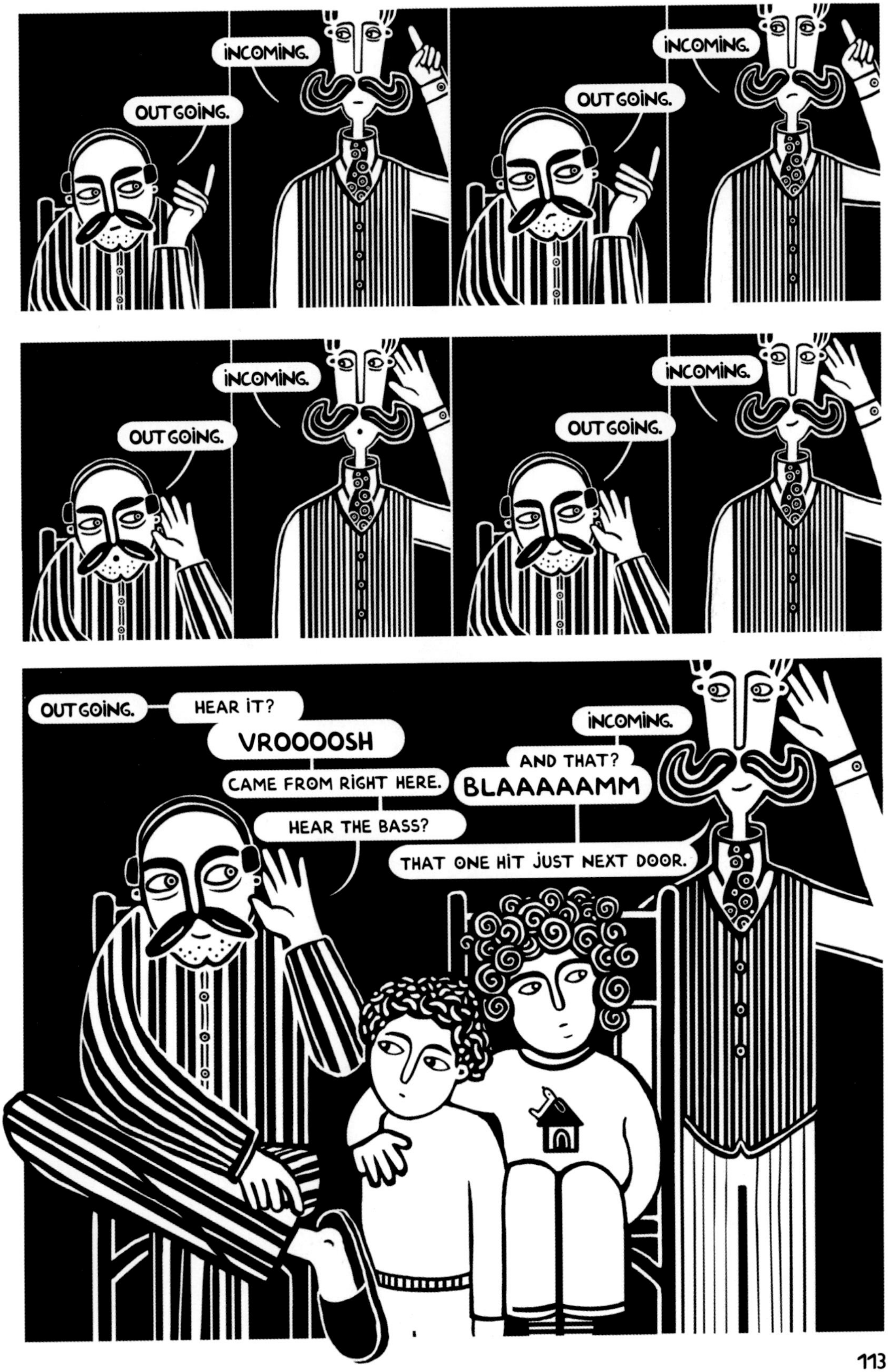
OUTGOING.
INCOMING.
OUTGOING.
INCOMING.
OUTGOING.
INCOMING.
OUTGOING.
INCOMING.
OUTGOING.
HEAR IT?
VROOOOSH
CAME FROM RIGHT HERE.
HEAR THE BASS?
INCOMING.
AND THAT?
BLAAAAAMM
THAT ONE HIT JUST NEXT DOOR.

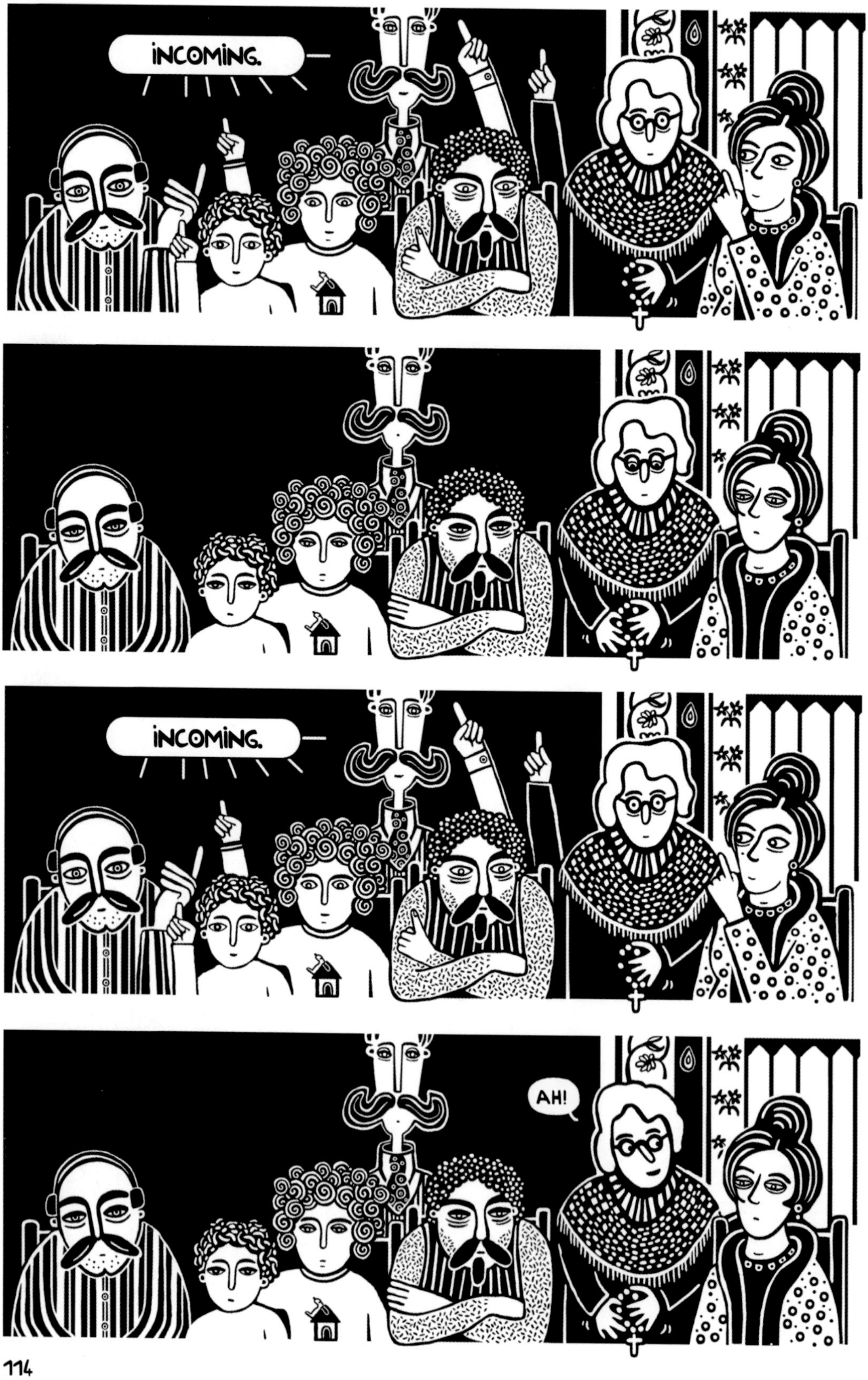
INCOMING.
INCOMING.
AH!

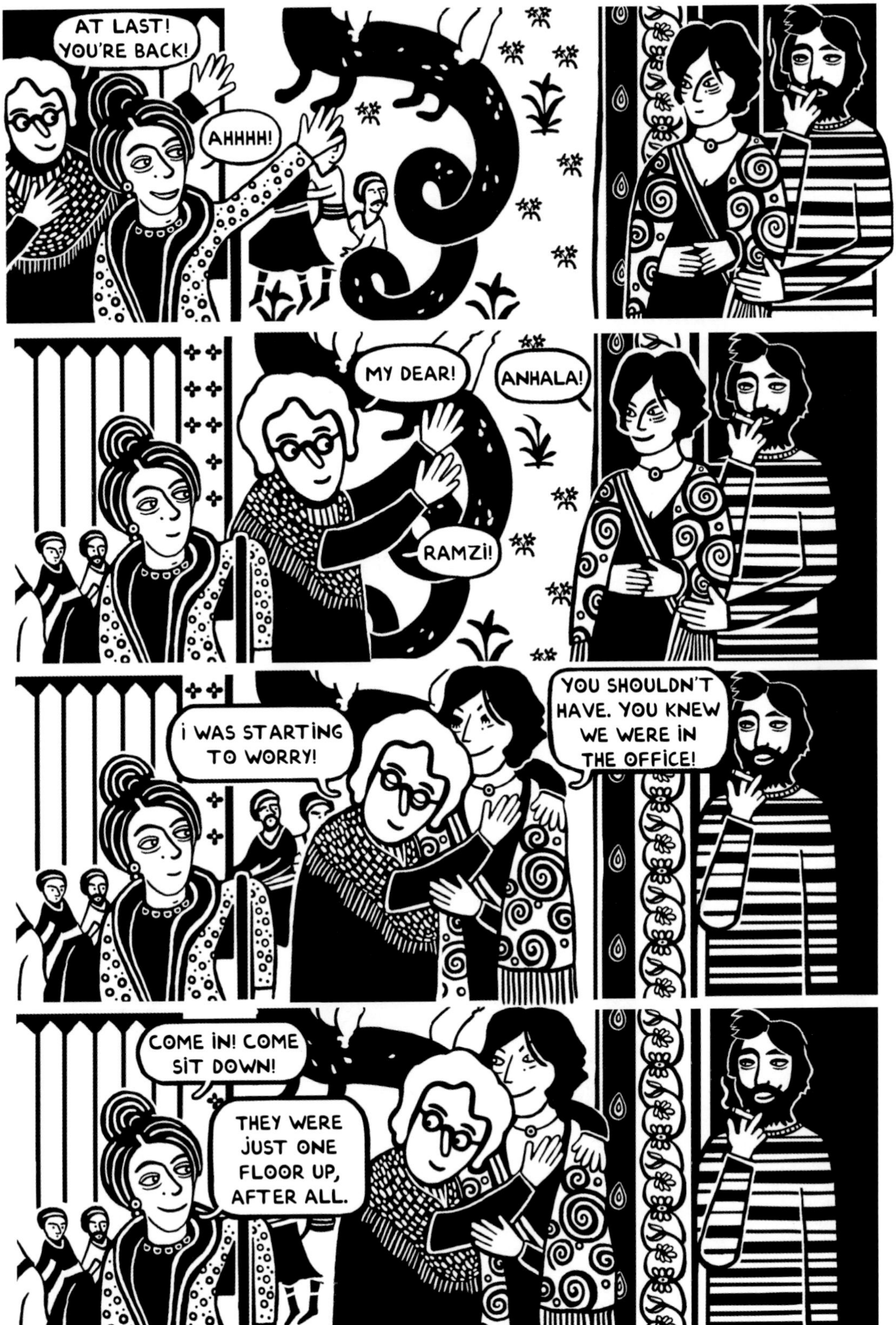
AT LAST! YOU'RE BACK!
AHHHH!
MY DEAR!
ANHALA!
RAMZI!
I WAS STARTING TO WORRY!
YOU SHOULDN'T HAVE. YOU KNEW WE WERE IN THE OFFICE!
COME IN! COME SIT DOWN!
THEY WERE JUST ONE FLOOR UP, AFTER ALL.

WHEN RAMZI AND FARAH MOVED INTO THE BUILDING WITH ANHALA, THEY DIDN'T THINK THEY'D HAVE TO LIVE IN RAMZI'S FATHER'S OFFICE FOR SO LONG.

THEY EXPECTED TO GET THEIR VISAS AND JOIN RAMZI'S BROTHER WALID, WHO HAD FLED TO CANADA WHEN THE WAR STARTED AND OPENED AN ARCHITECTURE OFFICE IN MONTREAL.

MUCH BETTER, THANKS! THIS MORNING I FELT HIM MOVE IN MY BELLY FOR THE FIRST TIME!

AH, MY DEAR!

I'D NEVER HAVE THOUGHT I'D HAVE MY FIRST CHILD IN AN OFFICE FULL OF SUITCASES...

THERE, THERE.

FARAH ALWAYS WORE A LITTLE BAG ON HER SHOULDER WITH BOTH THEIR PASSPORTS AND READY CASH.

USUALLY, WHEN FARAH AND RAMZI SHOWED UP IN THE FOYER, IT MEANT THAT THE BOMBARDMENT WAS ABOUT TO GET WORSE.

THE OFFICE, WHICH THEY'D TURNED INTO A BEDROOM, OVERLOOKED A VACANT LOT WHERE A CANNON HAD BEEN SET UP.

THROUGH THE OFFICE WALL, RAMZI COULD HEAR THE GUNNERS BEING GIVEN INSTRUCTIONS. HE WAS ALWAYS THE FIRST TO KNOW WHEN THINGS WERE ABOUT TO BECOME UNBEARABLE.

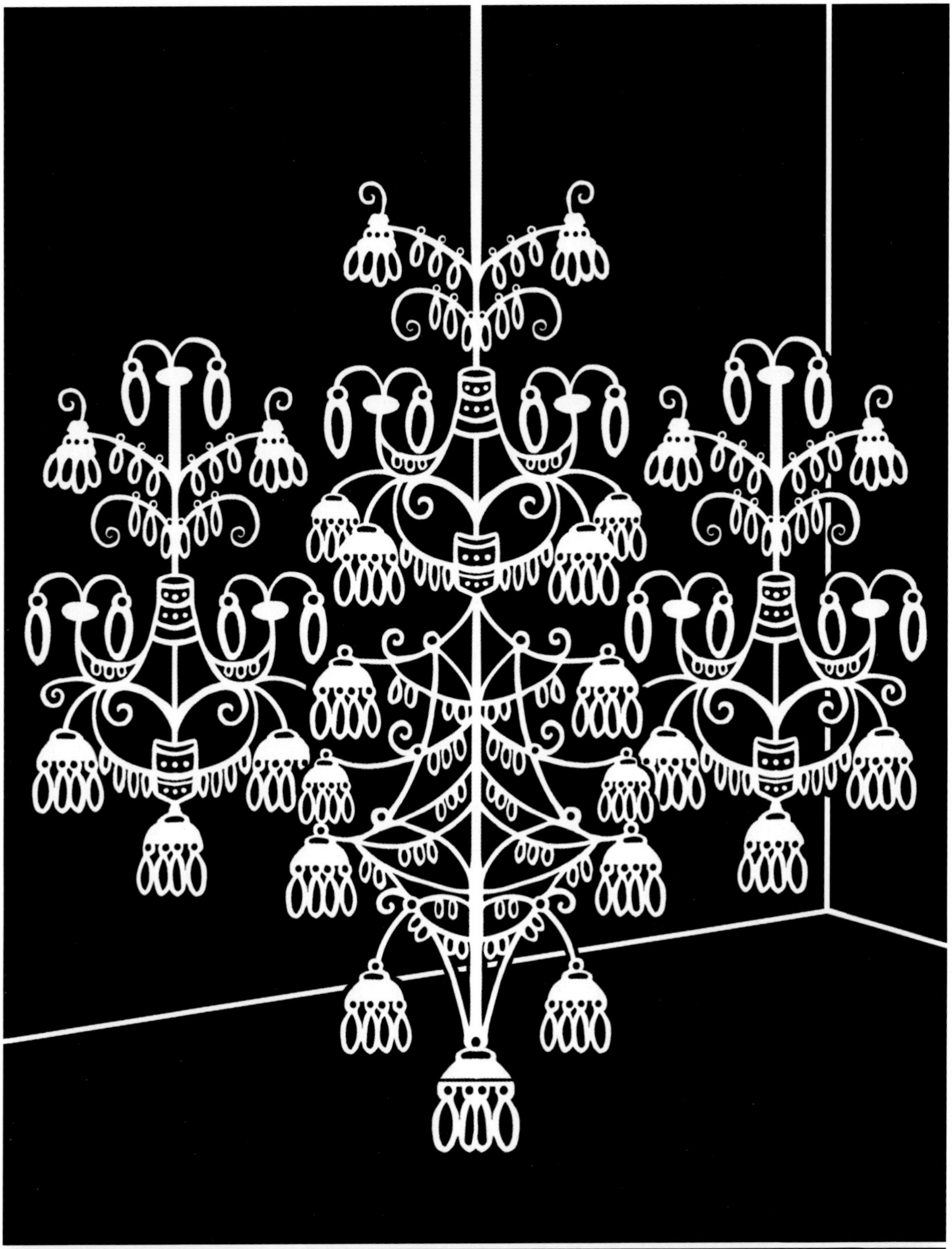

WHERE ANHALA SLEPT, A CRYSTAL CHANDELIER THAT BELONGED TO RAMZI'S FATHER'S CLIENTS HUNG ALMOST TO THE FLOOR.

ALTHOUGH ALL THE BUILDING'S WINDOWS HAD LONG SINCE BURST INTO PIECES, THE CHANDELIER—USELESS BECAUSE THERE WAS NO ELECTRICITY—HAD REMAINED INTACT.

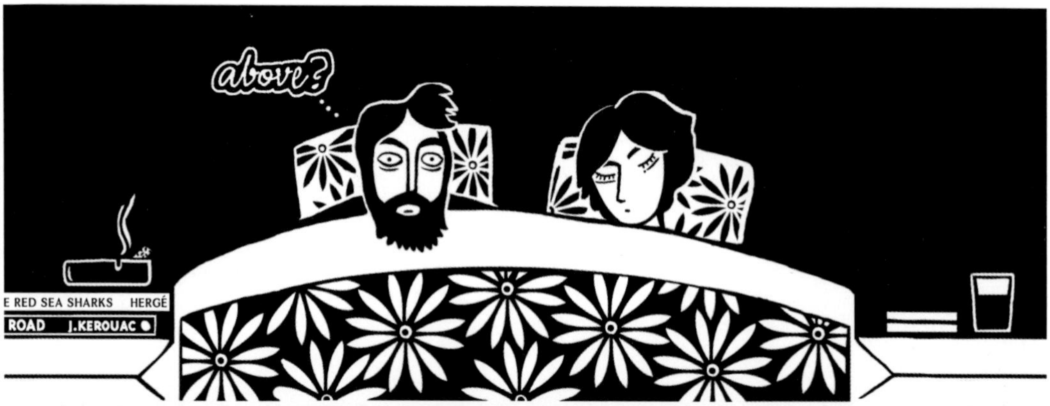
above?
E RED SEA SHARKS HERGÉ
ROAD J.KEROUAC

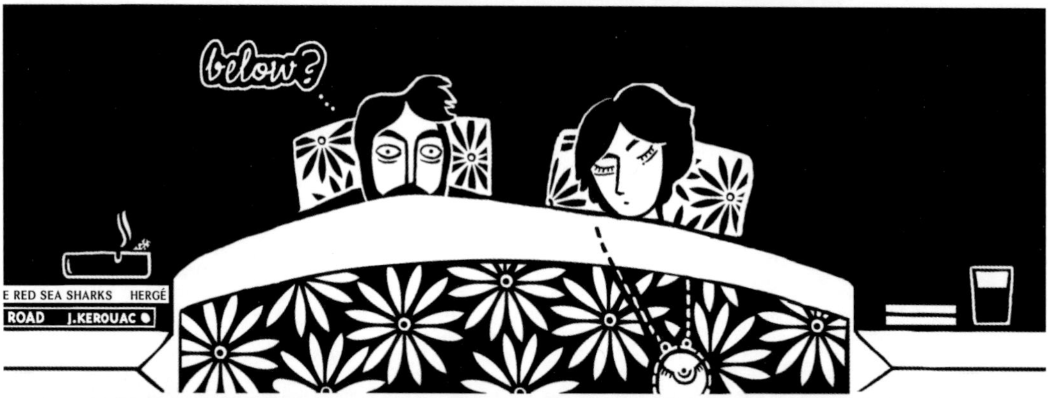
below?
E RED SEA SHARKS HERGÉ
ROAD J.KEROUAC

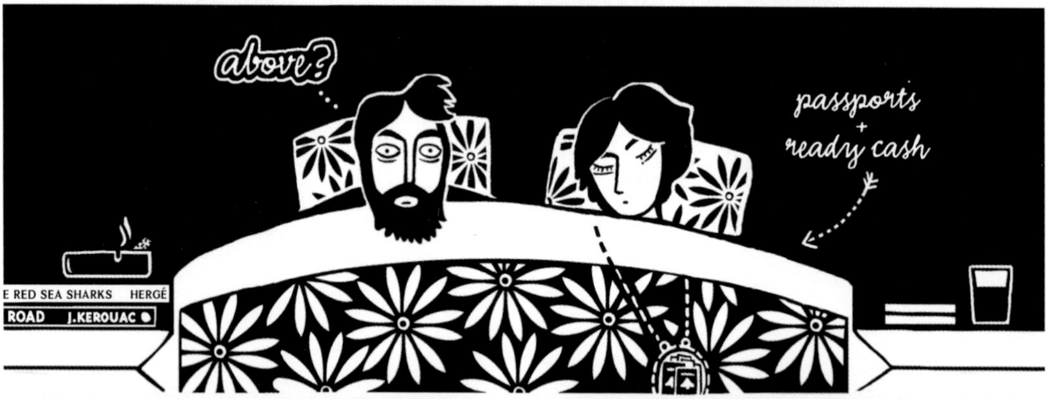
above?
passports
+
ready cash
E RED SEA SHARKS HERGÉ
ROAD J.KEROUAC

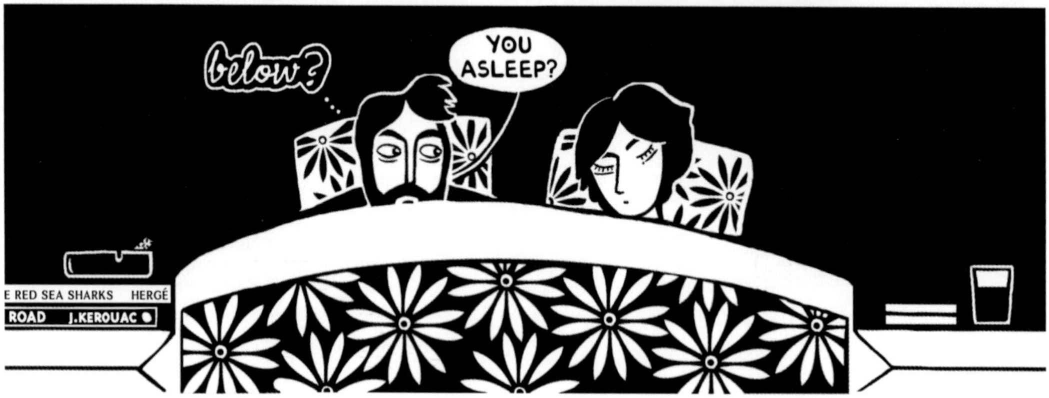
below?
YOU ASLEEP?
E RED SEA SHARKS HERGÉ
ROAD J.KEROUAC

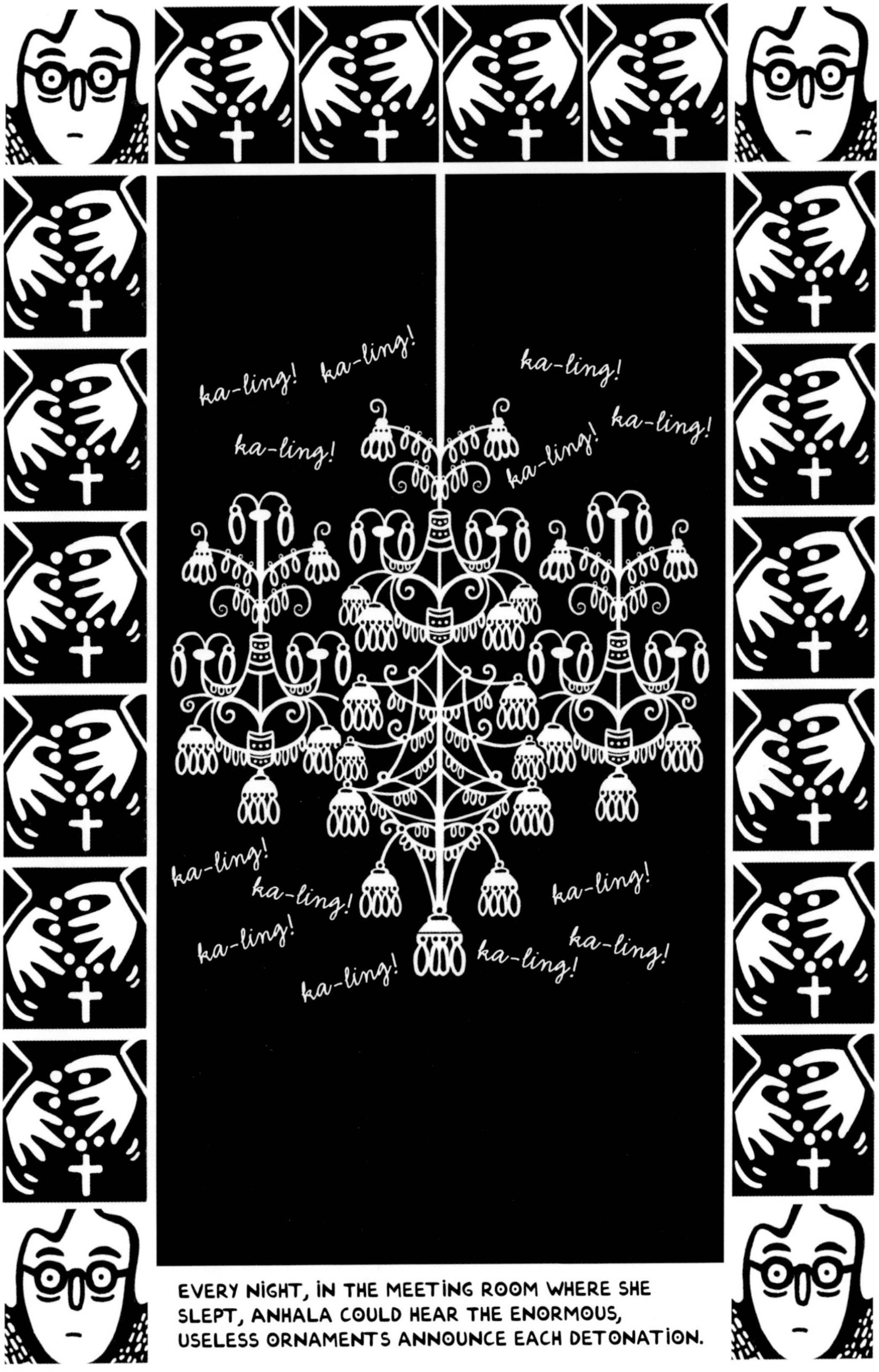
ka-ling!
ka-ling!
ka-ling!
ka-ling!
ka-ling!
ka-ling!
ka-ling!
ka-ling!
ka-ling!
ka-ling!
ka-ling!
ka-ling!
ka-ling!
EVERY NIGHT, IN THE MEETING ROOM WHERE SHE SLEPT, ANHALA COULD HEAR THE ENORMOUS, USELESS ORNAMENTS ANNOUNCE EACH DETONATION.

125

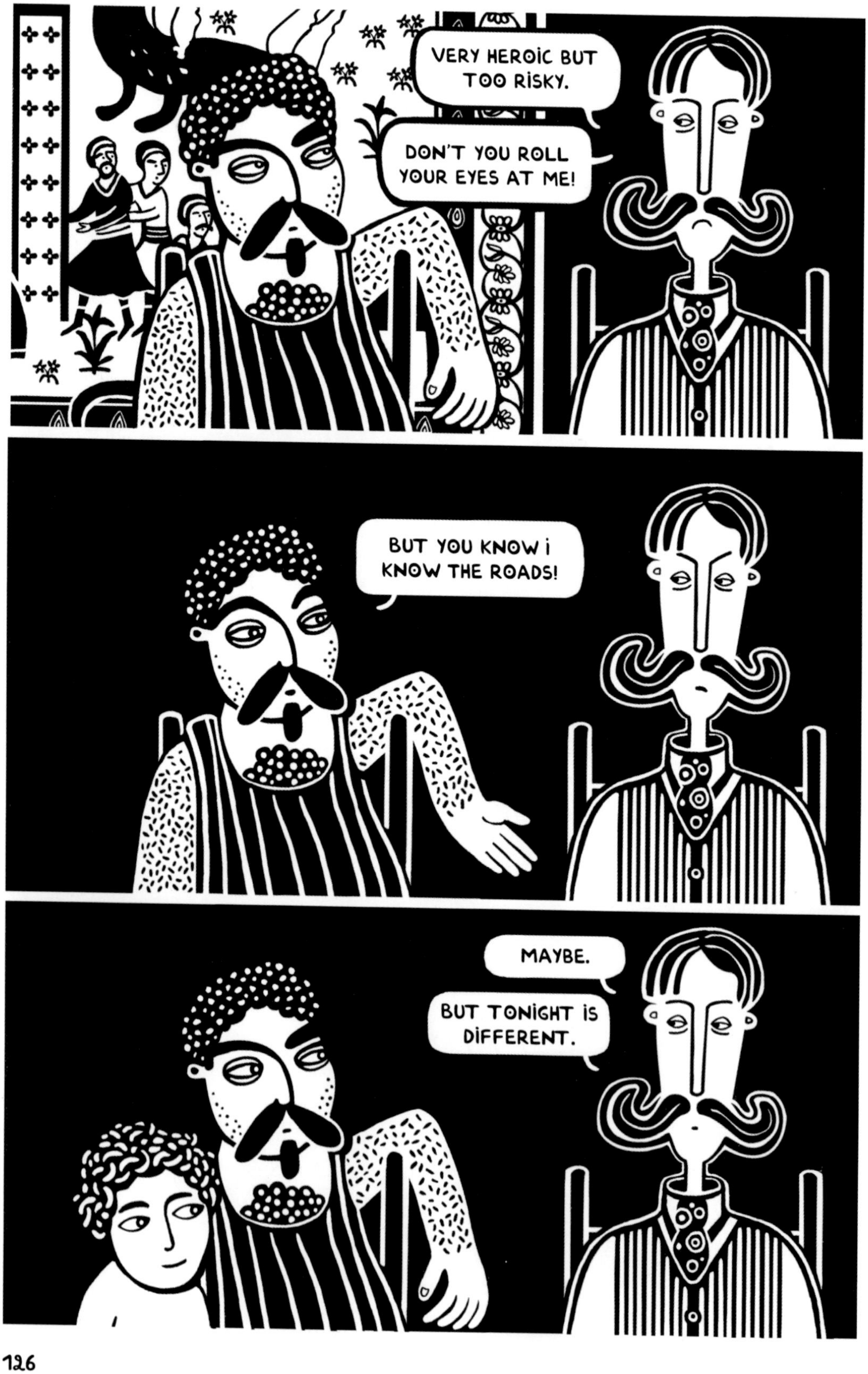
VERY HEROiC BUT TOO RiSKY.
DON'T YOU ROLL YOUR EYES AT ME!
BUT YOU KNOW i KNOW THE ROADS!
MAYBE.
BUT TONiGHT iS DiFFERENT.

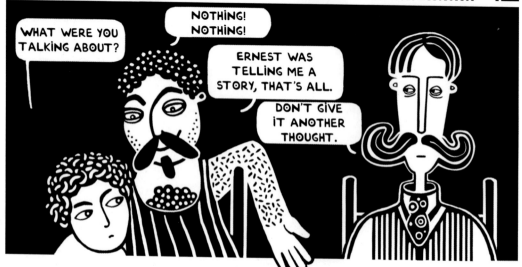

129

"ANHALA HAD PREPARED A BUFFET TO MATCH HER AFFECTION!
SINCE SUPERMARKETS WEREN'T YET EQUIPPED WITH SUFFICIENTLY POWERFUL
GENERATORS BACK THEN, THEY WOULD PUT ALL THE PRODUCTS THEY COULDN'T FIT
IN THEIR FREEZERS ON SALE.
A FEAST LIKE THAT WAS UNBELIEVABLE... AND IN THE MIDDLE OF WARTIME!"

"MAMA INSISTED WE HAVE MY DRESS MADE BY THE EMINENT DESIGNER COUSSA, WHO'D DESIGNED HER OWN WEDDING DRESS. BACK THEN IT WAS HIM, THAT IS. NOW HIS SON HAD TAKEN OVER THE STUDIO.
NEXT, JEAN, THE SHOEMAKER ON GHANDOUR EL-SAAD STREET, DESIGNED WHITE SHOES WITH BUTTON STRAPS THAT MATCHED MY DRESS. HE STUDIED IN ITALY, YOU KNOW! ON THE WEDDING DAY, FOUAD, THE STYLIST AT THE MA BELLE SALON, CAME TO THE HOUSE TO DO MY HAIR.
I WAS TREATED LIKE A REAL PRINCESS!"

"MAMA ABSOLUTELY INSISTED ON ACTING AS IF EVERYTHING WERE NORMAL—WHEN SHE WAS THE ONE WHO'D RALLIED EVERYONE!
JAMAL, THE BEAUTICIAN AT MA BELLE, CAME TO DO MY MAKEUP. HIS YOUNGER SISTER PATRICIA CAME WITH HIM, WITH HER TWEEZER KIT AND OTHER INSTRUMENTS OF TORTURE...
AND SAMIA, WHO'D TAKEN CARE OF MAMA'S NAILS FOREVER, GAVE ME A MEMORABLE MANICURE AND PEDICURE, IN MY ROOM AT MY PARENTS' HOUSE!"

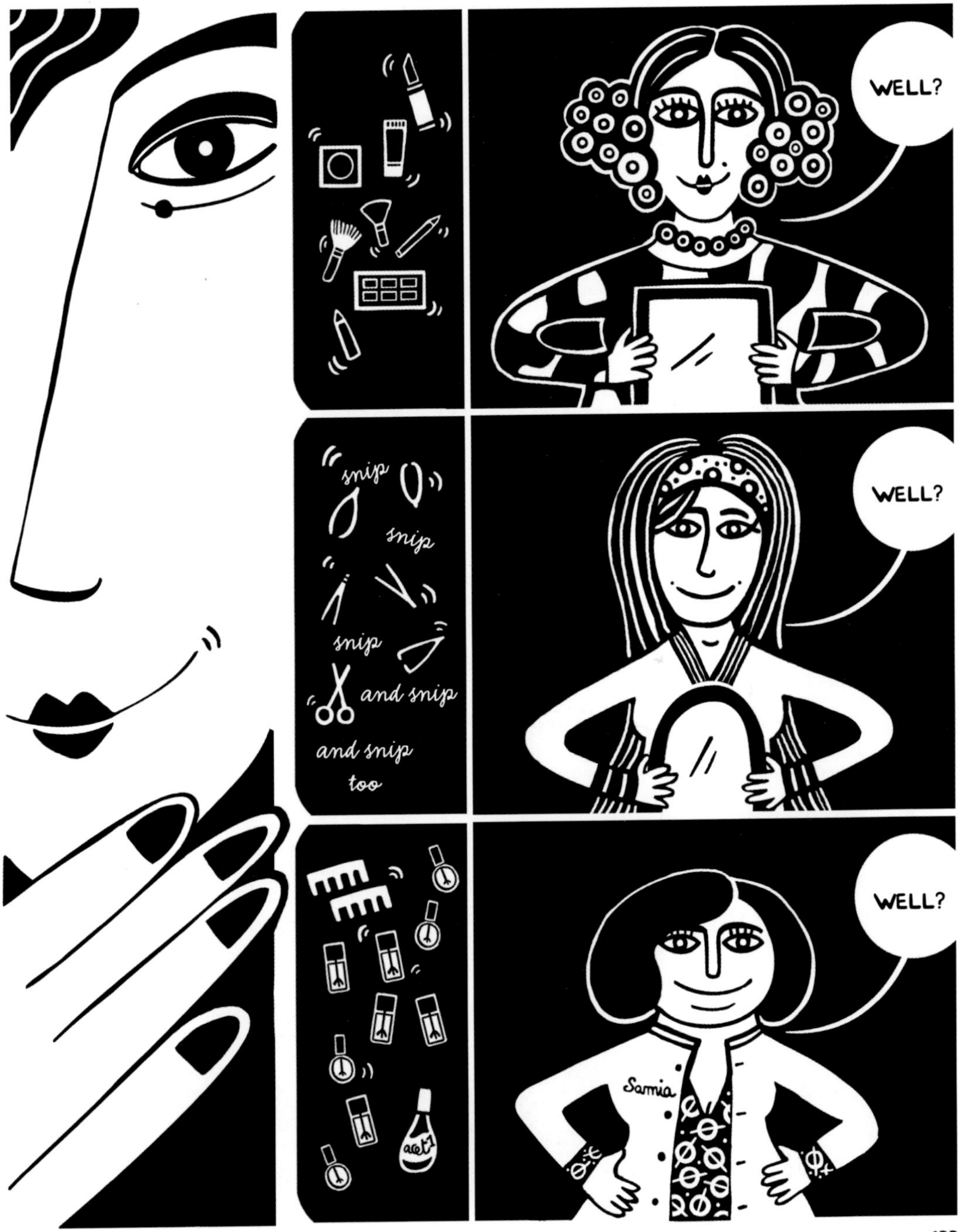
WELL?
snip
snip
snip
and snip
and snip too
WELL?
WELL?
Samia

"I DON'T REMEMBER THE RELIGIOUS CEREMONY VERY WELL ANYMORE.
SINCE RAMZI WAS A MARONITE, WE WERE MARRIED ACCORDING TO THE MARONITE RITE. QUITE PRACTICAL, IN THE END!
FIRST OF ALL: BECAUSE THERE WAS A MARONITE CHURCH RIGHT ACROSS FROM MY PARENTS' HOUSE.
NEXT: BECAUSE THE CEREMONY WAS SHORTER THAN THE ORTHODOX ONE.
IT REASSURED ALL THE GUESTS TO KNOW WE WOULDN'T SPEND MUCH TIME OUTSIDE THE HOUSE!

I REMEMBER THAT TO AVOID THE SNIPER, WE HAD TO RUN FROM MY PARENTS' HOUSE TO THE CHURCH AND THEN FROM THE CHURCH BACK TO MY PARENTS.

MAMA WAS SO STRESSED OUT BY THE CROSSING BACK AND FORTH THAT SHE STARTED FIXATING ON MY DRESS!"

"EVERYONE WAS MORE RELAXED WHEN WE GOT TO THE HOUSE. ANHALA CALLED US TO THE TABLE, MY FATHER UNCORKED THE CHAMPAGNE, AND SOMEONE PUT ON AN ENRICO MACIAS RECORD."

"WHEN I THINK BACK...I REALIZE WE NEVER SUSPECTED A THING."

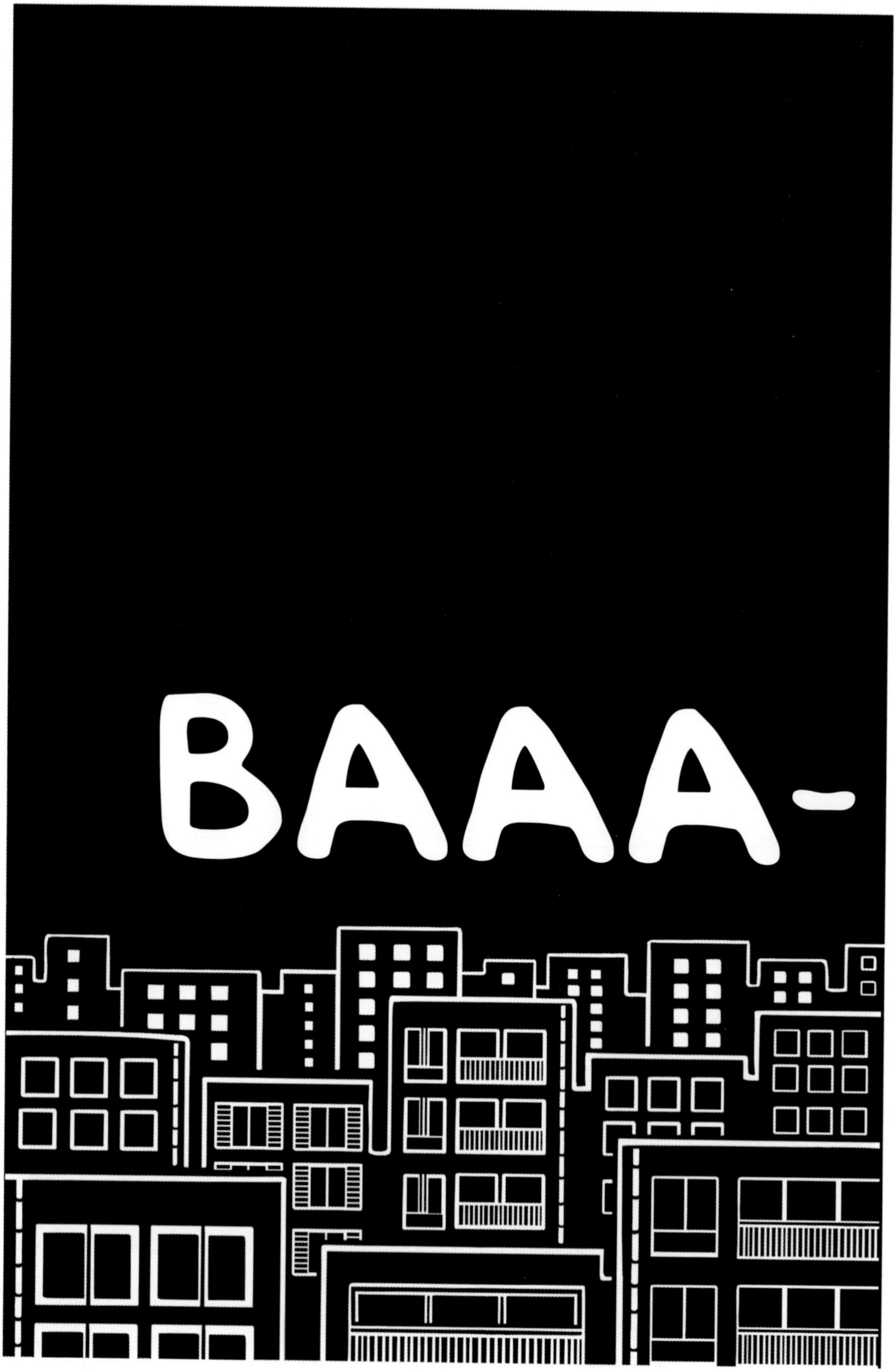
BAAA-

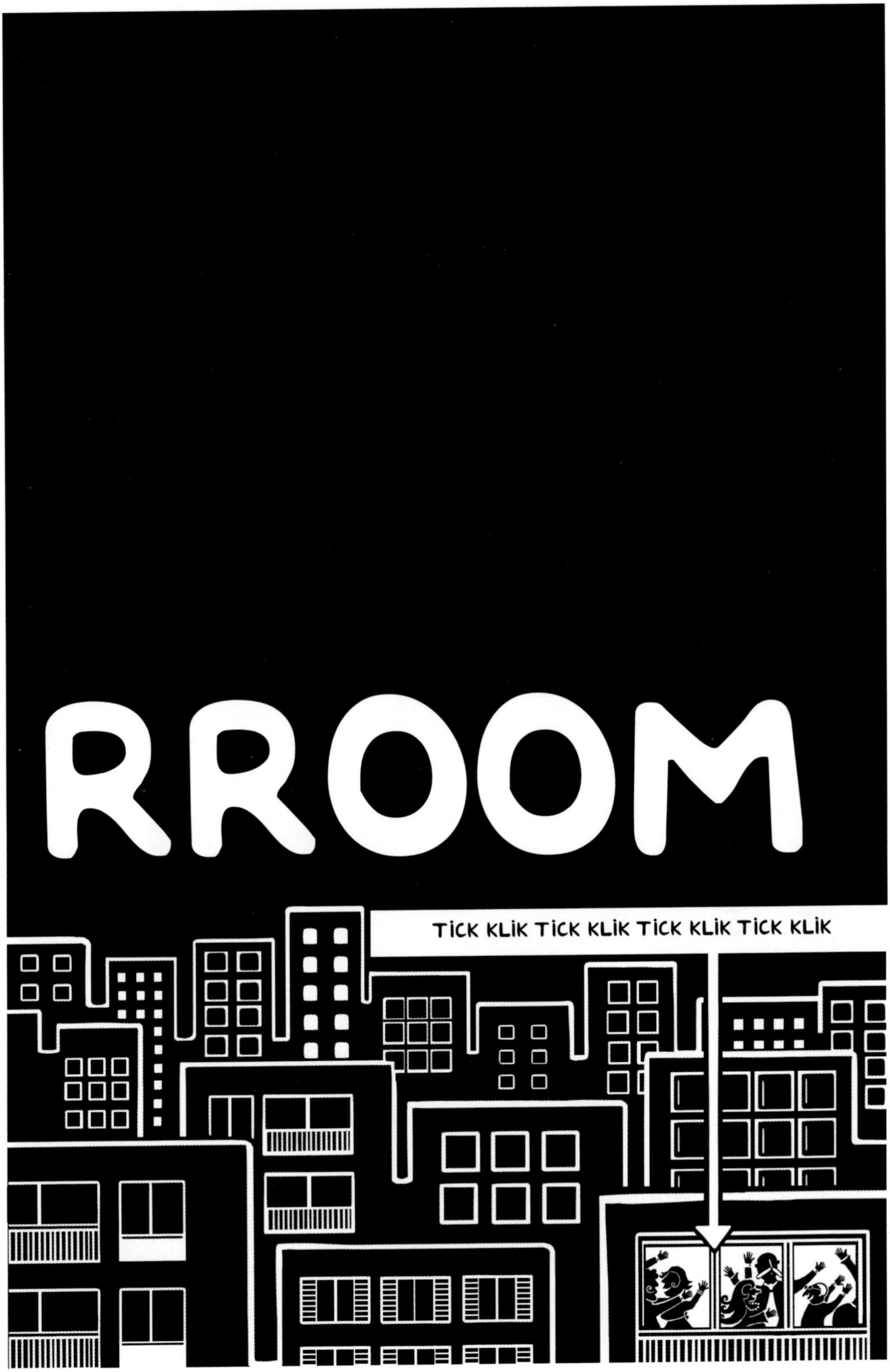
RROOM
TICK KLIK TICK KLIK TICK KLIK TICK KLIK

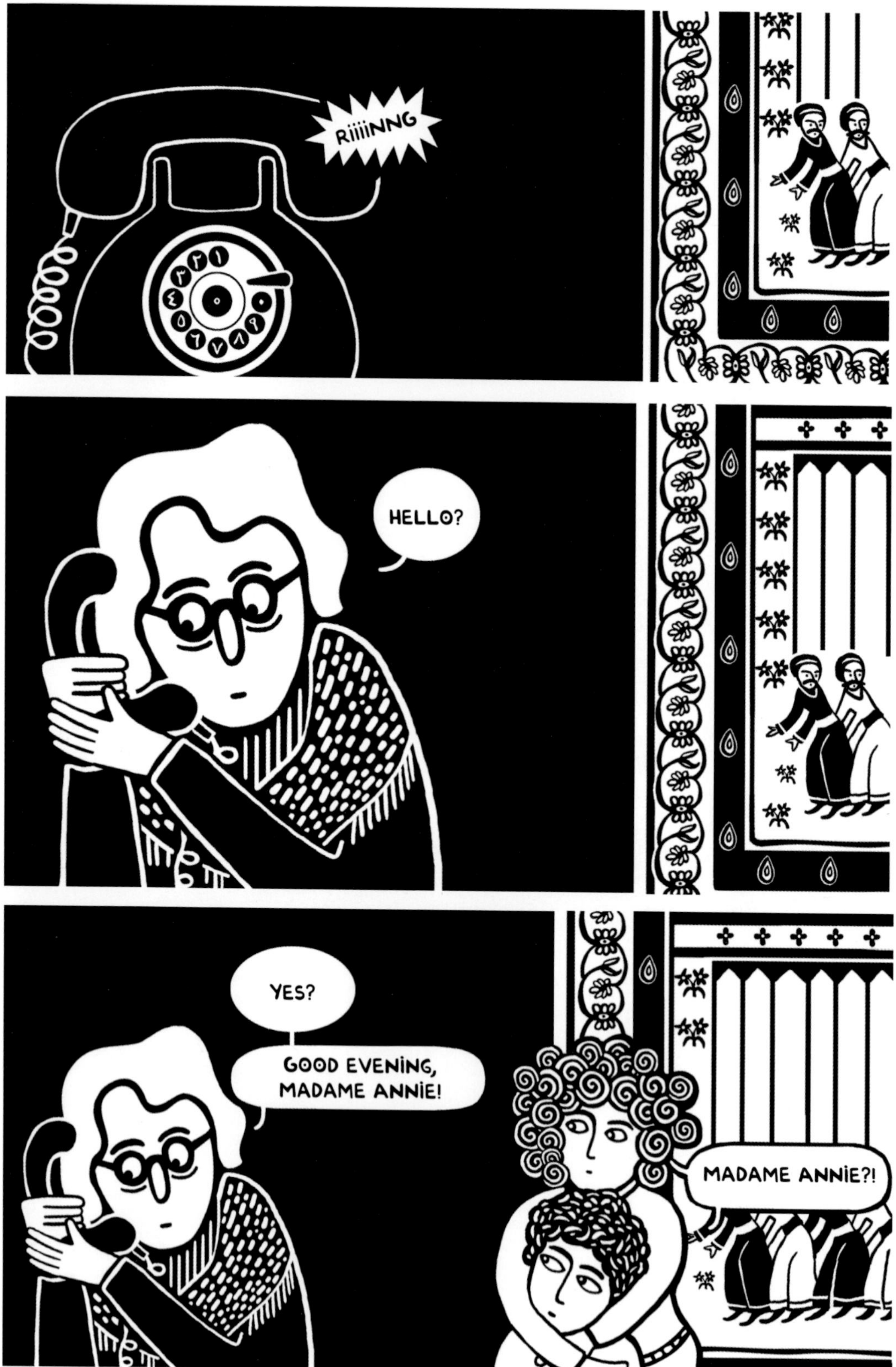
RiiiiNNG
HELLO?
YES?
GOOD EVENiNG, MADAME ANNiE!
MADAME ANNiE?!

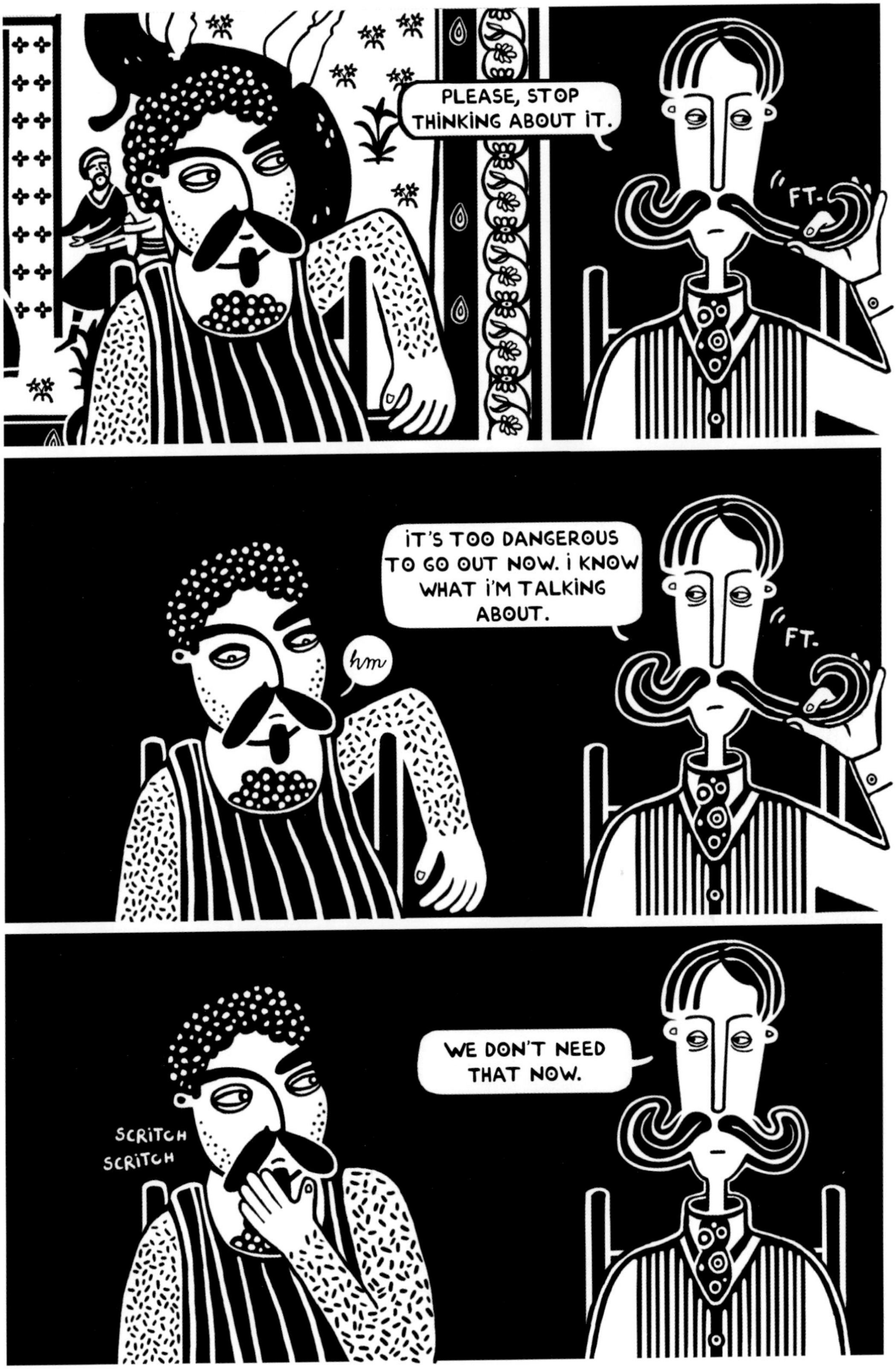
PLEASE, STOP THINKING ABOUT IT.
FT-
IT'S TOO DANGEROUS TO GO OUT NOW. I KNOW WHAT I'M TALKING ABOUT.
hm
FT-
WE DON'T NEED THAT NOW.
SCRITCH SCRITCH

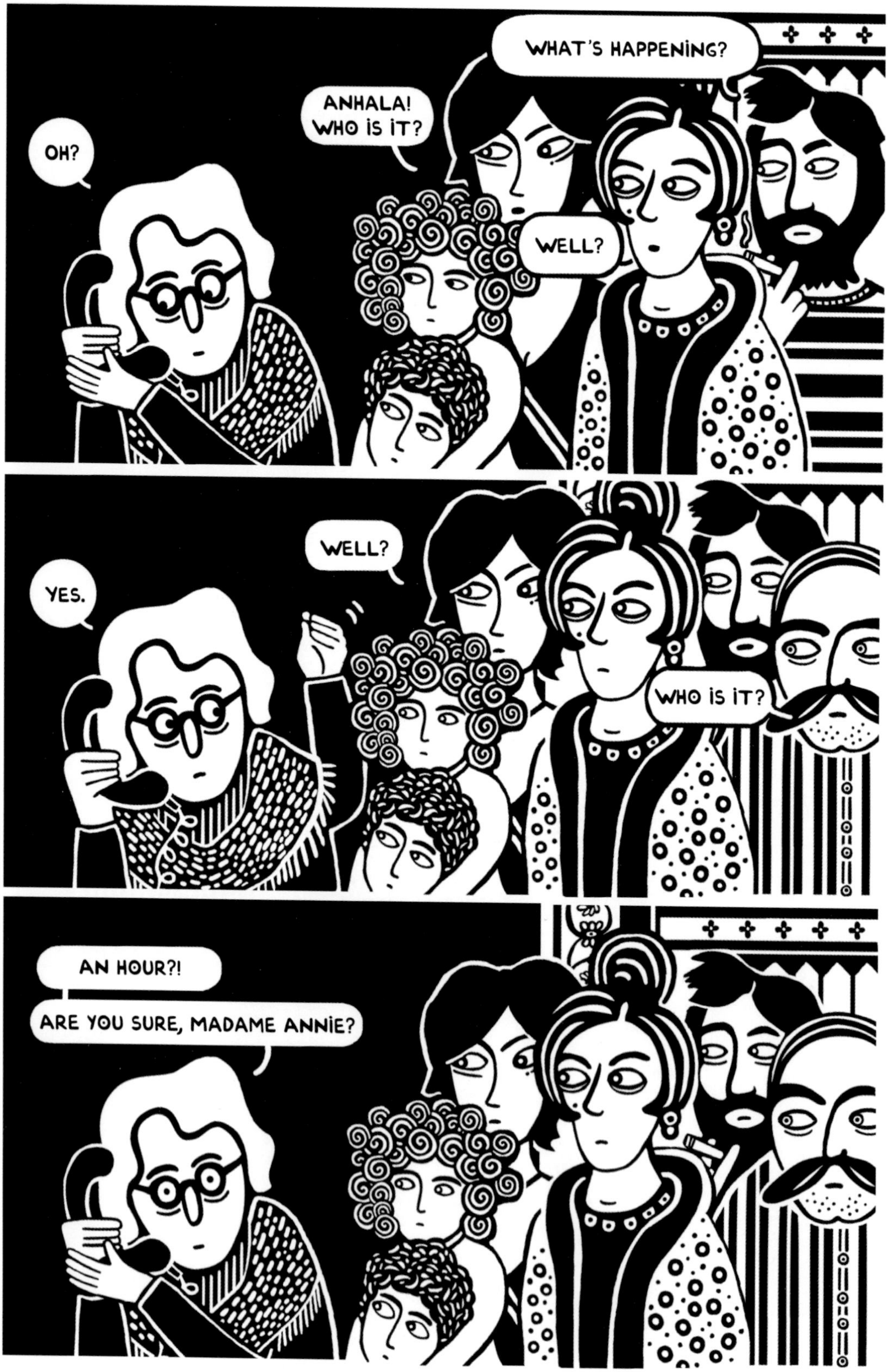
OH?
ANHALA! WHO IS IT?
WHAT'S HAPPENING?
WELL?
YES.
WELL?
WHO IS IT?
AN HOUR?!
ARE YOU SURE, MADAME ANNIE?

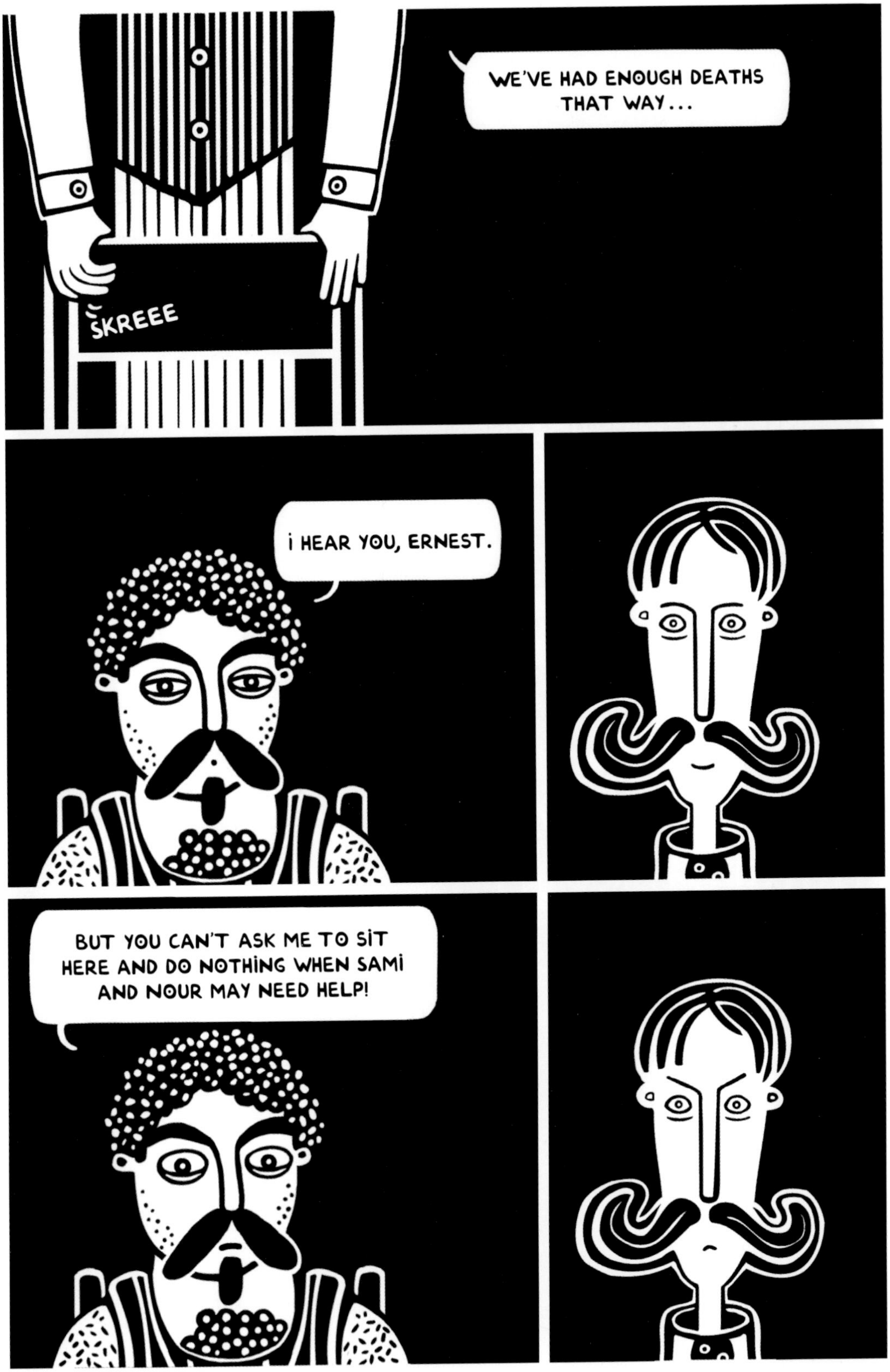
WE'VE HAD ENOUGH DEATHS THAT WAY...
SKREEE
i HEAR YOU, ERNEST.
BUT YOU CAN'T ASK ME TO SiT HERE AND DO NOTHiNG WHEN SAMi AND NOUR MAY NEED HELP!

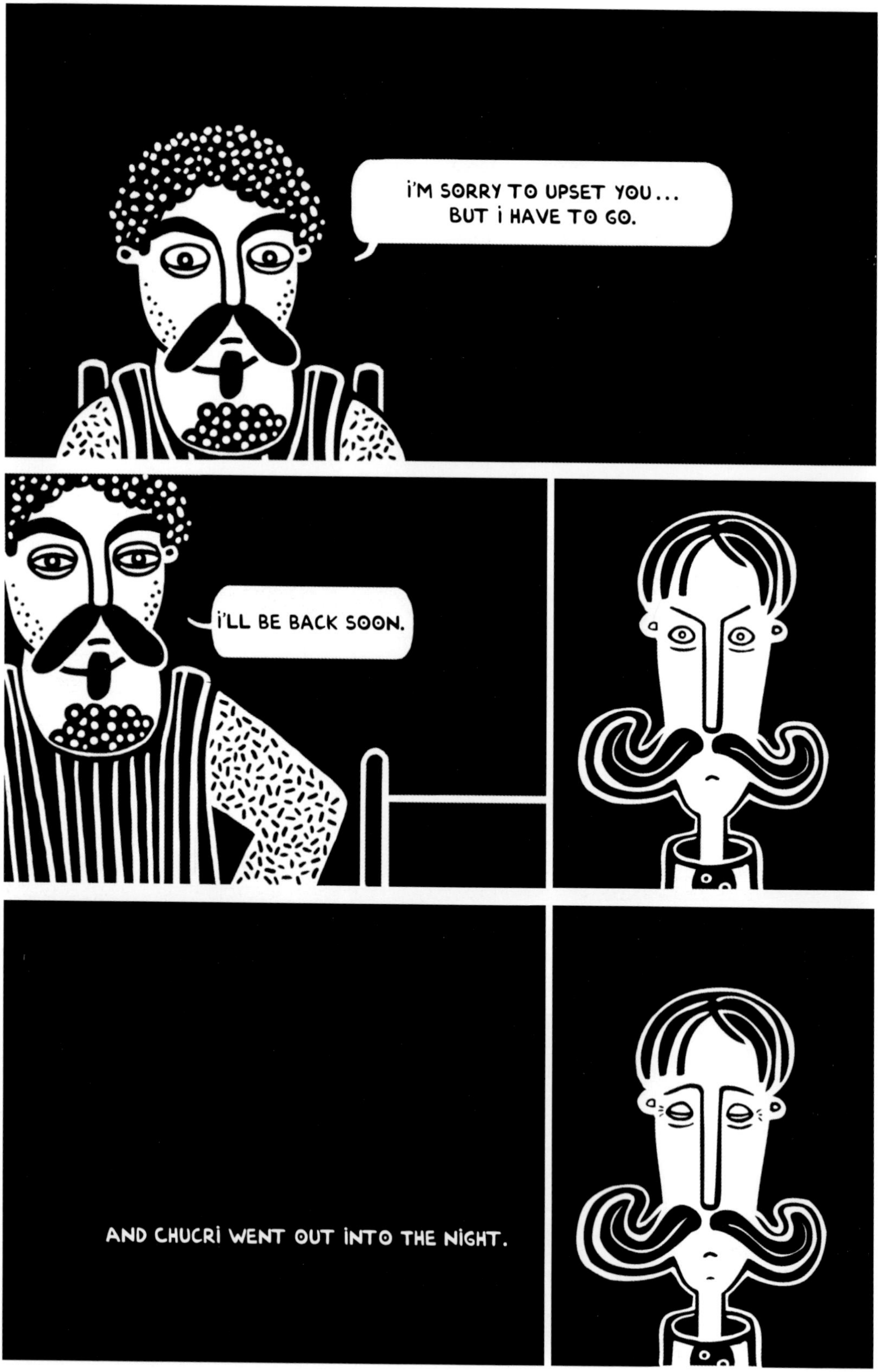
I'M SORRY TO UPSET YOU...
BUT I HAVE TO GO.
I'LL BE BACK SOON.
AND CHUCRI WENT OUT INTO THE NIGHT.

151

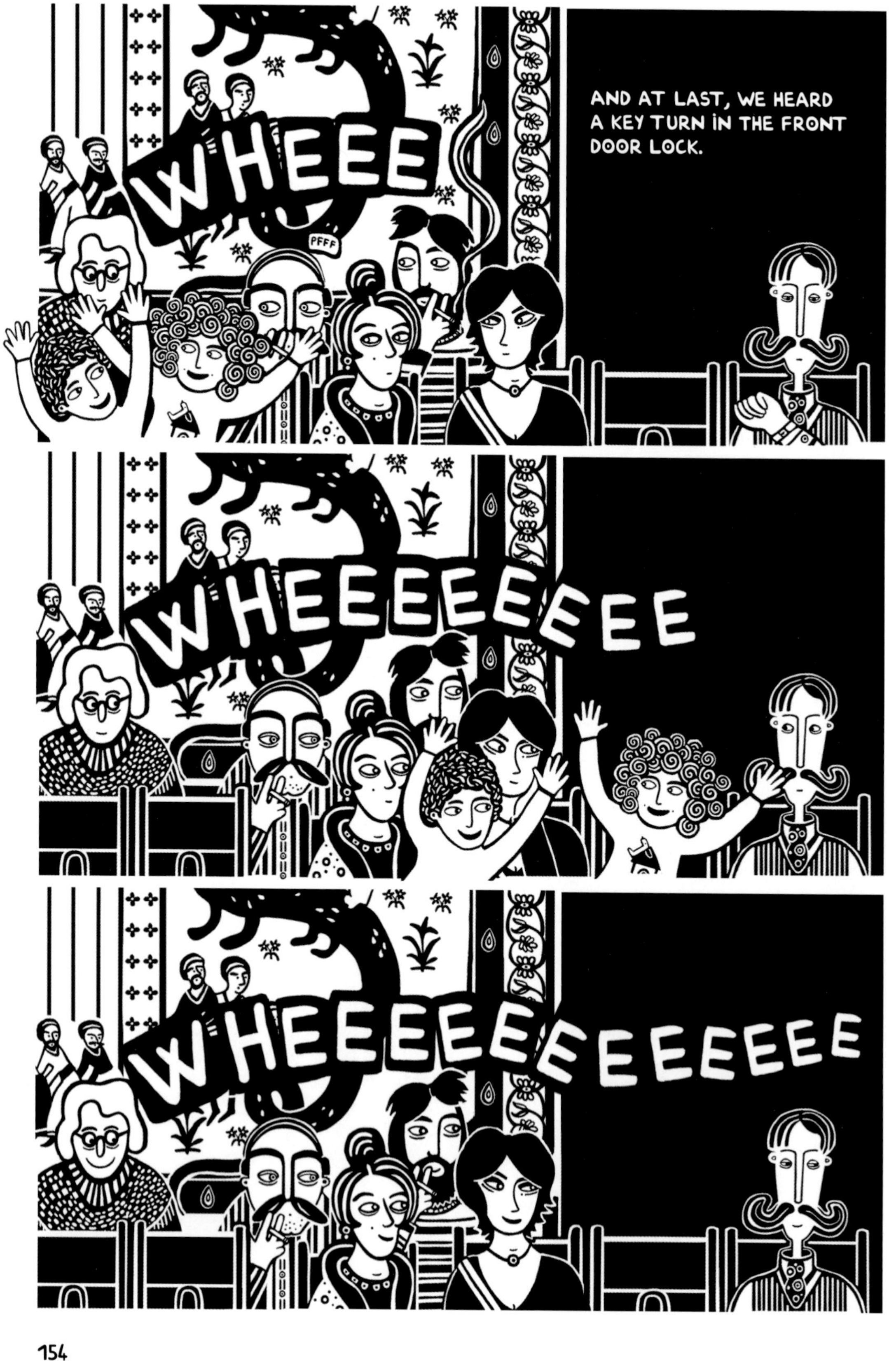
WHEEE
PFFF
AND AT LAST, WE HEARD A KEY TURN IN THE FRONT DOOR LOCK.
WHEEEEEEEE
WHEEEEEEEEEEEEE

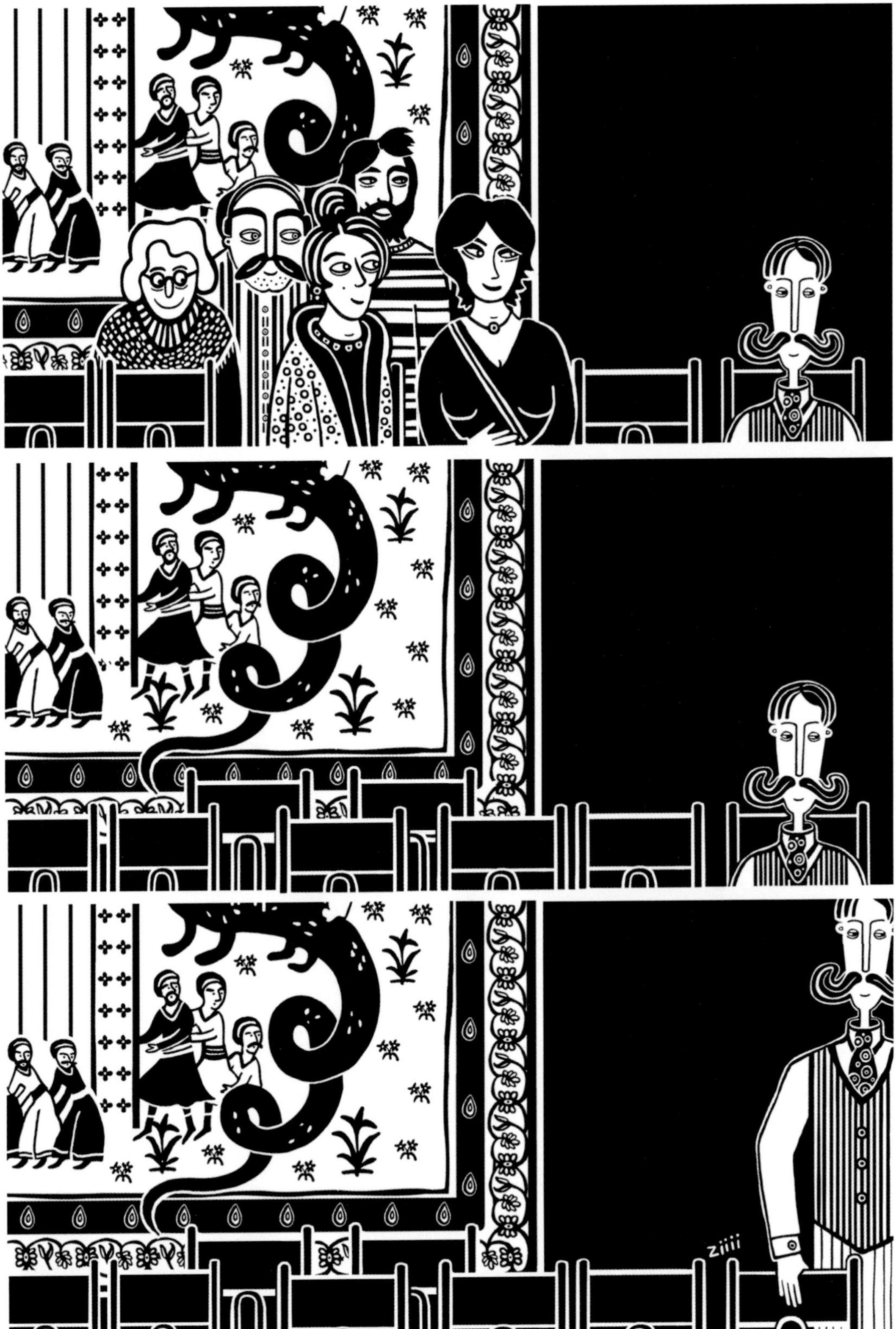
ziiii

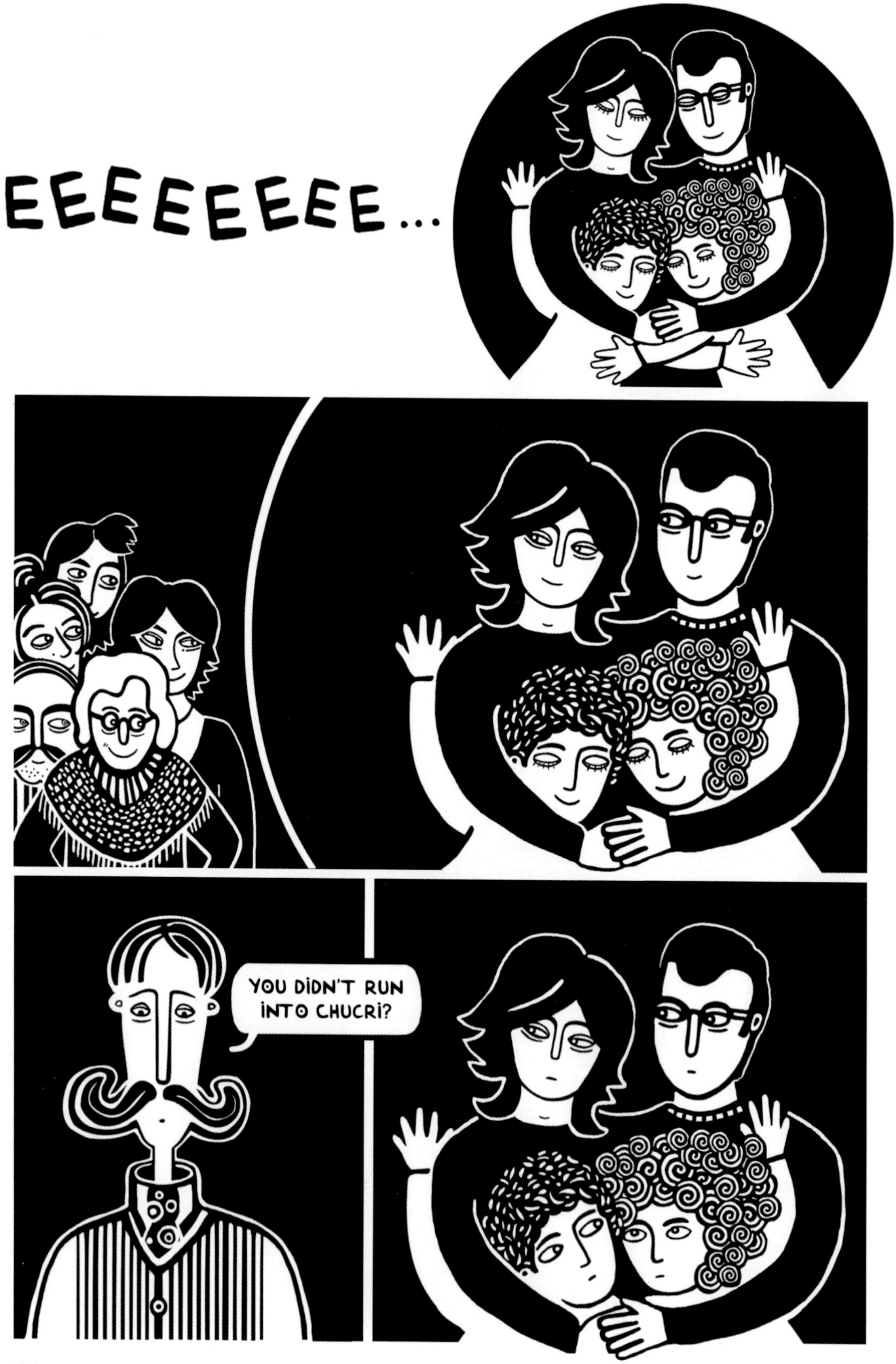
EEEEEEEE...
YOU DIDN'T RUN INTO CHUCRI?

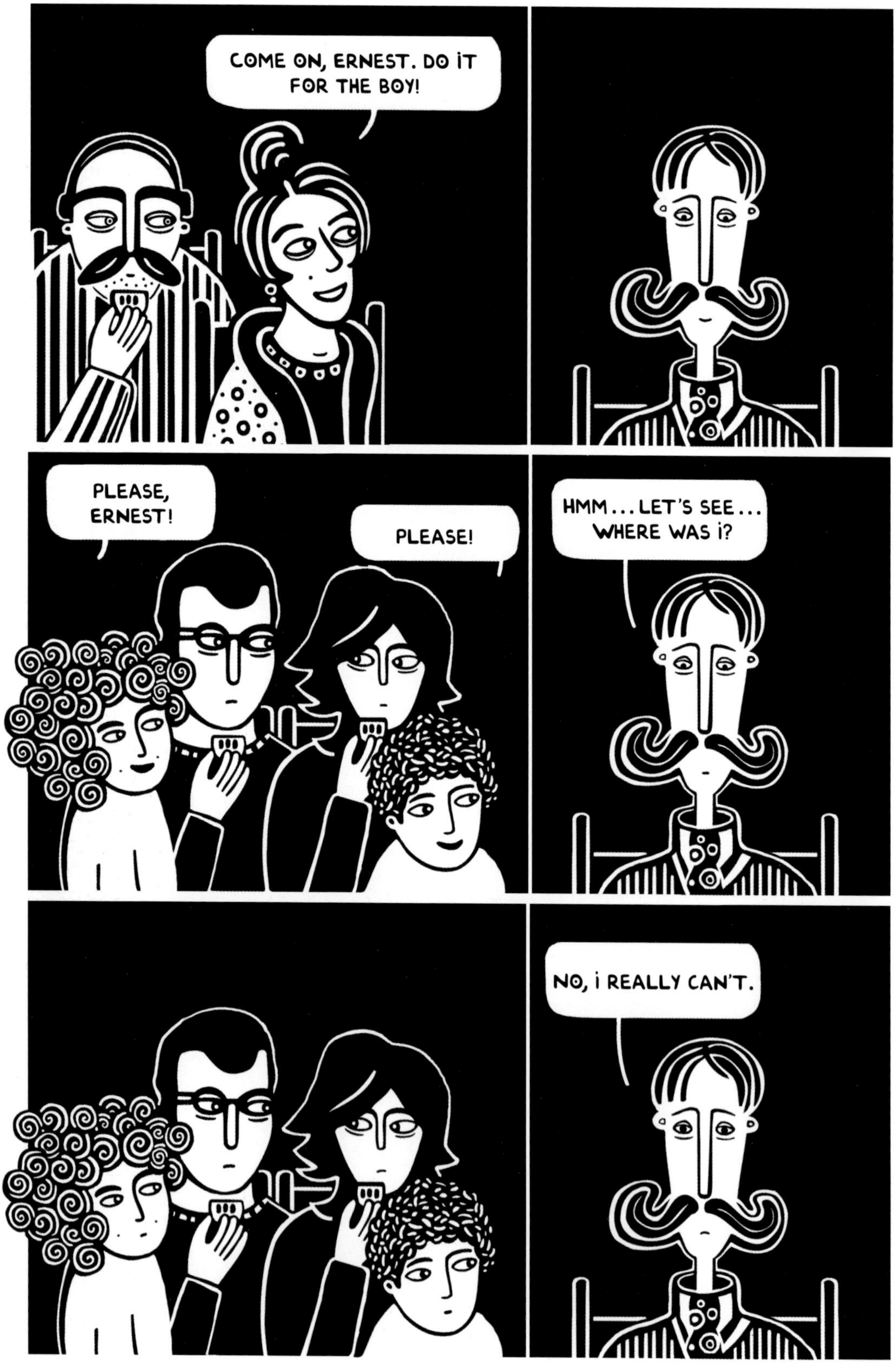
COME ON, ERNEST. DO IT FOR THE BOY!
PLEASE, ERNEST!
PLEASE!
HMM... LET'S SEE... WHERE WAS I?
NO, I REALLY CAN'T.

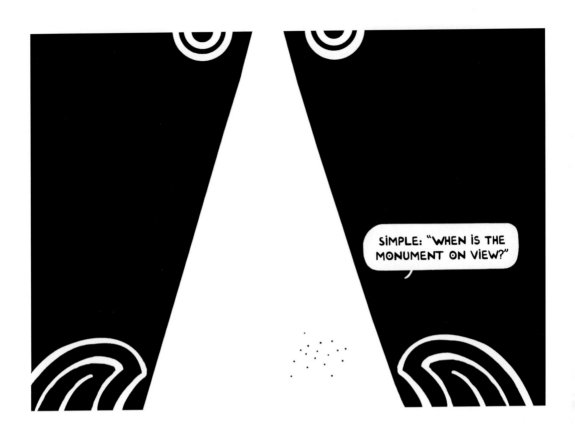

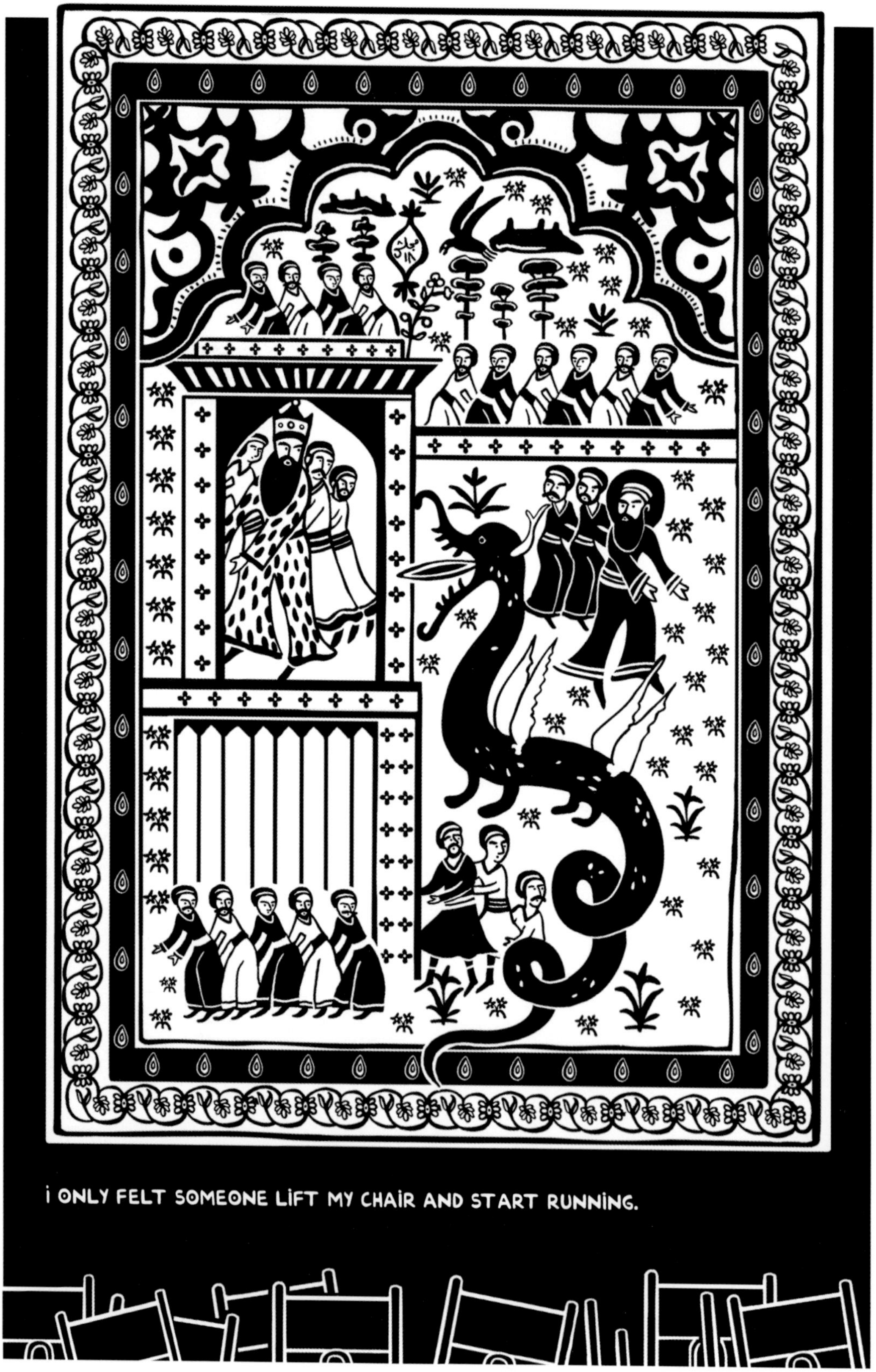
I ONLY FELT SOMEONE LIFT MY CHAIR AND START RUNNING.

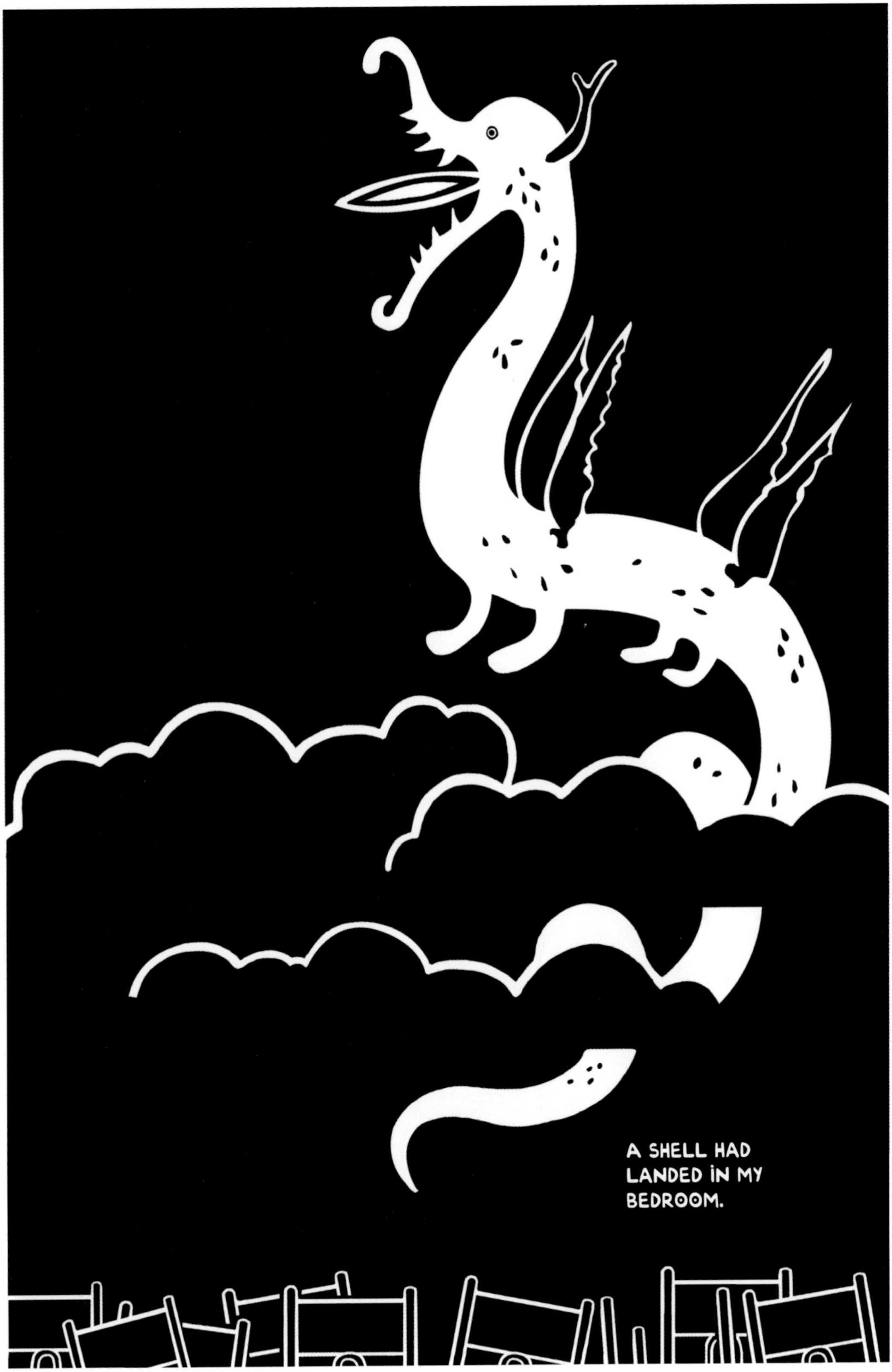
A SHELL HAD
LANDED IN MY
BEDROOM.

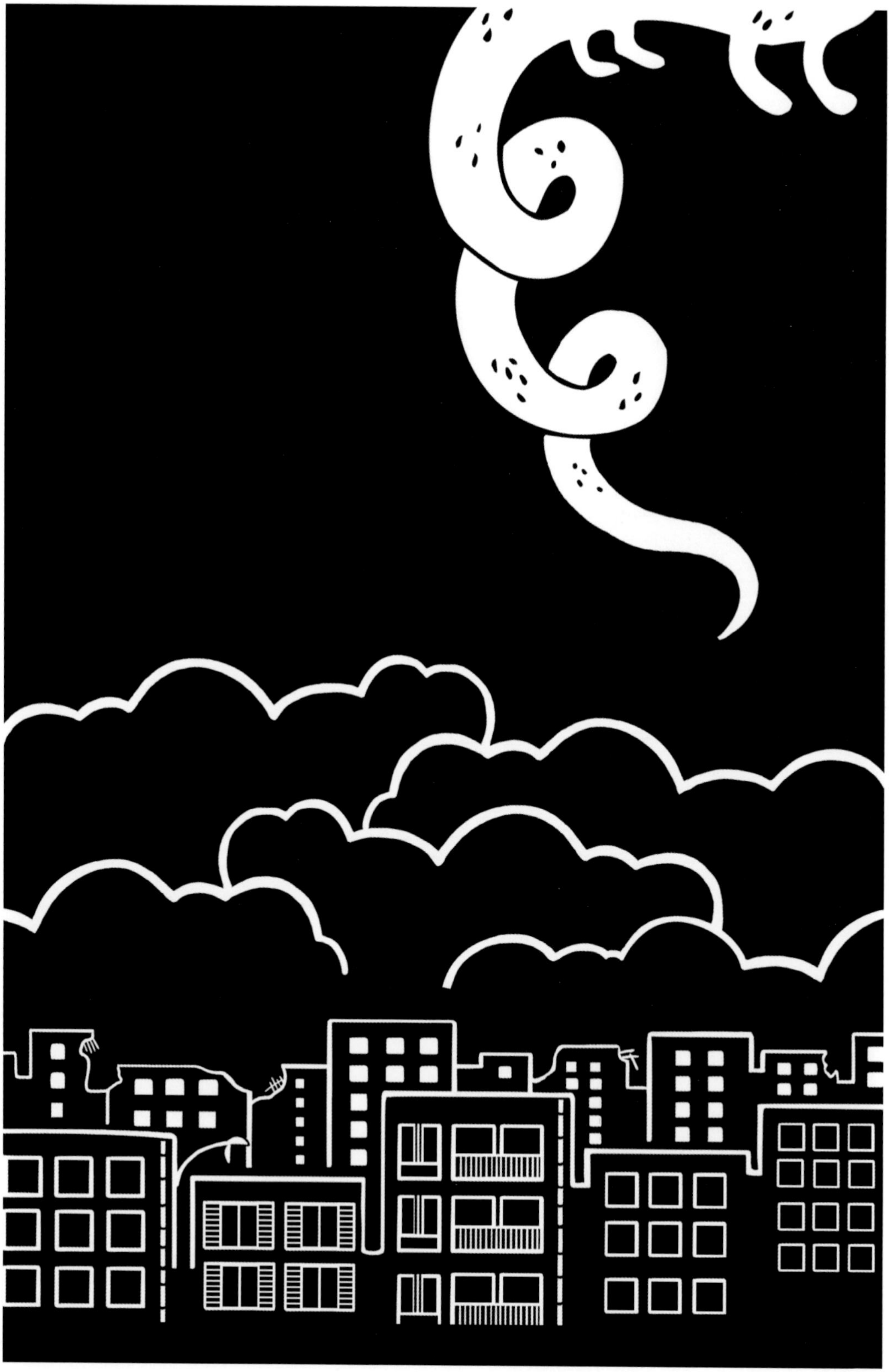

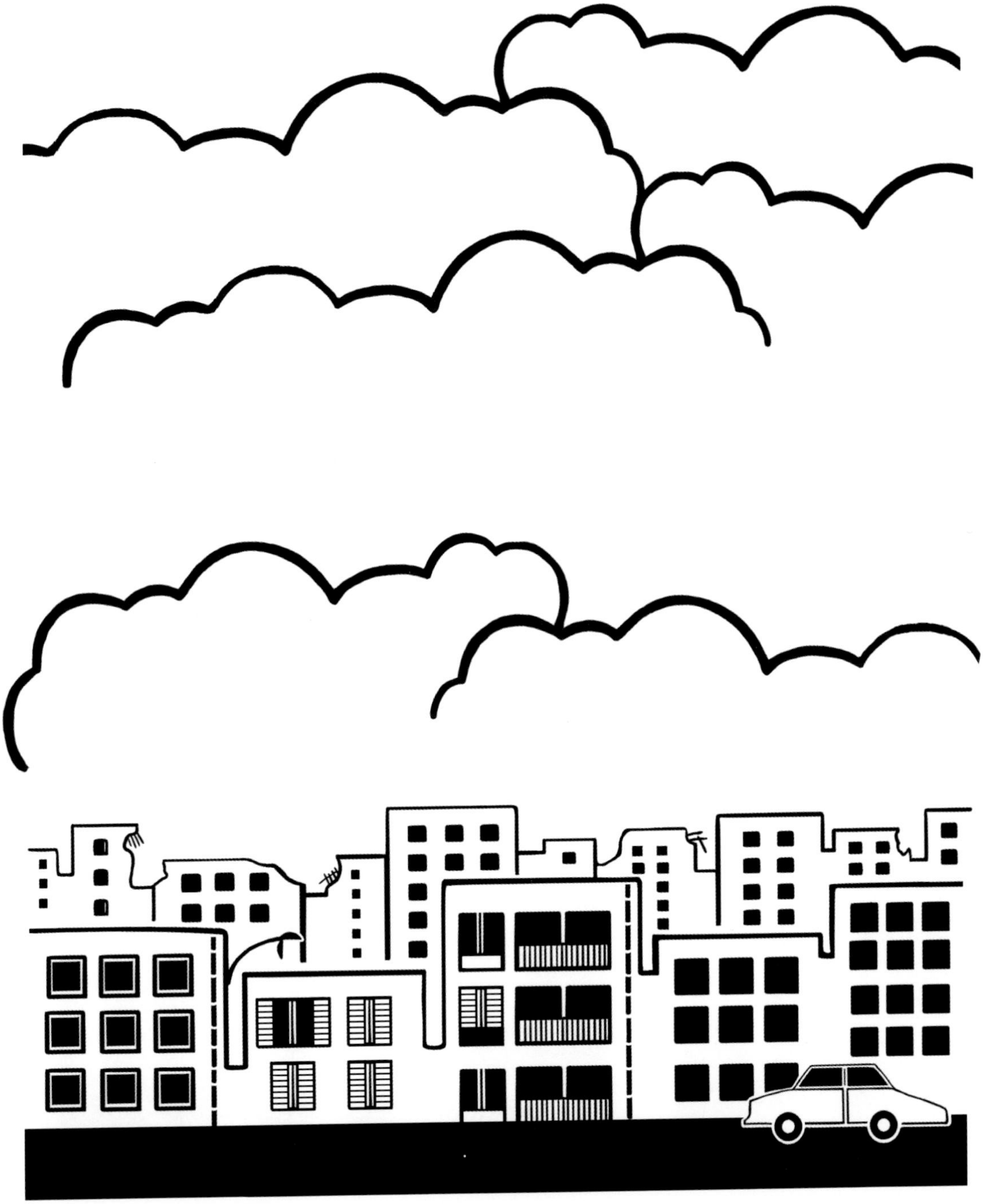

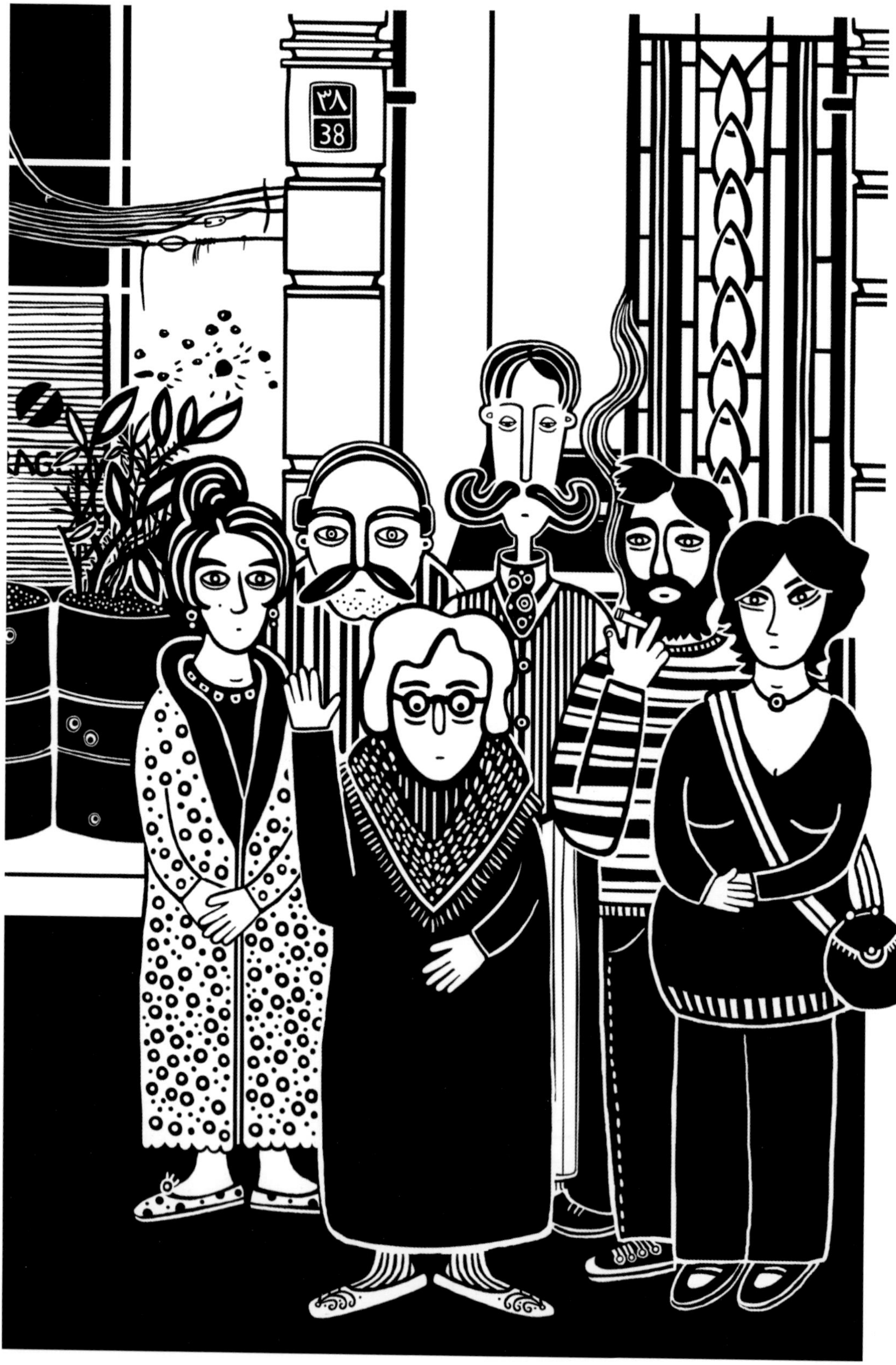
٣٨
38

AND THE NEXT MORNING, WE HAD TO LEAVE.

TO DIE   TO LEAVE   TO RETURN
IT'S A GAME FOR SWALLOWS
          —FLORIAN

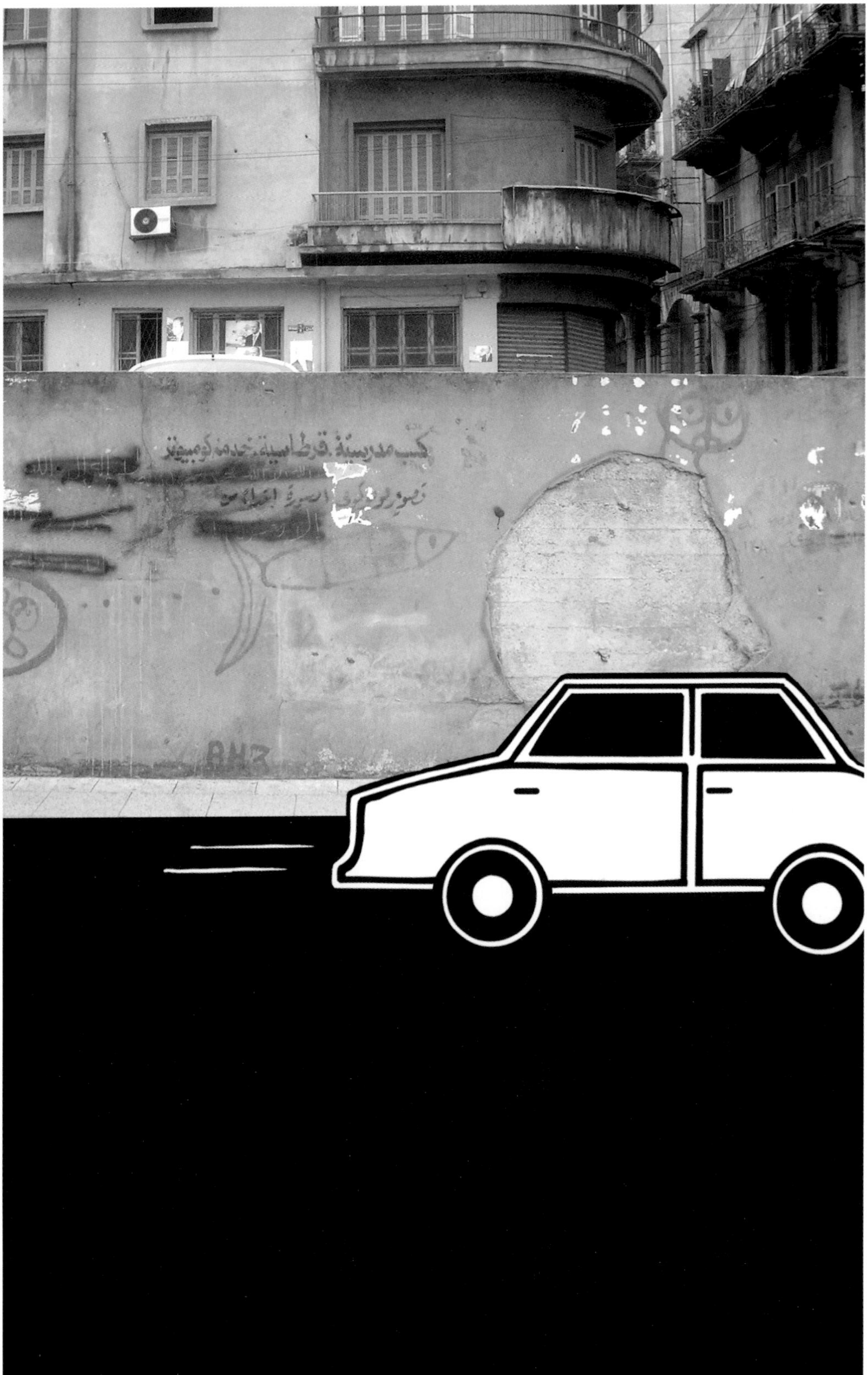
كتب مدرسية. قرطاسية. خدمة كومبيوتر

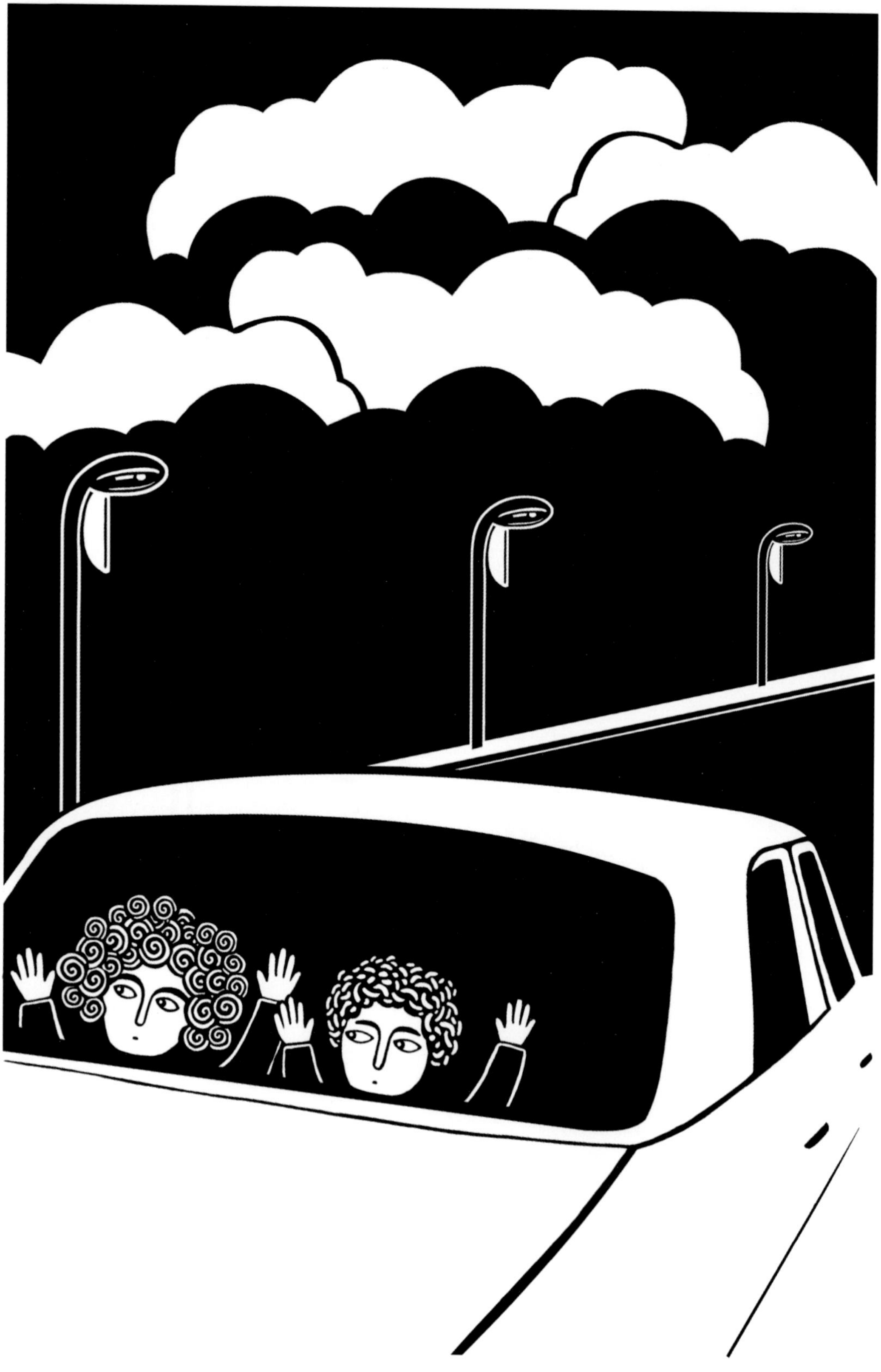

A WEEK LATER, MY PARENTS WENT BACK TO OUR APARTMENT TO GATHER A FEW THINGS.

THE BUILDING WAS EMPTY.

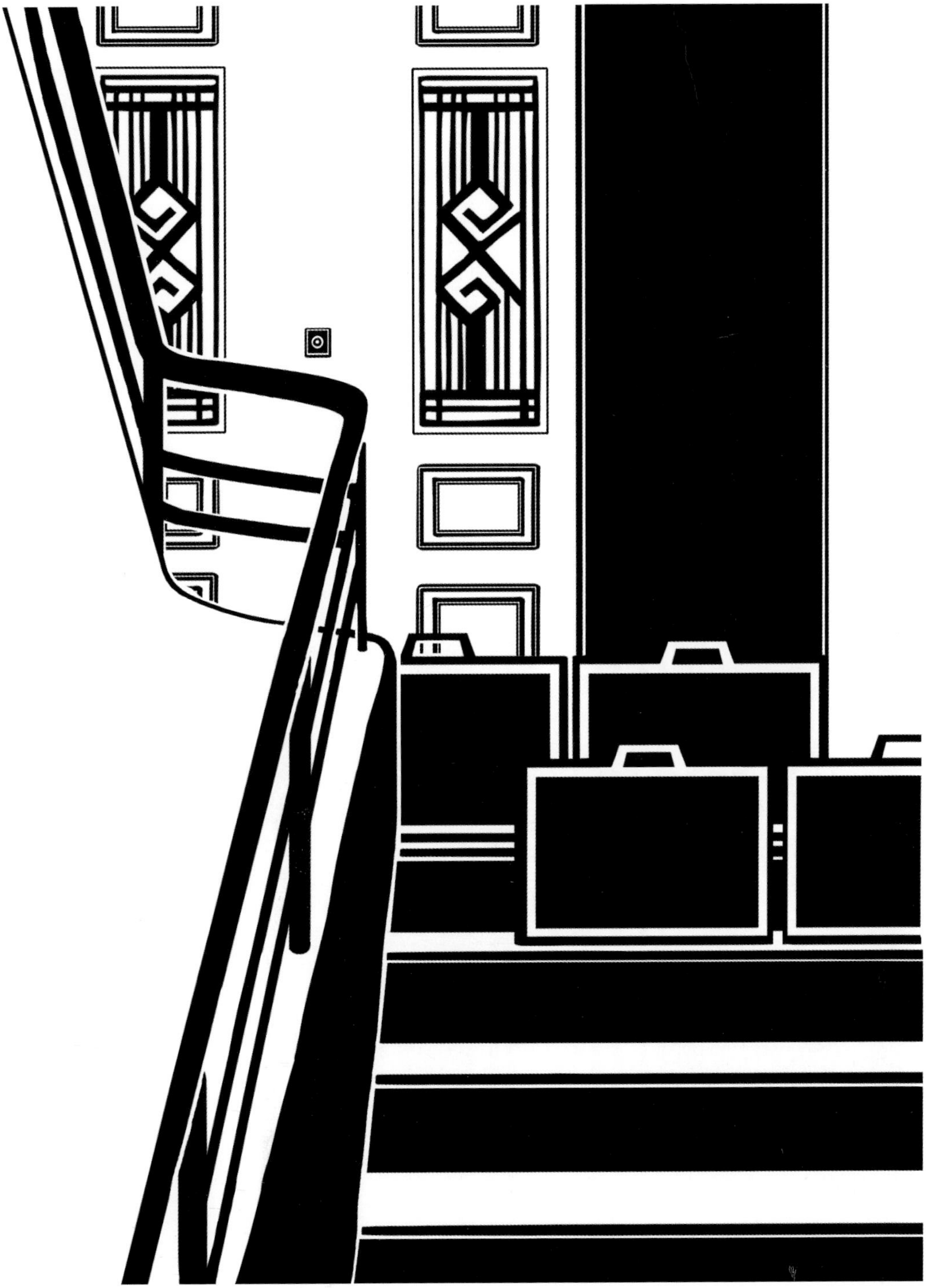

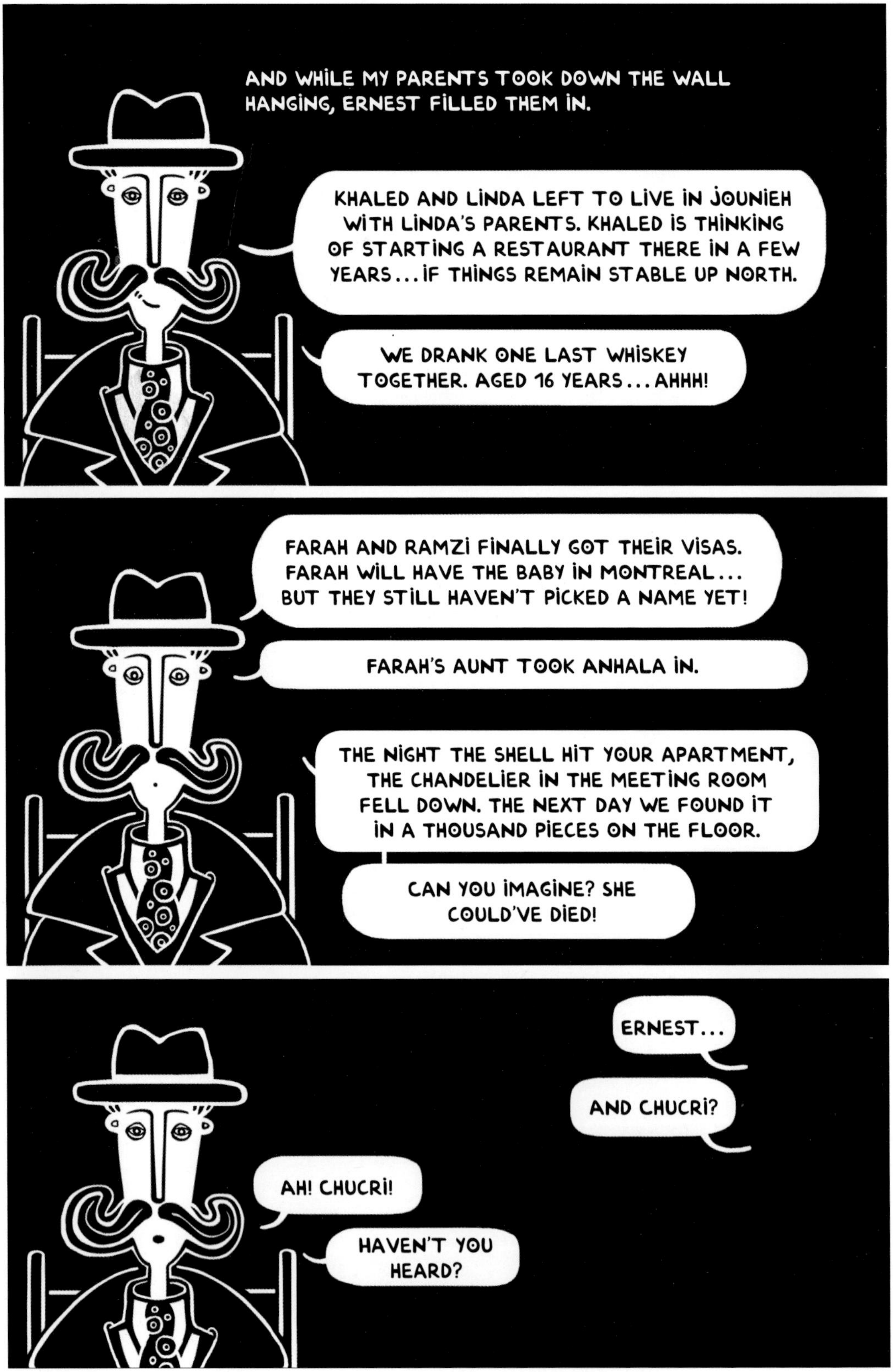
AND WHILE MY PARENTS TOOK DOWN THE WALL HANGING, ERNEST FILLED THEM IN.
KHALED AND LINDA LEFT TO LIVE IN JOUNIEH WITH LINDA'S PARENTS. KHALED IS THINKING OF STARTING A RESTAURANT THERE IN A FEW YEARS... IF THINGS REMAIN STABLE UP NORTH.
WE DRANK ONE LAST WHISKEY TOGETHER. AGED 16 YEARS... AHHH!
FARAH AND RAMZI FINALLY GOT THEIR VISAS. FARAH WILL HAVE THE BABY IN MONTREAL... BUT THEY STILL HAVEN'T PICKED A NAME YET!
FARAH'S AUNT TOOK ANHALA IN.
THE NIGHT THE SHELL HIT YOUR APARTMENT, THE CHANDELIER IN THE MEETING ROOM FELL DOWN. THE NEXT DAY WE FOUND IT IN A THOUSAND PIECES ON THE FLOOR.
CAN YOU IMAGINE? SHE COULD'VE DIED!
ERNEST...
AND CHUCRI?
AH! CHUCRI!
HAVEN'T YOU HEARD?

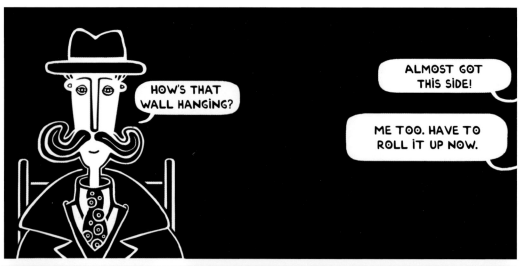

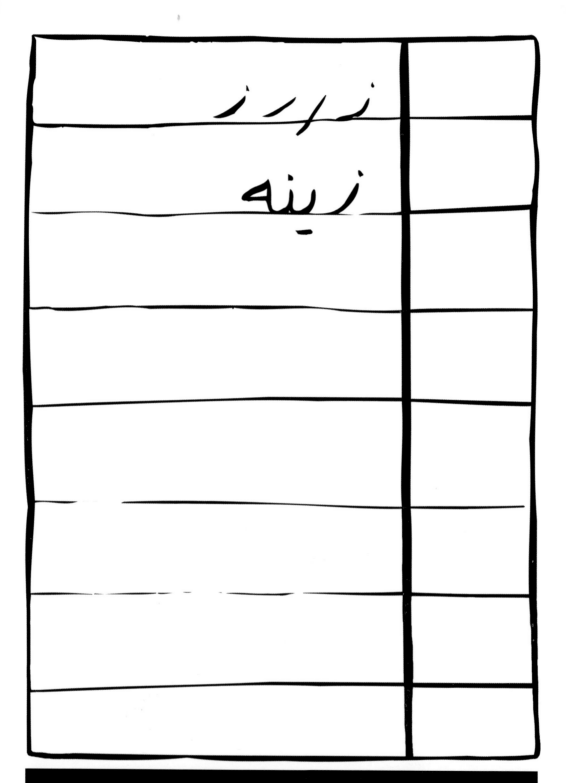

MY FATHER READ US THE REST OF *CYRANO* IN THAT HOUSE.
A YEAR LATER, I LEARNED TO WRITE MY NAME.

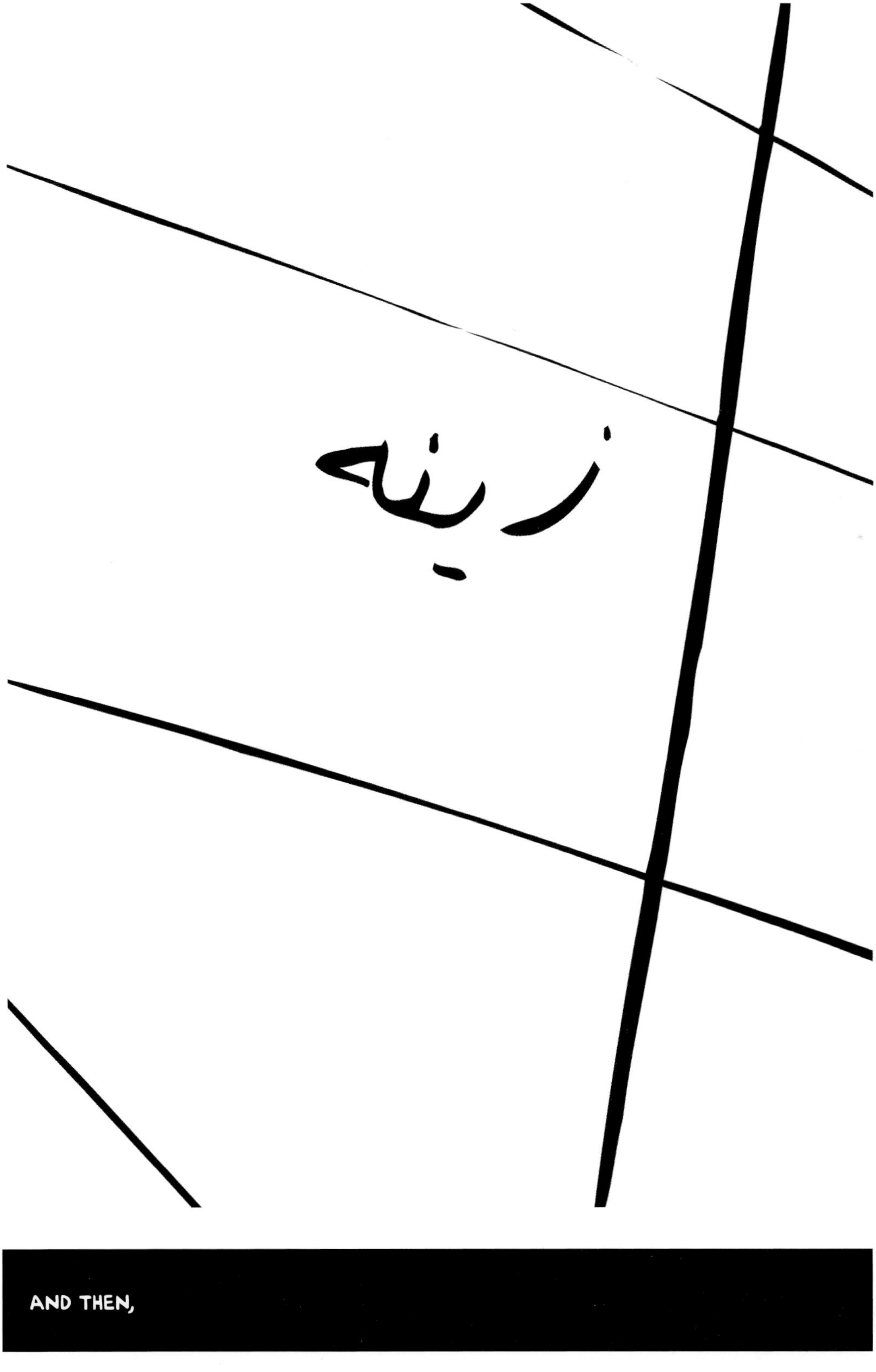
زینه
AND THEN,

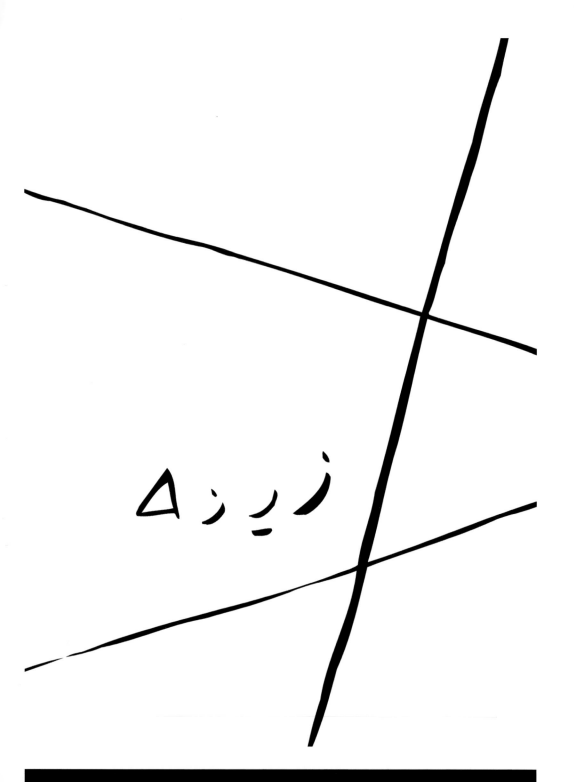

ONCE MORE,

WE HAD

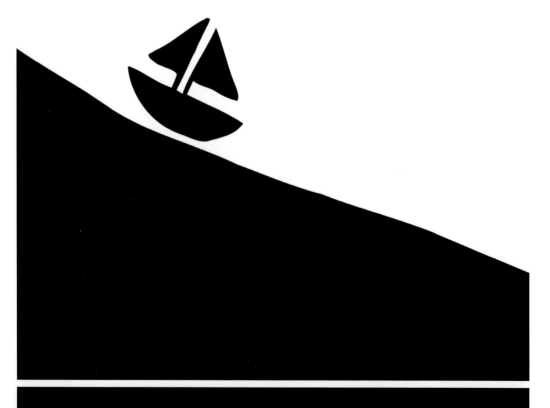

TO LEAVE.